Leigh Hunt and the London Literary Scene

Leigh Hunt's contributions to English literature, although downplayed for several decades, are now acknowledged by scholars as key to our understanding of the Romantic period. Hunt was not only a facilitator, in his support for Keats's and Shelley's poetry, but was also a major contributor in his own right to the literary and political world of the nineteenth century. *Leigh Hunt and the London Literary Scene* underscores the literary innovations in Hunt's writing during the first three decades of the nineteenth century and explores his independent critical approach and use of poetic language.

This book focuses specifically on selected works which serve to complement the current view of Hunt as a Romantic writer, and that are key instances in which Hunt strove to maintain his literary independence. Using an episodic, chronological approach Michael Eberle-Sinatra reassesses Hunt's substantial contributions to several different genres and offers an account of the significant impact of his works on audiences during the Romantic period.

Michael Eberle-Sinatra is Assistant Professor of Nineteenth-Century British Literature, with a specialization in British Romantic literature. After earning a D.Phil. at Oxford and a period as Research Associate at the Northrop Frye Centre, University of Toronto, he joined the University of Montreal in 2001. His publications include a dozen articles on Romantic authors in such journals as *European Romantic Review*, *Byron Journal*, *Keats–Shelley Journal*, and *Keats–Shelley Review*. Eberle-Sinatra is the editor of *Mary Shelley's Fictions: From Frankenstein to Faulkner* (Macmillan, 2000), the general editor, with Thomas Crochunis, of the forthcoming *Broadview Anthology of British Women Playwrights, 1777-1843* (Broadview P, 2006), and one of the general editors of the six-volume edition of *The Selected Writings of Leigh Hunt* (Pickering & Chatto, 2003). He is also founding editor of the electronic peer-reviewed journal, *Romanticism on the Net*.

Routledge Studies in Romanticism

1 **Keats's Boyish Imagination**
Richard Marggraf Turley

2 **Leigh Hunt**
Life, poetics, politics
Edited by Nicholas Roe

3 **Leigh Hunt and the London Literary Scene**
A reception history of his major works, 1805–1828
Michael Eberle-Sinatra

4 **Tracing Women's Romanticism**
Gender, history and transcendence
Kari E. Lokke

5 **Metaphysical Hazlitt**
Bicentenary essays
Uttara Natarajan, Tom Paulin and Duncan Wu

6 **Romantic Genius and the Literary Magazine**
Biography, celebrity, politics
David Higgins

Leigh Hunt and the London Literary Scene

A reception history of his major works, 1805–1828

Michael Eberle-Sinatra

NEW YORK AND LONDON

First published 2005 in the USA and Canada
by Routledge
711 Third Ave, New York, NY 10017

Simultaneously published
by Routledge
2 Park Square, Milton Park,
Abingdon, Oxon OX14 4RN

Routledge is an imprint of the Taylor & Francis Group

First issued in paperback 2013

Typeset in Garamond by
GreenGate Publishing Services, Tonbridge, Kent

Library of Congress Cataloging in Publication Data
A catalog record for this book has been requested

British Library Cataloguing in Publication Data
A catalogue record for this book is available from the British Library

ISBN 978-0-415-31676-7 (hbk)
ISBN 978-0-415-86002-4 (pbk)

To Wendy and Edward John Eberle-Sinatra

Vous êtes tous les deux la force de ma vie

Contents

Acknowledgments

This book began as a DPhil thesis and my work benefited from the comments of various scholars while I was at Oxford, especially David Chandler, Jon Mee, Tom Paulin, Seamus Perry, Fiona Stafford, and Duncan Wu. Jonathan Wordsworth suggested that I work on Leigh Hunt, and supervised my research with care. Lucy Newlyn and Nicholas Roe examined my thesis and made numerous suggestions for revisions. Roe's own extensive work on Hunt and other Romantic writers remains a constant source of inspiration for me. Particular thanks are due to three friends and fellow scholars from my Oxford days who contributed to this project and my life in more ways than I can properly acknowledge: Matthew Scott, Joel Pace, and Julia Saunders.

I am grateful to my fellow editors involved in *The Selected Writings of Leigh Hunt*: Greg Kucich, Jeffrey N. Cox, John Strachan, Charles Mahoney, and Robert Morrison. I owe a particular debt to Kucich and Cox, who have remained a source of Huntian cheer over many years. I have also benefited from the questions, comments, suggestions, and general encouragement of the following individuals: Alan Bewell, Thomas C. Crochunis, Nora Crook, Patricia Eberle, Dino Felluga, Neil Fraistat, Michael Gamer, Tim Fulford, Nicholas Halmi, Heather Jackson, Steven E. Jones, Laura Mandell, Jeanne Moskal, Michael O'Neill, Donald H. Reiman, Charles E. Robinson, David H. Stam, and Susan Wolfson. I also want to single out Anthony Holden, who gave me access to his biography in manuscript form. My editors at Routledge, first James Whiting and then Terry Clague, supported this project from the beginning and remained very patient with me for nearly two years.

My research in Oxford was made possible thanks to the moral and financial support of my family in France and in Canada. I also benefited from the financial support of St. Catherine's College, Oxford, and the Keats–Shelley Memorial Association which funded trips to deliver conference paper versions of Chapters 1 and 4. The Keats–Shelley Association of America awarded me a Carl H. Pforzheimer, Jr., Research Grant in 1999 to travel to the University of Iowa and work on the best collection of Hunt material in the world. The Northrop Frye Centre, Victoria University, granted me the status of Research Associate for two years, which allowed me to start the revisions of my DPhil thesis; I am particularly grateful to its director, Brian Merrilees. I also want to acknowledge the financial support of the Université de Montréal, and the constant encouragement of my former chair Robert K. Martin and my colleagues Joyce Boro, Lianne Moyes, and Heike Härting, as well as the hard work of my research assistant Jennifer Beauvais. Financial support from the Social Science and Humanities Research Council of Canada and from the Fonds québécois de la recherche sur la société et la culture helped me complete the final revisions.

For permission to reprint from manuscript letters in the Dove Cottage Library, I would like to thank Jonathan Wordsworth, chairman of the Wordsworth Trust. For granting me access and permission to quote from manuscripts and association copies in the Brewer–Leigh Hunt special collection, University of Iowa, I would like to thank Robert McCown and Sidney F. Huttner. Parts of Chapters 1, 3, and 4 appeared in *Keats–Shelley Journal*, L (2001), The *Charles Lamb Bulletin,* 116 (2001), and *Byron Journal,* XVI (2001) respectively; I am grateful to the editors for permission to reprint. I also want to thank Jonathan Mulrooney and Ken J. Bugajski for permission to quote from their unpublished PhD theses.

Finally, this book would not have been possible without the support of my wife Wendy J. Eberle-Sinatra who made everything easier (and this is no small task) thanks to her generosity, support, and constant encouragement. This book is dedicated to her and our son Edward John. Needless to say, I am solely responsible for any errors and shortcomings to be found in this book.

Introduction

> [Hunt] is likely to be honoured with more love from posterity, than he ever received, or can hope to receive, from his contemporary public.
>
> Richard H. Horne, *A New Spirit of the Age* (Horne 1907: 227)

James Henry Leigh Hunt (1784–1859) was one of the most prolific and influential writers on British culture and politics in the first half of the nineteenth century. He was an essential member of the literary circle that included Percy Bysshe and Mary Shelley, John Keats, Charles Lamb, and William Hazlitt, and he knew everyone from William Wordsworth and William Hone to Jeremy Bentham and Henry Brougham. A passionate and outspoken participant in the London political scene, he was imprisoned for seditious libel against the Prince Regent in 1813 and became a hero of the left. Although he is now most often remembered as the editor of the radical weekly newspaper the *Examiner* (1808–22) and the leader of the 'Cockney School of Poetry', Hunt's contribution to Romantic literature was as extensive as it has proven to be durable, in matters as various as prosodic experimentation and the modernization of the magazine essay.

Downplayed for several decades, Hunt's contributions to English literature are now acknowledged by scholars as a key element to our understanding of the Romantic period. Hunt was not only a facilitator (in his support of Keats's and Shelley's poetry, for instance), but also a major contributor to the literary and political world of the early nineteenth century. The main aim of *Leigh Hunt and the London Literary Scene* is to underscore the literary innovations made in Hunt's writing during the first three decades of the nineteenth century, and to show how Hunt was independent in his critical approach and his use of poetic language. This study consequently focuses on Hunt's literary and critical works, and the case for Hunt's significant positive impact on contemporary writing. Hunt's contributions included altering the format of theatrical criticism commonly found at the time, and offering a new approach to poetic language. Hunt's independence of mind distinguishes him from his contemporary fellow critics, as is manifest in both his insistence on the importance of 'mental theatre' alongside performance, and in his critical response to Wordsworth's poetry.

This study focuses specifically on selected works which complement the current view of Hunt as a Romantic writer and serve as key instances in which Hunt strove to create and maintain his literary independence. A parallel consideration is equally relevant to understanding the analysis of the historical reception of these works, the context of Hunt's public life, and how these factors functioned to reinforce or undermine his literary innovations. Grounding this study in the specific contemporary reception of the works under consideration demonstrates Hunt's importance for any discussion of the Romantic period that takes into consideration socio-historical conditions. Indeed, as Paul Magnuson persuasively argues in his book *Reading Public Romanticism*,

> [M]uch of the poetry published between 1789 and 1830 is public poetry, but … one cannot discover its public nature by reading individual works of literature apart from the public discourse that literature enters when it is published. Justice cannot be done to a work's literary and cultural significance by disregarding its various locations in collections of the author's own poetry, collaborative publications with several authors, reviews, newspapers, or anthologies.
>
> (Magnuson 1998: 3)

Contemporary reviews of Hunt's work are an integral part of this study, since these reviews offer one of the best means of contextualizing the publication and reception of his productions, even though, as Jane Stabler remarks, reviewers' 'varying degrees of critical objection depended on a number of factors including the political affiliation of the periodical and its intended readership' (Stabler 2002: 21).[1] Romantic authors were in general quite hostile to reviewers, especially anonymous ones, since reviewers seemed to wield too much power.[2] Reacting to a series of negative reviews of his *Biographia Literaria*, published in the second half of 1817, Coleridge, in an unpublished manuscript fragment 'On Anonymous Reviewing' (dated December 1817–January 1818), sharply questions,

> To what purpose should we reason with a Critic, who without affording a single proof of his competence or perhaps in spite of the most glaring proofs of the contrary; (nay, in spite of his own consciousness that he has never made himself master even of the means of studying the question;) will yet ~~dare hazard a blank assurance~~, assure the Public, that a writer's arguments are nonsense and his ~~facts~~ inductions false~~ness~~hoods?
>
> (Coleridge S. T. 1995: I, 697)

Hunt complained in equally bitter terms about the cover of anonymity which seemed to give the reviewer the right to utter calumny without having to be personally responsible for his comments, especially during the 1816–22 series of attacks on the Cockney School. He also criticized the practice of writing positive reviews in exchange for favors or friendship, in particular in the theatrical milieu where he began his career as a journalist. Ironically enough, William Gifford wrote against this kind of biased criticism in one of the notes to his 1795 *Maeviad*:

> It is to be wished that Reviewers, sensible of the influence their opinions necessarily have on the public taste, could divest themselves of their partialities, when they sit down to the execution of, what I hope they consider as, their solemn duty. We should not find them recommending a work to favour, deserving universal reprobation and contempt.
>
> (Gifford 1795: 75)

Hunt took great pains to differentiate himself from that kind of reviewing practice when he wrote for the *News*. He announced and adhered to this principle of independence in reviews, as in other writings, when he launched the *Examiner* in 1808 with his brother John.

Even when it constituted negative criticism, however, a review could also boost the sales of a volume in ways that publishers were certainly grateful for, as Edward Moxon wrote to Wordsworth on 9 April 1842: 'A review, even with a sprinkling of abuse in it, is, in my opinion, worth a hundred advertisements' (Moxon 1842: n. pag.). Of course more than 'a sprinkling of abuse' in more than a few reviews would have quite a negative impact on sales. Neither Keats's nor Shelley's poems sold well during their lifetimes,[3] nor did Hunt's own volumes, including *The Story of Rimini*, his most famous poem. The political malice that lay behind the most severe attacks in reviews unfortunately succeeded in preventing these authors from being recognized by the public at the time. The climate of reception changed during the Victorian period, especially for the poetry of Keats and Shelley, although their new promoters generally downplayed the extent of the poets' engagement with political issues in their works. Hunt's writings, however, did not benefit from this resurgence of interest in Romantic poetry. By the time of the publication of Cosmo Monkhouse's biography in 1893, Hunt was remembered primarily for his friendships with Keats and Shelley, for his attack on Byron, for his role in political journalism in the *Examiner*, and for but a select few poems and some essays. The focus of Monkhouse's biography is on the 'Romantic Hunt', and he glosses over Hunt's last three decades in only a chapter and a half. Modern Romantic studies have inherited this Hunt, who is worthy only by association, not on his own merits. Thus, James R. Thompson's assertion that '[b]ecause of his close literary and personal associations with the great writers of his day [Hunt] is continually in someone's shadow', remained true until a few years ago (Thompson 1977: 18).

Throughout the twentieth century, in most articles focusing on Hunt, or on Hunt in relation to Keats and Shelley, one can trace a tendency to move away from a study of Hunt's life per se to more contextualized discussions of Hunt's importance to a circle of writers and to his continuing involvement in contemporary issues. The last three decades have seen a resurgence of interest in Hunt as a leading figure in the Romantic period, particularly with regard to his political engagement and his literary importance. Nicholas Roe's collection of essays *Leigh Hunt: Life, Poetics, Politics* is a fitting example of a recent substantial scholarly reassessment of Hunt's work, and Anthony Holden's *The Wit in the Dungeon* challenges previous biographies with its enriching portrayal of Hunt and his many achievements over a literary career that lasted for close to sixty years. The present book owes much to many of these studies of Hunt and his circle, and proposes to add to their work by exploring some of the specific innovations of Hunt's works and their contemporary reception.

Leigh Hunt and the London Literary Scene: An overview

In the first quarter of the nineteenth century, Leigh Hunt was at the centre of the London literary scene. He knew many visual, dramatic, and literary artists, as well as political figures, and this knowledge gave him an unusual status among his contemporaries. His theatrical criticism anticipated the concept of dramatic character that Coleridge, Lamb, and Hazlitt would develop at greater length, and his essays are early examples of the new genre of personal literary essays, later taken up in different ways by Lamb and Hazlitt. Because his career involved a number of literary and political circles and genres which are usually treated in isolation, a study of the range of his work and interests during this period should provide valuable insight into the links between the Romantic movement and the growth of an expanded and more socially diversified audience for poetry and serious literary journalism.

Hunt's critical, journalistic, and editorial work remained steady until his death on 28 August 1859. His post-1828 output is quite impressive in its quantity, if not always in its quality: he edited several newspapers, including the *Tatler*, *Leigh Hunt's London Journal*, and the *Monthly Repository*;[4] he wrote a play, *A Legend of Florence*, which was successfully staged in 1840; he published a novel, *The Palfrey: A Love-Story of Old Times*, in 1842; he edited three volumes, with important critical commentaries, in the 1840s: *Imagination and Fancy* (1844), *Wit and Humour* (1846), and *Stories from the Italian Poets* (1846); and he published a new edition of his 1832 religious treatise *Christianism* under the title of *The Religion of the Heart* in 1853. These numerous publications are not only proof of his creative mind, but also serve as a reminder that Hunt was a professional writer, and not an author writing at his leisure. His high productivity reflects his need of a steady income, punctuated by his recurring financial difficulties, most famously illustrated in Dickens's fictionalized portrait of Hunt as Harold Skimpole in *Bleak House*.[5] Yet the period spanning the years 1801 to 1828 seems the best place to begin a fuller reappraisal of Hunt's writings because of the variety of work he produced and its contemporary reception. Whether negatively or positively received, none of the works under consideration in *Leigh Hunt and the London Literary Scene* went unnoticed by reviewers at the time of publication.

Because they were much less noticed, for various reasons, three other periodicals Hunt edited during these three decades, namely, the *Reflector*, the *Indicator*, and the *Companion*, are not discussed here, even though some of Hunt's best essays were published in the latter two publications. Because of its nature as a pocket diary and appointment book, *The Literary Pocket-Book*, edited by Hunt between 1819 and 1823, is referred to here only indirectly.[6] Furthermore, since the emphasis of *Leigh Hunt and the London Literary Scene* is on introducing new Hunt material and on contextualizing Hunt's contributions to the Romantic period, this study is neither intended as a new biography of Hunt, nor as a reevaluation of his relationships with individual writers such as Shelley, Keats, Hazlitt, or Lamb. Scholars have already covered these relationships well, either in biographies or in critical studies. The present book is a companion piece to these studies, and complements present biographies of Hunt and his circle with a greater emphasis on the socio-historical reception of a selection of his works. Although a study of Hunt's familiar and professional circles, not only in the Romantic period—a topic that Jeffrey N. Cox addresses expertly (Cox 1998)—but throughout his entire life would prove to be a most enriching subject of research, such is not the present concern of this work.

The focus of the first chapter of *Leigh Hunt and the London Literary Scene* is on Hunt's first major contribution to criticism: his theatrical essays for the *News*, later reprinted in *Critical Essays on the Performers of the London Theatres*. A comparison of mid-eighteenth-century dramatic criticism with Hunt's early theatrical writings demonstrates how Hunt's emphasis on the actors and the stage direction of the plays he reviews is new to the genre of theatrical criticism. This chapter also shows how much Hunt's innovative journalistic style differs from that of other contemporary writers, such as Samuel Taylor Coleridge and Charles Lamb, although modern scholars rarely discuss his work as a theater critic.

The Feast of the Poets is Hunt's first major poem, and the focus of chapter two. First published in March 1812 in the *Reflector*, *The Feast of the Poet*s reappeared in 1814, 1815, and 1832, with important revisions to each new edition. This poem is especially important for an understanding of Hunt's place in the contemporary literary scene because it presents his opinions of writers—in particular Southey, Coleridge, and Wordsworth—during the first two decades of the nineteenth century. Hunt's revisions to the poem, and the addition of numerous notes to the 1814 version, document his evolving view of his fellow writers and demonstrate affinities with his literary criticism published in the *Examiner*. Hunt presents his readers with a satirical view of the London literary scene between 1811 and 1815 in the various versions of The Feast of the Poets. The poem offers Hunt's independent critical view of his fellow writers, but does not display the poetic innovations of *The Story of Rimini*.

With the publication of *The Story of Rimini* in 1816—Hunt's most important poetical contribution to the Romantic period—Hunt became the subject of a controversy that centered on linguistics and politics, as emerges in the third chapter through an analysis of Hunt's debt to Dante's Rimini episode at the end of the fifth book of *The Inferno* and the nature of Hunt's greatly expanded version of this story. The focus on language by contemporary reviewers, especially in *Blackwood's* and the *Quarterly*, responds directly to concern about the poetic productions of middle-class writers who deliberately assert their difference from a more aristocratic tradition. Hunt's own writing was part of his innovative literary criticism on Wordsworth, insofar as it criticizes the reviewers who think Wordsworth's lower-class language is unpoetic and beneath their contempt. Hunt's use of common language indicates his poetical and political allegiance to the Wordsworth of the *Lyrical Ballads*, as opposed to the epic, high-flown Wordsworth of *The Excursion*. The focus on language in the reception of *The Story of Rimini* underscores not only the importance of socio-political values in contemporary reviews, but also Hunt's important contribution to Romantic literature within a period that routinely associates poetic innovations with names such as Wordsworth and Keats.

As is well known, Hunt's stay in Italy turned out to be a difficult time for him. The death of Shelley in 1822 affected him strongly, and his collaboration with Byron on the *Liberal* proved to be challenging. Since it had a large impact on public opinion of Hunt in the 1820s, Hunt's work on this publication and its reception in England is explored in the fourth chapter of this study, along with four rarely discussed essays Hunt wrote about Italy. In order to put Hunt's Italian essays in perspective, some references to the major fictional and non-fictional travelogues of the period devoted to Italy are also provided. Hunt's other descriptions of Italy, written for *The Literary Examiner*, and the articles he published on London while still in Italy, also form part of this discussion. The articles on London reflect the lifetime attachment to the city that he would express in many of his other works. They also illustrate his disappointment with the Italy of his personal experience, as opposed to the imagined land based on travelogues and various literary descriptions; his reaction is similar to that of other contemporary travelers such as Wordsworth and Hazlitt. These essays also attest to Hunt's involvement in the popular genre of travel literature in the 1820s.

In all, the following pages attempt to reassess Hunt's substantial contributions to several different genres and to offer an account of their significant impact on audiences during the Romantic period through an episodic, chronological approach. The period 1801 to 1828 witnessed Hunt's rise to political and literary fame with the creation of the *Examiner* in 1808 and the publication of *The Story of Rimini* in 1816. This period also saw the development of Hunt's lifelong interest in theater and the innovations he brought to the genre of theatrical criticism with his work on the *News*, and in the *Critical Essays*. The third decade under scrutiny also contains some of Hunt's lesser-known work in the genre of travel literature. As a whole the period covered in this book illustrates the range of literary interests that Hunt pursued, as well as the evolution of his position within the London literary scene over a thirty-year timespan. However, this phase of Hunt's life is obviously too complex to be rendered fully in any single study. Thus the idea here is not to attempt an exhaustive history, but rather to present a starting point for further enquiry into both the first part of Hunt's career as a Romantic writer and public figure, and the second part of his life, under the reign of Queen Victoria. Ultimately, I hope that the process of re-reading the texts selected for this study in light of their contemporary reception will serve to open up further areas for re-examination, both for Hunt scholars as well as for Romanticists at large.

1 1805–1811

> [F]orty or fifty years ago, people of all times of life were much greater play-goers than they are now. … Nobility, gentry, citizens, princes,—all were frequenters of theatres, and even more or less acquainted personally with the performers.
>
> (Hunt 1850: I, 249–50)

The years 1801 to 1808 saw the emergence of Leigh Hunt as a public figure on the London literary scene, first with the publication of his 1801 collection of poetry, *Juvenilia*, and then with his work as theater critic for the *News* between 1805 and 1807. Although rarely mentioned by modern critics, Hunt's early theatrical reviews, which provided the basis for his volume *Critical Essays on the Performers of the London Theatres*, deserve to be reevaluated and placed in his corpus of theatrical writings, which, until the publication of *The Selected Writings of Leigh Hunt* in 2003, were typically taken to consist chiefly of his articles in the *Examiner* and the *Tatler*. In his introduction to *The Selected Writings of William Hazlitt*, Tom Paulin describes Hazlitt as 'the first major art critic in English' (Hazlitt 1998: I, xii). I argue in what follows that Hunt was the first major Romantic theater critic. Hunt changed the way plays were reviewed in periodicals at the beginning of the nineteenth century by writing longer reviews than was the practice at the time. He also focused in greater detail than was common at the time on the performances of actors, as well as on the scenery, costumes, and music of specific stagings.

At the same time, Hunt is arguably the first Romantic critic to develop the concept of a 'mental theatre'. An examination of the pieces included in his *Critical Essays on the Performers of the London Theatres* reveals that Hunt devoted as much attention to the actors as to the debate on the question of reading versus performing plays—a question that would preoccupy other Romantics during the following two decades.[1] Alan Richardson argues that '[i]f the process of reading is emphasized, it is because the Romantics found their own response to Shakespearean tragedy strongest in reading' (Richardson 1988: 19). As an active theater critic, Hunt addresses this issue by insisting on the importance of the imagination. He introduced the role of the readerly imagination as a critical tool, a way to re-examine not only the way one approaches the texts of Shakespeare's plays, but also how performances of these plays should be judged. Although other major Romantic critics (principally Hazlitt, Coleridge, and Lamb) would later write extensively about the importance of the imagination in drama and about the superiority of reading Shakespeare over seeing his plays performed, Hunt's criticism (dating from 1805 to 1807) anticipates these three critics by several years. Even if there are valid questions about the absolute primacy of these ideas, it is certainly reasonable to argue for Hunt's relative originality in terms of their publication history.[2]

Scholars have of course recognized the value of Hunt's dramatic criticism, although this recognition is primarily based on his reviews for the *Examiner*. Discussing these review articles in their edition of Hunt's dramatic criticism, Lawrence Huston Houtchens and Carolyn Washburn Houtchens observe that '[o]ne interesting feature of Hunt's criticism … is the fact that he gave impetus to the English Romantic movement by his adoption of romantic criteria in certain reviews for the *Examiner*, an influential London newspaper which disseminated his ideas widely' (Hunt 1949b: viii). Without diminishing the importance of Hunt's articles in the *Examiner*, I would argue that the theatrical criticism published in the *News* laid the foundation for many of his later views on drama and acting. Hunt's writings on the actors of his time in *Critical Essays*, like the reviews and extended articles on theatrical subjects in the *News*, marked a distinct change in direction at the outset of his literary career. In many ways, the essays make an original contribution to dramatic criticism and literary journalism of the period. They also provide the opportunity for Hunt to declare his 'independence' as a writer, a stance he struggled all his life to maintain.

Theatrical criticism and the *News*

When in 1805 Hunt came to write theatrical criticism for the *News*, a weekly published by his brother John, most other periodicals of the time did not pay much attention to drama. Although the tradition of periodicals devoted to the theater began in 1720 with Richard Steele's the *Theatre* and continued in the nineteenth century with publications such as Thomas Dutton's *Dramatic Censor; or, Weekly Theatrical Report*,[3] and Thomas Holcroft's *Theatrical Recorder*,[4] most of these publications included short and medium-length articles rather than detailed reviews. In this respect, they were similar to the major 'generalist' daily newspapers, such as the *Times*, the *Morning Post*, or the *Morning Herald*, which included only short notices about drama and representations of new plays, usually brief descriptive pieces. Evening newspapers such as the *Sun*, the *Star*, the *Courier*, or the *Lloyd Evening Post* did not discuss drama at all. Weekly papers such as William Cobbett's *Weekly Political Register* also did not contain dramatic reviews. Monthly publications of the early nineteenth century did tend to include brief summaries of new plays appearing in the London theaters. To mention only two, the *European Magazine and Review* and the *Monthly Mirror* presented some general comments on new plays, more extensive in length than those included in the dailies but still without serious critical commentary. The important exception is *Bell's Weekly Messenger*, a newspaper that enjoyed a substantial circulation for more than twenty years after its launch in May 1796. *Bell's Weekly Messenger* devoted an unusual amount of attention to actors and the general atmosphere of the plays, including the audiences' reactions. Louis Landré suggests that these articles might have inspired Hunt, who most certainly read this weekly. Indeed, Hunt had been introduced to John Bell in 1804, and, as he recalls in the *Autobiography*, Hunt 'used to hear of politics and dramatic criticism, and of the persons who wrote them' during his regular visits to Bell's house (Hunt 1850: I, 276). Landré notes, however, that Hunt's criticism is more detailed and extensive (Landré 1936: II, 101). I would add that Hunt's distinctive strength lies in his close reading of the actors' performances and in his emphasis on acting as a dramatic art in its own right.

Although, like his contemporaries, Hunt focuses his attention on famous actors and their favorite roles, he self-consciously avoids the habits of name-dropping and flattery that were becoming customary at the time. John Taylor evokes this culture of theater criticism in his autobiography *Records of my Life* (Taylor 1832), where he discusses numerous actors and playwrights with whom he was regularly in contact, including Kemble, Hull, Siddons, O'Keefe, and Sheridan. Taylor records the trend of praising friends, the various favors that theater managers asked of newspaper editors, and the general practice of biased journalism at the turn of the century (Taylor 1832: II, 138; 271–2), a practice Hazlitt draws attention to in his 1821–2 essays 'Whether Actors ought to sit in the boxes?' and 'On Patronage and Puffing' (Hazlitt 1930–4: VIII, 272–9; 289–302).

Hunt also discusses the practice of 'puffing' in his *Autobiography*:

> Puffing and plenty of tickets were ... the system of the day. It was an interchange of amenities over the dinner-table; a flattery of power on the one side, and puns on the other; and what the public took for a criticism on a play, was a draft upon the box-office, or reminiscence of last Thursday's salmon and lobster-sauce. The custom was, to write as short and as favourable a paragraph on the new piece as could be; and to say that Bannister was 'excellent' and Mrs. Jordan 'charming'; to notice the 'crowded house' or invent it, if necessary; and to conclude by observing that 'the whole went off with *éclat*'.
>
> (Hunt 1850: I, 282)

Forty years previous to this comment, Hunt had given a sarcastic definition of 'a crowded house' in an article in the *News*, and included in the appendix of *Critical Essays* as 'a theatre on the night of a performance, when all the back seats and upper boxes are empty', and of a good actor as 'the general term for an actor who gives good dinner' (Hunt 2003: I, 15). He also emphasizes the link between a good meal and a good review when he writes about

> those amiable journalists, who will abuse one performer merely to please another, who after getting drunk at an actor's table will come and tell us what power he possesses over their senses, and what a want of solidity there is in that man who never invites them to eat his roast beef.
>
> (Hunt 1807a: 181)

Although Theodore Fenner rightly remarks that Hunt was not the first to voice a complaint against the practice of puffing (Fenner 1994: 7), Hunt's independent stance in theatrical criticism is worth underscoring because it had a direct impact on his political writings in the *Examiner*.

Between 19 May 1805 and 13 December 1807, Hunt reviewed plays performed in London for the *News*. These essays were unusual for their length and for their serious attention to what were, after all, ephemeral events. In his articles Hunt not only describes each play from a critical perspective—he never refrains from criticizing actors and playwrights, unlike many other journalists—but he also pays close attention to costumes, stage direction, and musical accompaniment. What is new and distinctive in the criticism Hunt published in the *News* is his dedicated attention to acting and its socio-educational aspect. Hunt is interested in performances that bring something to the audience, whether an emotional experience or an education—or an improvement in their manners. The relevance of the performance to the audience is thus, for Hunt, the basis for an intelligent appraisal of acting.

Hunt did not have a strong interest in the abstract theory of drama that Joanna Baillie had discussed several years before in the 'Introductory Discourse' to her *Series of Plays* (1798) and that Coleridge, Lamb, and Hazlitt also debated in the 1810s and 1820s, although he does consider certain generic categories of drama, such as comedy and tragedy. His serious critical attention was devoted to major actors of the time, and these essays analyze at length specific performances as well as more general qualities and defects of the actor under consideration, especially in relation to the new style of acting then being adopted by many. The expanded stages of London theaters at the end of the eighteenth century reduced the sense of intimacy between audience and actors, and as a result, any subtle acting skill was lost in barely audible performances for those audience members sitting furthest away from the stage. As Jeffrey N. Cox notes, '[i]t was now impossible for an actor or actress to rely upon small effects of voice or movement in such cavernous halls' (Cox 1992: 9). Actors were to perform in a style very different from that of the mid-eighteenth century, which was suited to smaller, more intimate stages. This physical change in the theaters encouraged an exaggerated style tending toward the grand effect, a style repeatedly criticized by Romantic writers, including Hunt.

Hunt is generally more critical of new plays and favors classical works, particularly those of Shakespeare.[5] He deplored the excessive adulation given to certain popular actors and the consequent treatment of plays as mere vehicles for stars or future stars. Playwrights wrote plays tailored to satisfy the demands of both actors and audience. An author himself, Richard Cumberland acknowledges the influence actors had on playwrights:

> Perhaps it is to be lamented, that their influence is such, as to induce an author to make greater sacrifices, and pay more attention, to the particular persons, whom he has in view to represent the characters of his play, than to the general interests of the play itself.
>
> (Cumberland 1807: 63)[6]

The full development of the star system indeed reconfigured the theatrical scene of the early nineteenth century. For instance, the famous actors Kean and Kemble were personally involved in the choice and the adaptation of the plays put on stage at Drury Lane and Covent Garden. Kemble was also the manager of Drury Lane, and then of Covent Garden at the time of the 'Old Price' Riots; the example of Kemble serves well to illustrate Stanley Jones's observation concerning actor-managers:

> When the theatres were managed by men of business who were not actors, their object was, first, to get as good a play as they could, and then to find the best possible actors for the part. With the actor-manager it is different. The first thing is to find a play in which he shall have a good part, and the second is to look to it that nobody else shall have so good a part as himself.
>
> (Jones 1899: 20–1)

Yet, fame and success alone would not assure a positive review from Hunt.

However little appreciated by members of the theatrical world for the frankness of his criticism,[7] Hunt quickly established himself as a major theater critic in London during the three years he wrote for the *News*. Early in 1808,[8] a number of his essays based on his pieces in the *News* appeared under the title *Critical Essays on the Performers of the London Theatres, including General Observations on the Practice and Genius of the Stage* in a volume printed by, and dedicated to, John Hunt. As Fenner remarks,

> [Hunt's] skill as an experienced critic is clearly evident in *Critical Essays*, with which he culminated his work for [the *News*]. Its very appearance is testimony to that skill, for theatrical essays were not considered the kind of matter to be distinguished by placing them between hard covers.
>
> (Fenner 1972: 47)

When Hunt publishes *Critical Essays*, he is by that very gesture arguing that theater reviewing as a literary form (or at least his own theater reviewing) is deserving of serious attention. That he chooses to put out such a volume also attests to his popularity as theatrical reviewer at the beginning of 1808, and the publication of *Critical Essays* marks the next step in establishing him as a major theater critic.[9]

Critical Essays on the Performers of the London Theatres

As the title of the volume indicates, Hunt's principal focus in *Critical Essays* is on actors, virtually to the exclusion of all other aspects of dramatic performance. But Hunt also refers throughout the essays to eighteenth- and nineteenth-century playwrights, the politics of the London theaters, and even the political aspects of drama as suggested by the xenophobic dimensions of some characters, as he does in his essay on 'Mr. Blanchard' where he comments on the presence of French characters in some plays and their political use to assert the superiority of England and reinforce English nationalism (Hunt 1807a: 122).[10] In addition, he includes two theoretical introductions to the sections on tragedy and comedy. Numerous details serve to lend the volume an air of literary authority, from the detailed index (organized both thematically and by the names of individuals cited), and the references to established, respected authors such as Congreve, Shakespeare, Johnson, Racine, Milton, Voltaire—'the writer who made the greatest impression on me' (Hunt 1850: I, 261)—, and Addison, to the quotation from Horace's *De Arte Poetica* on the cover: 'Respicere exemplar vitae morumque jubebo/Doctum imitatorem, et veras [for vivas] hinc ducere voces'. Hunt judiciously chooses a quote relevant to his ideal readers: 'I would advise one who has learned the imitative life to look to life and manners for a model, and draw from thence living words' (Horace 1929: 476–7).

Contemporary reviews such as the *Anti-Jacobin Review and Magazine* praised the depth and sharpness of Hunt's criticism ([Anon.] 1809b: 191), and the *Critical Review* also announced,

> Upon the whole, these essays are sensible, ingenious, and amusing; and the instructions which they contain, the merits which they extol, and the defects which they censure, constitute a dramatic monitor, whose wholesome counsels we earnestly recommend to the male and female performers of the English stage.
>
> ([Anon.] 1808: 379)

This is an indication of the contemporary appreciation of Hunt's prose style, but also of his objective and critical stance *vis-à-vis* the London stage. Hunt's monitoring attitude also earned him praise from the anonymous reviewer of the *Cabinet*, who commends Hunt for introducing impartiality and objectivity to theatrical criticism, qualities that the reviewer says are absent from most such criticism at the time ([Anon.] 1809a: 142). Hunt had stated in his first article for the *News* that impartiality was to be the keyword of his criticism:

> One novelty at least, it is trusted, will always gratify our Readers in their perusal of *THE NEWS, – an impartiality of Theatrical Criticism.* On this entertaining subject we shall usually bestow a considerable proportion of

> our time and of our Paper, and shall embrace in our strictures not only the merits of the Actors and Dramatic Writers, but the management also of the Stage itself, and all those little local proprieties, so requisite to a finished Actor, which go under the general denomination of the business of the Stage. By these means we presume that while we are entertaining our Readers, we may offer some useful hints to those who so often entertained us, and who form one of the most delightful enjoyments of a great city.
>
> (Hunt 2003: I, 4)

Hunt emphasizes once again the lack of impartiality of the contemporary press in his essay on the actor Alexander Pope: 'As to the newspapers, and their praise of this gentleman, I do not wish to repeat all the prevailing stories. Who does not know their corruption?' (Hunt 1807a: 23).[11] Hunt judiciously inserts an asterisk after 'As to the newspapers' which refers the reader to the appendix for a longer attack on the art of theatrical criticism as currently found in other newspapers; Hunt also echoes here Samuel Johnson's negative comment on the importance of actors in comparison with the freedom of critics in his *Idler* essay 'New Actors on the Theatre' (Johnson 1963). This is obviously a topic of importance for Hunt, who would still comment upon it in his 25 July 1831 *Tatler* column 'The Play-Goer': 'We do not *attack* players, dead or alive; we only criticise, and express an opinion' (Hunt 1830–2: III, 83).

Critical Essays make clear how different Hunt's style is from the standard criticism published in contemporary newspapers. Whereas the typical review is superficial in its treatment of performances, Hunt reveals a finely tuned attention to the details of an actor's performance and stage direction. Performances were more commonly described in terms of the actors' relationship with the critics than with what happened on stage, but Hunt pays scrupulous attention to the actors and the quality of their acting. In fact, as Joseph Donohue remarks, Hunt can be said to excel at describing the power of an actor's performance (Donohue 1975: 146). The choice of the actors under discussion is also innovative. Hunt declares in the preface to the *Critical Essays*:

> The second and third sections [of the *Critical Essays*] are confined to those performers, whom I regarded as the possessors of some exclusive originality. Somebody perhaps will still miss his favourite king or his favourite footman; but I have endeavoured to criticise those only who deserve applause, not those who merely obtain it.
>
> (Hunt 1807a: viii–ix)

Earlier on in the preface, Hunt comments:

> If any man, not very fond of music, will reflect a little between the acts of one of the modern comedies, he will find that his chief entertainment has

> arisen from the actors totally abstracted from the author. … It was this strange superiority of the mimetic over the literary part of the stage, of the organ in fact over it's inspirer, that determined me to criticise the actors.
>
> (Hunt 1807a: vi–viii)

The distinction between the mimetic and the literary aspects of the stage is a crucial element in Romantic re-assessment of contemporary drama. It is in this context that Hunt remains consistently interested in the actors in a play, as Lamb does in several of his theatrical essays, including his 1822–3 pieces 'On Some of the Old Actors' and 'On the Acting of Munden' (Lamb & Lamb 1903–5: II, 150–61; 175–81). In his discussion of actors, Hunt puts into practice his stated critical principles, as in this extract from his essay on the actor Pope:

> If we have just had an example of almost perfect tragedy [in the preceding essay on Siddons], we have now an instance of every fault that can make it not only imperfect but disgusting. Mr. POPE has not one requisite to an actor, but a good voice, and this he uses so unmercifully on all occasions, that it's value is lost, and he contrives to turn it into a defect. His face is as hard, as immovable, and as void of meaning as an oak wainscot, his eyes which should endeavour to throw some meaning into his vociferous declamation he generally contrives to keep almost shut, and what would make another actor merely serious is enough to put him into a passion.
>
> (Hunt 1807a: 22)

Hunt's style is sharp and straightforward; his description of Pope's defects is simultaneously witty and imaginative—and ruinous for Pope. Hunt's suggestive image of the oak wainscot, coupled with his colorful choices of words and turns of phrase, vividly recreate for his readers an experience of the performance.

Recalling this part of his career in his *Autobiography*, Hunt regrets some of the comments he made about actors in *Critical Essays*, with the striking exception of the frequent criticisms he made of John Philip Kemble: 'I think I was right … about Kemble; but I have no regret upon that score. He flourished long enough after my attacks on his majestic dryness and deliberate nothings' (Hunt 1850: I, 285). Kemble's first major theatrical work, *Macbeth Reconsidered; An Essay: Intended as an Answer to Part of the Remarks on Some of the Characters of Shakespeare*, was published anonymously in 1786 in response to Thomas Whately's *Remarks on Some of the Characters of Shakespeare* (Whately 1785). Kemble's *Macbeth Reconsidered* presents a detailed counter-argument to Whately, principally attacking Whately's characterization of Macbeth as a coward, and attempting to counter this characterization with one of Macbeth as a complex, intrepid character in the vein of Richard III.[12] The main interest of the work lies in Kemble's reading of *Macbeth* from an actor's point of view. When the book appeared, Kemble was a rising star at Drury Lane, having made his debut as Hamlet two years before.[13] He would then replace David Garrick as the leading actor of his time,[14] before being replaced himself by Edmund Kean several years later.[15] Because of Kemble's fame at the beginning of the nineteenth century, rivaled only by that of his sister Sarah Siddons, it comes as no surprise to find him as the subject of Hunt's first essay in *Critical Essays*. For Hunt, Kemble is an actor whose personal faults at times intrude in his performances, yet at other times are advantageous. Referring to Kemble's playing Penruddock in Richard Cumberland's *The Wheel of Fortune*, Hunt describes it as 'his greatest performance, and I believe it to be a perfect one' (Hunt 1807a: 8). Significantly, however, it is only a great performance because of Kemble's tendency to overact and to impose an overbearing seriousness on the character he performs: '[T]he very defect which hurts his general style of acting, that studious and important preciseness ... contributes to the strength, to the nature of *Penruddock*' (Hunt 1807a: 8). The essay then continues:

> Wherever this air of self-importance or abstraction is required, Mr. KEMBLE is excellent. It is no small praise to say of an actor that he excels in soliloquies: these solitary discourses require great judgment because the speaker has no assistance from others, and because the audience, always awake to action, is inclined during a soliloquy to seek repose in inattention. Indeed to gain the attention of an audience is always in some degree to gain their applause, and this applause must cheerfully be given to Mr. KEMBLE, who by his busy air and impressive manner always attaches importance to a speech of whatever interest or length.
>
> (Hunt 1807a: 9)

The subtlety of Hunt's criticism is evident as he cleverly disguises a negative comment on Kemble's attitude on stage as an apparent compliment. Hunt then asserts that Kemble's exaggerated attention to minute details is 'the great fault of his acting' (Hunt 1807a: 10), and ends the essay with a discussion of Kemble's very personal delivery, a topic that Hunt and others would tackle again in later articles.[16] Although Hunt praises Kemble for an understanding of the author's text, he also reproaches him for his self-indulgent effort to pronounce the words in his own manner. For the sake of novelty, and under the pretext of linguistic improvement, Kemble alters the pronunciation of certain words and the consequent result, in Hunt's view, is an amusing but pointless exercise. Furthermore, by using an apparently learned and careful system of pronunciation—what Hunt describes as a 'studious and important preciseness'—Kemble disassociates himself from the more common, popular form of expression. This, for Hunt, is a grave mistake, since it alienates a large part of the audience.[17]

Hunt's style in these essays often anticipates Hazlitt (though it does not quite rise to the level of Hazlitt's brilliant prose) and the resemblance in style hints at Hunt as a possible influence on Hazlitt, who was familiar with Hunt's criticism. One may hear such resemblance in the following extract on critics, one of the most effective passages in the *Critical Essays*:

> CRITICS are without doubt the most unpolite beings upon earth; they have no more tenderness for the faults of ladies than of gentlemen, arguing very singularly that if ladies chuse to become public characters they must endure public examination and sometimes public reproof; they say curiously enough, that their peace is not to be disturbed merely because a writer is called Mistress instead of Mister, and that they cannot be delighted even though it is an actress that plays badly and not an actor. All this is very shocking and ungallant, but then it would be more shocking if these ladies were to lose their wits for want of a little rational advice.
>
> (Hunt 1807a: 44)

Hunt is both playful and direct, here. He pretends to attack 'unpolite' critics only to reassert that theatrical criticism should always be free of any gender bias. He cleverly demonstrates that male and female actors are to be treated on the same level because they share a public status. Hunt also wittily defends his own position as an independent writer, free from the influence of the actors' popularity or the gender deference commonly found in other critics' works, as well as from personal acquaintance, a topic Hazlitt would expand upon in his 1822 essay 'Whether Actors ought to sit in the boxes?', where he declares virulently: 'Spare me this insight into secrets I am not bound to know. The stage is not a mistress that we are sworn to undress. Why should we look behind the glass of fashion? Why should we prick the bubble that reflects the world, and turn it to a little soap and water?' (Hazlitt 1930–4: VIII, 279).

Hunt's 'Rules for the Theatrical Critic of a Newspaper', first published in the *News* on 25 May 1806 and included in the appendix to the *Critical Essays*, is another instance of his sarcastic style, sharply critical. The rules consist of five sections describing what a theatrical critic 'should' do.

> *In the first place*—Never take any notice whatever of the authors of a play or of the play itself, unless it be a new one: if the author be living, it is most probable you will have no reason to speak of him more than once, and if he be not living, you have no reason to speak of him at all, for dead men cannot give dinners.
>
> (Hunt 2003: I, 14–15)

In this rule, as in the other four, Hunt's ironic tone undermines any serious reading of these rules as something other than what they are: a strong criticism of the current practices of puffing and bribery. The rules underscore the defects of theatrical critics that Hunt attacks throughout his writings on theater.

Behind this criticism lies a positive view of the role of the theater critic in influencing the popular reception of drama. Hunt has considerable confidence in the power of responsible journalism to educate a public that has not had the benefit of the kind of education afforded to the privileged classes. If the journalist can either be a conduit for popular opinion or attempt to shape that opinion, Hunt advocates the latter role, attempting to make himself something of a public educator. His style reflects this engagement; he aims principally to enrich the public's critical opinions about acting in a style that is learned but with a diction that is not elevated, to prove accessible to any audience. In addition, he repeatedly provides the reader with entertaining humorous comments, evoking familiar scenes and events from various plays performed on the London stage with which contemporary theater audiences would have been familiar. It is worth remembering that the actors under consideration in *Critical Essays* were all well known and popular. Therefore, Hunt would have found a sympathetic audience for the opening of his essay on Bannister:

> WHEN I write the name of BANNISTER, a host of whimsical forms and humourous characters seems to rise before me, and I had much rather lay down my pen and indulge myself in laughter. But there is a time for all things; laughter is a social pleasure, and as I have got nobody to laugh with me, I had better be composed.
>
> (Hunt 1807a: 60)

The last part of this passage also underscores the social element of theater going, a popular activity that drew hundreds of people together under one roof to share the ephemeral experience of a performance.

The organization of the *Critical Essays* into chapters focused on individual actors suggests how seriously Hunt treats acting as a dramatic art. In his essay on comedy, he asserts, 'I am writing not upon authors, but actors' (Hunt 1807a: 48), and he declares in the preface, 'I have endeavoured to criticise those [actors] only who deserve applause, not those who merely obtain it' (Hunt 1807a: ix). Hunt's main goal throughout *Critical Essays* is a detailed analysis of the qualities and defects of the actors under consideration, classified by genre to illustrate how their strengths and weaknesses play in certain roles. Hunt considers it his duty 'to literature and to the public' to point out failings in actors who lack one or more of the qualities necessary to the art (Hunt 2003: I, 22). Thus, he describes Henry Johnston as 'invariably too lofty, his mien becomes haughty when it should merely be steadfast, and as he possesses a very expressive countenance and a commanding figure this haughtiness has an effect peculiarly observable' (Hunt 1807a: 36). Hunt acknowledges the fact that a great character may be proud and affected and performed as such, but points out that an actor should not emphasize this character trait too much, for this excess can easily diminish the actor's performance.

Hunt's essay on Elliston is one of the best instances of the critic's independent stance. Elliston is, in Hunt's view, the greatest actor discussed in the collection, in itself a sign of Hunt's critical independence since Elliston primarily excelled at comedy at a time when tragedy was considered the highest dramatic art, and Kemble, a tragic actor, was universally praised as exemplary. Hunt goes so far as to assert that Ellison is 'the only genius that has approached [Garrick] in universality of imitation' (Hunt 1807a: 180–1), one who 'in the true inspiration of his art … excels [Kemble]' (Hunt 1807a: 182). He particularly praises Elliston's original acting style, his ability to express a feeling with his body language, which at the same time is perfectly attuned to his speech, and yet also to move from one emotion to another easily. Elliston's versatility and enthusiasm differentiates him from other actors, although his choice of comic roles diminishes his standing amongst other actors in the eye of the public: '[I]f Mr. ELLISTON performed in tragedy only, he would be thought a much better tragedian, not only because the critics would more willingly allow him his single claim, but because his comic powers would no longer present their superior contrast' (Hunt 1807a: 203).

The effective rhetoric displayed throughout *Critical Essays* is part of a prose style that was to prove characteristic of Leigh Hunt for the rest of his career. A good example of his talent as a writer in full control of his style can be found in the third introductory essay, in which Hunt discusses *Hamlet*:

> The character of Hamlet however seems beyond the genius of the present stage, and I do not see that it's personification will be easily attained by future stages; for it's actor must unite the most contrary as well as the most assimilating powers of comedy and tragedy, and to unite these powers in their highest degree belongs to the highest genius only. With all the real respect I have for a true actor, I must rank him in an inferior class both to the great painter and great musician; and neither of these inspired ones has united comic and tragic excellence. It is the pen alone, which has drawn a magic circle round the two powers, and rendered them equally obedient to the master's hand.
>
> (Hunt 1807a: 183–4)

Here Hunt sums up the inherent difficulty of performing a complex character such as Hamlet when he notes that the actor 'must unite the most contrary as well as the most assimilating powers of comedy and tragedy'.[18] Hunt views the musician and the painter as superior in their creative powers to the actor; but he argues masterfully for the supreme creativity of the writer. Hunt, who considered himself a poet above all else, unsurprisingly advocates literature over drama, painting, and music.

According to most Romantics, to perform some of Shakespeare's plays, particularly *Hamlet*, in a way that did the text justice was an impossible task.[19] Hazlitt declares that '[t]here is no play that suffers so much in being transferred to the stage' (Hazlitt 1930–4: IV, 237). Similarly, Lamb famously asserts, 'It may seem a paradox, but I cannot help being of the opinion that the plays of Shakespeare are less calculated for performance on a stage, than those of almost any other dramatist whatever' (Lamb & Lamb 1903–5: I, 99).[20] Lamb also states that he is 'not arguing that *Hamlet* should not be acted, but how much *Hamlet* is made another thing by being acted' (Lamb & Lamb 1903–5: I, 101). As Alan Richardson notes, 'Charles Lamb's paradoxical and deliberately perverse argument that Shakespeare's tragedies are better read than performed helps clarify his contemporaries' turn from the stage' (Richardson 1988: 2). Because of the common practice in the early nineteenth century of adapting plays for performance, one must take into consideration the extent to which the Shakespeare performed and viewed by the Romantics was in fact not the Shakespeare they knew as printed texts. In fact, as Greg Kucich shrewdly notes, Keats 'seemed most invigorated by Shakespeare when "Sitting Down to *Read* (my italics) *King Lear* Once Again" not when jostling into the theater to *watch* compromised versions of the play' (Kucich 1992: 65). Indeed, actors themselves often edited texts of plays to promote their interpretations of the characters, a common theatrical practice that seems to have become more common during the Romantic period. Kemble is certainly the best example of this practice since he arranged no less than forty plays, including all the Shakespearean plays he performed, making him the leading arranger of his time, with more than twice as many arrangements as Kean would make.[21]

Lamb's and Hazlitt's comments express a prejudice in favor of the printed text of Shakespeare's plays over their performances, a view shared by Hunt and Coleridge. In fact, all four writers questioned whether the stage ever could do justice to Shakespeare's greatest plays, an argument principally based on the supreme importance of the role of imagination (Bate J. 1989: 134). In Hunt's case, imagination is to be interpreted not in the Coleridgean epistemological sense, nor in Shelley's moral sense, but in a more general sense. For Hunt, imagination constitutes both a creative and interpretive process, as he points out in *Critical Essays*.

> Imagination then is the great test of genius; that which is done by imagination is more difficult than that which is performed by discernment or experience. It is for this reason, that the actor is to be estimated, like the painter and the poet, not for his representation of the common occurrences of the world, not for his discernment of the familiarities of life, but for his idea of images never submitted to the observation of the senses.
> (Hunt 1807a: 51)

Here we see the explicit articulation of Hunt's emphases upon the need to look beyond the actor's physical appearance in terms of his gestural style, his costume and his make-up. In this sense, Hunt's treatment of the actor is more concerned with a positive sense of the capacity of the audience for creative response than with the actor's mimetic ability. Furthermore, the need for the actor to internalize his role leads to an exploration of the role of imagination in performance, on the part of the actor as well as the audience. To credit actors with imagination is not the received opinion of most Romantic writers, who identify imagination with poetic creation, which in turn was historically contrasted with mimesis. Hunt's originality thus lies in his assertion that actors ('mimes') must have the creative imagination to do justice to the plays they perform. Imagination is a key term for Hunt, who also asserts the need for the audience's interpretive imagination in order to enhance the rendition of a play. Hunt explains at greater length the role of the imaginative audience in his criticism of the actor Pope's limited range of facial expression:

> [W]hen an actor's face is not exactly seen, an audience is content to supply by its own imagination the want of expression, just as in reading a book we figure to ourselves the countenance of the persons interested. But when we are presented with the real countenance, we are disappointed if our imagination is not assisted in its turn; the picture presented to our eyes should animate the picture presented to our mind; if either of them differ, or if the former is less lively than the latter, a sensation of discord is produced, and destroys the effect of nature which is always harmonious.
>
> (Hunt 1807a: 25)

Hunt exhibits a dialogic understanding of how the imagination of audience and performer interact. The parallel between imagining the actor's expression on stage and imagining 'the countenance of the persons interested' when reading clearly underscores the pre-eminence of imagination in his dramatic theory.

In asserting that actors must have the creative imagination to do justice to the plays they perform, and in including references to actors whenever he discusses dramatic theory, Hunt differs significantly from Hazlitt, Lamb, and Coleridge. In fact, Coleridge's own emphasis on reading and theorizing about Shakespeare's plays led him to focus on Shakespeare's texts rather than the performances. Coleridge's sustained interest in dramatic theory, as opposed to performance, in his lectures and in the *Biographia Literaria* is matched by the virtual absence of references to actual contemporary actors in his writings.[22] It is thus worth underscoring that in the chapter on *Bertram* in *Biographia Literaria*, Coleridge chooses not to reproduce the section of his letter to the *Courier* where he discusses Kean's performance in the role. In the letter, Coleridge acknowledges Kean's interpretation of the leading role as in accordance with the part as written (and therefore worthy of praise), but also asserts that the same excess in style in a performance of *Othello* or *Richard III* he would condemn as 'extravagance and debasement' (Coleridge S. T. 1987: I, 261).

Similarly, Lamb's strong criticism of the decision to perform a Shakespeare play rather than read it is most forceful in his comment on *Lear*, first published in Hunt's *Reflector* in 1811:

> But the Lear of Shakespeare cannot be acted. ... On the stage we see nothing but corporal infirmities and weakness, the impotence of rage: while we read it, we see not Lear, but we are Lear,—we are in his mind, we are sustained by a grandeur which baffles the malice of daughters and storms.
> (Hunt 1812a: II, 308)

Hazlitt's view is that actors cannot properly perform Shakespeare's words, as he asserts, for instance, in his *Examiner* review of Kean's performance as Richard II: 'the reader of the plays of Shakspeare is almost always disappointed in seeing them acted; and, for our own parts, we should never go to see them acted, if we were not found as critic to do so' (Hazlitt 1930–4: V, 222). Hunt, on the other hand, offers a new approach to the question of performance versus reading by associating the actors with the audience in realizing the imaginative potential of the plays. In other words, Hunt anticipates the debate on reading versus performing in his theatrical essays by stressing the importance both of active involvement on the part of the audience and of appropriate performance by the actors.

However, as Jonathan Bate observes, once imagination is considered as pre-eminent for a proper understanding of the plays, one can argue that the plays are best rendered in the imagination of the individual reader and not on stage (Bate J. 1989: 129). To a certain extent, this was to be the opinion held by most Romantic writers. The beginning of the nineteenth century witnesses a shift from a tradition of acting *and* reading, as illustrated in David Garrick's and John Philip Kemble's comments, to a new tradition of skepticism about the capacity of contemporary theater troupes to perform Shakespeare's plays properly, a skepticism evident in the comments of Coleridge, Hunt, Lamb, and Hazlitt. The recourse to new technologies of stage illusion for many plays emphasizes the crucial distinction between the visual impact of a play and its imaginative impact. Stage illusion employs various props, such as lighting effects and scenery changes, which are meant to influence the audience's physical perception of the play and the corresponding sense of illusion. The actors contribute to this stage illusion by playing with these elements and integrating them into their acting—for instance, by moving into the shadows before reciting their lines to add a touch of Gothicism.[23]

Stage illusion differs, nevertheless, significantly from the dramatic illusion of most Romantic writers. For Coleridge, the aesthetic experience taking place during a performance is dependent, to a point, on the willing and active audience awareness of illusion as illusion (Burwick 1991: 222). Hazlitt and Lamb might be said to agree with Coleridge's view here, but not Hunt. Frederick Burwick declares that the interest of the Romantics in dramatic illusion has to do with the fact that '[t]he phenomena of illusion offer insight into the ambiguities of knowledge and the frail and fallible access we have to self, others, and the world' (Burwick 1991: 303). Although I agree with Burwick, I would suggest that Hunt stands apart from the other Romantics, and from Coleridge in particular, in at least one key respect: he does not share Coleridge's philosophical interest in dramatic illusion. As Janet Ruth Heller notes, Coleridge thought that,

> [l]ike many popular novels and waxworks, the theatre merely appeals to the senses when it tries to copy reality. In contrast, by reading good plays, one can use the imagination actively to transcend the senses and the ego, to become spellbound by ennobling concepts, and to sympathize with the sufferings of other people.
>
> (Heller 1990: 91)

The Coleridgean use of imagination as a way to 'transcend the senses and the ego' is, however, not a concept that appeals to Hunt. Hunt's decision to base his dramatic criticism on his own principled response to specific dramatic performances is part of what he takes as critical 'independence'. Unlike Coleridge, Hunt does not look to the authority of philosophy as a necessary foundation for his criticism. In fact, one of the characteristics of Hunt's theatrical criticism can be illustrated in his continuing engagement with dramatic performances. Hunt shares the doubts of Coleridge, Lamb, and Hazlitt about the possibility of properly performing Shakespeare's plays, but he remains interested in the actual physical performances of these plays, primarily because he saw this as part of his role as a dramatic journalist.

Hunt's essays in the *News* and *Critical Essays* clearly convey his views on the role of the dramatic critic. He is more 'independent' than Coleridge in conceiving the critic's role as not to endorse an established authority but, so to speak, to 'vote' for or against particular performances and to give sound reasons for his opinion. By encouraging his readers to reflect on their reasons for admiring a given actor's performance, Hunt aims to make them informed and responsible members of the theatrical audience, aware of their power in giving or withholding applause. As one who empowers his readers by informing them of the principles that guide his judgment, Hunt feels that the critic's role is fundamental to ensuring the quality of contemporary theatrical performances. In the face of the new focus of popular attention on the figure of the actor, and of the power of the actor as a drawing card for theater revenues, Hunt wants to ensure that drama criticism remains impartial, free of economic biases. The role of the critic becomes especially important in light of the greatly expanded audience, which gives theaters more economic importance and thus economic power *vis-à-vis* the critics and newspaper owners.

Criticizing the absence of standardized critical rules of judgment for this new kind of theater, Hunt regularly reasserts his wish for an independent criticism. The following is taken from an article published in the *News*, which was reproduced in the appendix to the *Critical Essays*:

> It is the boast of the writer of this article that his opinions have been guided by nothing but a regard for truth, for the real pleasure of the

town, and for the literary reputation of Englishmen; and it is his happiness that these opinions have been approved by the public. … It is time to rescue the critical character of the public prints from the charge of carelessness, of ignorance, and of corruption; they are the directors of the public taste and the correctors of it's depravation, and they should study to deserve the confidence of those whom they would instruct.

(Hunt 1807a: 'Appendix' 16–7)

Hunt is extremely direct in his attacks on the press; his own criticism certainly exemplifies his wish to improve 'the critical character of the public prints'. A few years later in the *Examiner*, Hunt writes,

The effect of the drama upon real life appears to us to be of a very general cast, not a particular one; and to keep alive a certain softness and sociality of spirit, without which, among other helps, a nation might relapse into brutality.

(Hunt 1816b: 435)

Hunt views drama as one of the major social influences on the citizens of a country. Many years later, he will again acknowledge the importance of the role of the theatrical critic, and its attendant responsibilities:

Never, after I had taken critical pen in hand, did I pass the thoroughly - delightful evenings at the playhouse which I had done when I went only to laugh or be moved. I had the pleasure, it is true, of praising those whom I admired; but the retributive uneasiness of the very pleasure of blaming attended it; the consciousness of self, which on all occasions except loving ones, contains a bitter in its sweet, put its sorry obstacle in the way of an unembarrassed delight[.]

(Hunt 1850: I, 249)

As Louis Landré observes, Hunt believes in the importance of his task: since the theater is a forum that can serve to educate the public's taste and inspire its further reflections, the task of the responsible theatrical critic is to assert the value of a performance with these criteria in mind (Landré 1936: II, 104).

Hunt concludes *Critical Essays* with 'An essay on the Appearance, Causes, and Consequences of the Decline of British Comedy'.[24] Having repeatedly attacked contemporary dramatists throughout the previous essays, he now presents, in detail, what he considers their faults, beginning with a disclaimer:

The vanity of these writers, who cannot imagine that any critic should unceasingly object to their manoeuvres without personal hostility, has rendered it necessary on our part to disclaim such a feeling entirely, and we repeat, that we know nothing of these men but their dramatic

> attempts: we hope and believe that they are good private characters; but they are doing all they can to ruin the British Drama, and they must be treated as the public violators of literature.
>
> (Hunt 1807a: 'Appendix' 48)

Having pre-empted any possible attack on the charge of personal hostility, Hunt then proceeds to establish the various failings of these writers, especially their use of puns instead of wit to win applause. He also reproaches them for writing prologues and epilogues that flatter the audience and thus assure a generous response in return. To explain the current popularity of what he considers bad comedy, Hunt brings into the discussion the lack of a sufficient critical presence in the newspapers. 'The great *existing* reason', he says, 'is the mere want of critical opposition. If the newspapers were unanimous, they might overthrow the farci-comic writers in a few months' (Hunt 1807a: 'Appendix' 55). Hunt suggests that the current absence of serious theatrical criticism is due in part to the relegation of drama criticism to mere short notices in most newspapers, in order to make way for extended articles on politics, and in part to the tendency of critics themselves to write short, positive reviews reflecting too great a sensitivity to the internal politics among playwrights, theater managers, and journalists.

Later, in his *Autobiography*, Hunt would comment on his youthful inexperience as a theatrical critic, but this modesty does not do justice to the pieces collected in *Critical Essays*. Despite this slight self-deprecation, Hunt acknowledges the fact that these early essays reveal his acquaintance with the styles of Voltaire and Johnson, two important influences on him, and that they are written with more care and attention than was customary for newspaper writing at that time (Hunt 1850: I, 291). Hunt's concern about and writing of theatrical criticism was to last for close to thirty years, both in periodicals he edited himself, such as the *Examiner*, the *Chat of the Week*, or the *Tatler*, and in others, such as the *Times* or *True Sun*. His interest in theater also led him to write biographical and critical notes to his editions *The Dramatic Works of Wycherley, Congreve, Vanbrugh and Fraquhar* (1840), *The Dramatic Works of Richard Brinsley Sheridan* (1840),[25] and *Beaumont and Fletcher* (1855). He also included chapters on Marlowe, Shakespeare, Ben Jonson, Beaumont and Fletcher, and Webster in *Imagination and Fancy* (1844) and *Wit and Humour* (1846), and eventually wrote plays himself, the most famous of which is *A Legend of Florence* (1840).

Hunt's early theatrical criticism arguably marks the creation of a new kind of writing about theater, a broadening of drama criticism to include a closer attention to acting and a more serious interest in comedy. It also empowered members of the theatrical audience to think about what they saw and heard, to reserve their praise and applause for good acting, and not to hesitate to criticize what insulted their intelligence or taste. Hunt thus strongly encourages the public to follow his example and to exercise a truly critical, independent judgment.

The *Examiner*

The importance of independent judgment, expressed in the *News* and *Critical Essays*, clearly influenced Hunt's journalistic career in the *Examiner*, as demonstrated in the prospectus for this periodical (included at the back of *Critical Essays* and reprinted in the first issue of the *Examiner*). This lengthy advertisement also serves as further evidence of the socio-political implications of Hunt's theatrical criticism, the way in which *Critical Essays* constitutes the first instance of Hunt's longstanding insistence on independence from external pressures, whether they be editorial, personal, or political, and his early engagement in social and cultural issues. Hunt links critical and political independence in his choice of motto for the *Examiner*: 'Party is the madness of many for the gain of a few'. He thus effectively advertises the impartiality of his new periodical by using his current reputation as an impartial theatrical critic:

> The Gentleman who till lately conducted the THEATRICAL DEPARTMENT in the NEWS, will criticise the Theatre in the EXAMINER; and as the Public have allowed the possibility of IMPARTIALITY in that Department, we do not see why the same possibility may not be obtained in POLITICS.
>
> (Hunt 2003: I, 31)

Hunt distinguishes the *Examiner* further by describing the contemporary tendency of the press: 'The newspaper proves to be like the generality of it's species, very mean in it's subserviency to the follies of the day, very miserably merry in it's puns and it's stories, extremely furious in politics, and quite as feeble in criticism' (Hunt 2003: I, 31).[26] Hunt asserts in the conclusion of the prospectus that, just as he had cleared the way for a new, unbiased drama criticism when he started writing for the *News*, so too would he change political journalism and provide a new, neutral voice within the contemporary press with the founding of the *Examiner*.

The *Examiner* rapidly rose to success, and the sales were very strong in the first decade of the newspaper's existence, with a circulation of approximately 2200 issues by November 1808, rising to a peak of between 7000 and 8000 in the 1810s. These circulation figures are quite impressive when one bears in mind the limited numbers of copies sold by all the publications of that period; for instance, the *Edinburgh Review*'s circulation was 12,000 and the *Times*'s 8000 (Deguchi 1996: vii). This success can be ascribed in part to the shared commitment to reform of both Leigh Hunt and his brother John, and in part to Hunt's personality as editor. Indeed, Jeffrey N. Cox and Greg Kucich rightly explains that part of the success of the newspaper, both in terms of longevity and its influence, comes 'from the power of Hunt's writing, which is by turn chattily erudite and aesthetic, cleverly satirical, and filled with political rage' (Hunt 2003: I, xxxvii).[27]

The *Examiner* played a major role in the London political scene, as well as in the literary periodical world. The new weekly also had an important impact on Leigh Hunt's life and career. As Kenneth Neill Cameron notes, 'the *Examiner* became not so much a weekly paper as an institution and Leigh Hunt was transformed from an obscure poet and essayist into an influential editor, a man whose opinions were read and admired by thousands of readers week by week for some thirteen years' (Cameron 1961–70: I, 263). Hunt's periodical came to have a major influence on an entire generation of writers in the early decades of the nineteenth century, from a political as well as a literary perspective.[28] Studies devoted to Shelley, Keats, and Hazlitt frequently include a discussion of Hunt's newspaper, since it played such an important role in their writing careers. The *Examiner* also provides modern readers with the proper contextual information for Keats's and Shelley's poems, as Roe and Cameron, amongst others, have persuasively argued.[29]

The years 1808 to 1812 show Hunt rising to the peak of his career as a political journalist. Politics was so much part of Hunt's life during these years that he created a second periodical, the *Reflector*, in an attempt to present more directly the reformist view on the political issues of the day.[30] It can be argued that Hunt's political views and his repeated attacks on the Prince Regent and the Government, as expressed week after week in the pages of the *Examiner*, were bound to send him to prison, as several of his friends feared at the time. It is worth remembering that, as Robert Southey writes in an article published in 1812, the impact of weekly newspapers on the population was taken seriously by the Government since

> It is the weekly paper which finds its way to the pot-house in town, and the ale-house in the country, inflaming the turbulent temper of the manufacturer, and disturbing the quiet attachment of the peasant to those institutions under which he and his fathers have dwelt in peace. He receives no account of public affairs ... but what comes through these polluted sources.
>
> (Southey 1832: I, 132–3)

In an attempt to quell one of these polluted sources, the Government finally succeeded in getting a guilty verdict in the case of 'The King *v.* John and Leigh Hunt', their fourth attempt at sending the Hunts to prison.[31] Although the Hunts had to wait two months for their sentence, they knew that, because of the repeated attacks of the Government against the *Examiner* in the preceding years, they could not expect the verdict to be a light one. Neither did the anonymous journalist for the *Universal Magazine*, who reported in the December 1812 issue: 'from the temper of the judge [Lord Ellenborough] on the bench in delivering his charge to the jury, little lenity is expected. ... [F]rom the temper displayed on the bench, [the Hunts] cannot expect other than a rigorous administration of the law' ([Anon.] 1812: 502–3).

On 3 February 1813, Lord Ellenborough's success in pursuing his severe charge was evident, and Justice Grose announced a harsh sentence: the Hunts were each to pay a fine of £500 and be imprisoned for two years. 'At the sound of two years' imprisonment in separate gaols,' Leigh Hunt writes in his *Autobiography*, 'my brother and myself instinctively pressed each other's arm. It was a heavy blow; but the pressure that acknowledged it, encouraged the resolution to bear it; and I do not believe that either of us interchanged a word afterwards on the subject' (Hunt 1850: II, 134–5). The Hunts accepted the sentence and refused all compromise with a government that had offered to modify the sentence if there were no further political attacks in the *Examiner*.[32] In the first 'Political Examiner' written from prison, Hunt proudly declares: 'I have done my duty; I am an Englishman setting an example to my children and my country; and it would be hard, under all these circumstances, if I could not suffer any extremity rather than disgrace myself by effeminate lamentation or worse compromise' (Hunt 2003: I, 282).[33] Hunt, who went on editing the journal while in prison, continued to question the Government's actions in numerous 'Political Examiner' articles.[34] Yet, it is clear that this severe judgment by the Government had a direct impact on the public expression of reproaches and complaints about the Prince Regent. In fact, as Saul David remarks, after the Hunts' imprisonment, 'the more outspoken criticisms of the Regent tended to be anonymous—like Tom Moore's *Intercepted Letters or the Two-Penny Bag*, a collection of political squibs published in March 1813' (David 1998: 331).

Hunt's imprisonment was obviously welcome news to periodicals in favor of the Government, such as the *Quarterly Review* and the *Satirist*. The latter published the following rather witty poem in January 1814, thus attesting to Hunt's continuing fame nearly a year after his imprisonment:

A SPORTING Journalist once *Hunted* Fame
  He at a distance saw;
And, though pursuing *legal game*,
  Was *hunted* down by *Law*.

His *course* was plain and clear he thought,
  'Twas neck or nothing clearly;
The pleasures of the *Hunt* he sought,
  But paid for pleasure dearly.

Examin'd by our sapient Law,
  Which no SUCH crimes excuses,
The sportsman's doom'd for *faut pas*, [*sic*]
  In *gaol* to HUNT—the *Muses*!

([Anon.] 1814a: 63–4)

Hunt's political enemies approved of his sentence, but they did not anticipate the positive impact that Hunt's stay in Surrey Gaol would have on his position within London literary circles, including, as Jeffrey N. Cox and Greg Kucich comment, the rise of 'a new public persona, Hunt as the insolent Cockney aesthete, which would condition the writing and social practices of the second-generation romantic era writers now beginning to gather around him' (Hunt 2003: I, 277). The anonymous author of '*The* Sporting Journalist' concludes his poem with a reference to Hunt chasing the Muses in prison, and Hunt did make the most of his imposed stay to write, or expand upon, poems that would make his reputation for a long time.

Although Hunt's involvement in the *Examiner* is not addressed directly in this study, it is worth underlining that Hunt retained a keen interest in politics after his stay in Surrey Gaol. From its inception until November 1820, except during the worst stages of recurring illnesses and occasional literary business outside London, Leigh Hunt was the editor of the *Examiner*, and the author of the 'Political Examiner' articles and the theatrical reviews ('Theatrical Examiner'). Nine of the sixteen pages of an average issue of the *Examiner* are concerned with politics and 'domestic economy', and thus attest to the newspaper's main subject. Although Hunt may not have had the proper background in political science when he began writing for the *Examiner*, he rapidly showed his developing expertise and enthusiasm for the subject, as his numerous references from treatises and tracts by Swift, Bolingbroke, Sydney, Milton, Fletcher, and Bentham indicate. Hunt also took pride in defying insular prejudice in favor of a more open relationship with Europe, including France. Hunt's attention to contemporary political issues remained constant until his departure for Italy in 1822, and even after. In fact, Hunt's work on the *Liberal*, in particular the preface to the first issue and what Kevin Gilmartin call its 'verbal warfare' (Gilmartin 1996: 213), indicates his sustained political awareness. Thus, although it is clear that literature became more prominent in Hunt's life after 1813, I disagree with critics such as Carl Woodring and Mark Garnett when they argue that Hunt's personal engagement in political discussions lessened following his two-year sentence (Woodring 1962; Garnett 1997). On the contrary, as Roe has demonstrated in *John Keats and the Culture of Dissent*, Hunt remained politically engaged in the years following his imprisonment, and politics had a part in his poetry and his other literary endeavors during that time. Politics also provided the main basis for criticism against Hunt, from the publication of *The Story of Rimini* in 1816 to that of *Lord Byron and Some of his Contemporaries* in 1828.

2 1811–1816

> Thou shalt believe in Milton, Dryden, Pope;
> Thou shalt not set up Wordsworth, Coleridge, Southey;
> Because the first is crazed beyond all hope,
> The second drunk, the third so quaint and mouthey[.]
>
> Lord Byron, *Don Juan* (I, 205; Byron 1980–92: V, 74)

Most critics now consider Hunt's imprisonment for seditious libel to have been one of the most positive events of his life. If, not surprisingly for Hunt in light of his lifetime difficulty with managing money,[1] his finances did not improve during this time, in other respects he found a number of unexpected advantages in adversity. He spent much of his time in Surrey Gaol surrounded by friends and well-wishers, and he devoted hours of his enforced leisure to reading and writing. As soon as he moved into his new quarters in a two-room suite in the prison infirmary on 16 March 1813, his family moved in to stay with him for most of the duration of his imprisonment. Additional comforts followed when, as Greg Kucich notes, Hunt transformed his outer room into

> an aesthetic bower of bliss featuring wall paper of trellised roses, a sky-blue painted ceiling dotted with meandering clouds, Venetian blinds over the barred windows, wall portraits of Milton and John Hunt, a lute, a pianoforte, busts of poets, multiple bookcases, couches, and flowers, flowers everywhere.
>
> (Kucich 1999: n. pag.)

Thus redecorated, Hunt's prison suite became one of the most popular literary salons in London. Even a partial list of Hunt's guests is impressive, including, among many others, William Hazlitt, Thomas Barnes (who contributed the 'Theatrical Examiner' articles in the *Examiner* during Hunt's imprisonment), Charles Cowden Clarke, Thomas Alsager (who wrote for the *Times*), Henry Brougham (who had been the Hunts' lawyer), Charles and Mary Lamb, John Scott (editor of the *Champion*), Benjamin Robert Haydon, and Maria Edgeworth. Thomas Moore was another regular visitor, and, on 20 May

1813, he introduced Lord Byron to Hunt. The day before his visit, Byron included in his letter to Moore these famous lines:

To-morrow be with me, as soon as you can, sir,
All ready and dress'd for proceeding to spunge on
(According to compact) the wit in the dungeon—
Pray Phoebus at length our political malice
May not get us lodging within the same palace!
(Byron 1973–94: III, 49)

Ultimately, as one Hunt biographer observes, 'Hunt's imprisonment was, publicly and personally, a triumph. Deriving maximum pleasure from his study and work, [and] enjoying an ever enlarging group of friends … , he escaped what had seemed an inevitable breakdown. Moreover, he emerged as the imprisoned champion of liberty' (Blainey 1985: 73). The apparent incongruity of Hunt's time in prison—a time spent entertaining friends and working assiduously on his poetry—is even more surprising when one realizes that he actually kept on writing political articles for the *Examiner*, the very activity that had led to his imprisonment in the first place. The Government's attempt to silence Hunt eventually led him to assume an even more important role within the London radical scene, and the sales of the *Examiner* rose accordingly. The paradoxical benefits of Hunt's imprisonment for libel were not atypical: as Kevin Gilmartin notes, '[w]riters and editors who managed to continue working through their trial and imprisonment emerged with an enhanced status in the reform movement' (Gilmartin 1996: 123). Keats's sonnet 'Written on the Day that Mr. Leigh Hunt left Prison' gives poetic expression to the paradox that Hunt's imprisonment gave him a new kind of freedom:

What though, *for showing truth to flattered state,*
  Kind Hunt was shut in prison, yet has he,
  In his immortal spirit, been as free
As the sky-searching lark, and as elate.
Minion of grandeur! think you he did wait?
  Think you he naught but prison walls did see,
  Till, so unwilling, thou unturned'st the key?
Ah, no! far happier, nobler was his fate!
In Spenser's halls he strayed, and bowers fair,
  Culling enchanted flowers; and he flew
With daring Milton through the fields of air:
  To regions of his own his genius true
Took happy flights. Who shall his fame impair
  When thou art dead, and all thy wretched crew?
(ll. 1–12; Keats 1988: 41; my emphasis)[2]

Thus, not only Hunt's friends welcomed his release from prison in February 1815 but also a greatly enlarged group of readers and radical sympathizers. From a political perspective, Hunt's stay in Surrey Gaol strengthened his voice within the radical milieu, and his own convictions were confirmed by the experience; he remained ardently opposed to the Government on many topics that were discussed at great length in the 'Political Examiner' articles he wrote during his two-year imprisonment, and which he continued to produce for several years afterwards.

From a literary perspective as well, Hunt made the most of his imprisonment. He discussed literature with old friends, and his network of literary acquaintances expanded while he read and wrote poetry extensively. Several poems were published in the *Examiner*, including his beautiful series of sonnets 'To Hampstead', as well as two political poems, 'The St. James Phenomenon. Being a Surprising New Ballad, on a Most Wonderful Creature now Exhibiting in Westminster' (20 March 1814) and his 'Ode for the Spring of 1814' (17 April 1814). Hunt wrote the latter poem on hearing the news of Napoleon's abdication, and this poem provided the basis for his drama *The Descent of Liberty: A Mask*, published the following year. While in Surrey Gaol, Hunt also drafted most of *The Story of Rimini* and revised his major satirical poem, *The Feast of the Poets*, as he announces to Moore in a letter dated 20 September 1813:

> [A]t present, I have advanced only thirty-four lines [in the composition of *The Story of Rimini*] beyond the place you saw last, and have found it necessary to relieve myself from that intentness of thinking which grave composition requires, by falling in with an old plea, 'the request of friends,' and busying myself in preparing for re-publication the 'Feast of the Poets,' with additional verses and notes.
>
> (quoted in Moore 1853–6: VIII, 156)

The revised version of *The Feast of the Poets* was certainly more than just a republication: Hunt revised the original poem extensively to reflect his growing knowledge of several of his contemporary writers, and he also added numerous notes that attest to his increasing confidence as a literary critic.

The Feast of the Poets

The first version of *The Feast of the Poets* appeared in the fourth issue of the *Reflector* on 23 March 1812 and ran for 334 lines.[3] As Edmund Blunden remarks, 'it records [Hunt's] principles and tastes in development; and it was one of his many pugnacious feats for the furtherance of what he thought truth and light' (Blunden 1930: 65). In subsequent editions, Hunt expanded the poem, first to 430 lines in 1814, and then to 534 lines in 1815, the version that Rodney Stenning Edgecombe qualifies as 'an entirely pleasant poem, free and relaxed in its conduct, but never so digressive as to lose its way'

(Edgecombe 1994: 164). Although Hunt revised the poem again, issuing several more editions during his lifetime, it is fair to say that the 1815 version is the most complete. The 1832 edition is somewhat abridged, to reflect his less critical views of some of his contemporaries in his later years, as Hunt himself notes in the preface to that edition:

> To omit this poem in the present collection, appeared to me, for various reasons, improper; but *it has been altered to suit my present feelings*; and if all the hostile passages have not been left out, the retention under the circumstances, is, I think, not unwarrantable.
>
> (Hunt 2003: VI, 91; my emphasis)

In 1815 Hunt was one of the leading figures of the London political and literary scene, the editor of a famous newspaper, and something of a political hero. By 1832 Hunt was a man whose public image had been damaged by the debacle of the *Liberal* and the numerous attacks on his 1828 memoir *Lord Byron and Some of his Contemporaries*. The two versions of *The Feast of the Poets* clearly indicate Hunt's awareness of his own public situation in each case: one version is confidently critical and satirical of his contemporaries, while the other shows a more temperate and modest attitude toward them. Hunt's revisions in 1832, both of his poems and of his stance toward his reading public, were on the whole successful, as the reviews in the *Literary Gazette* and the *National Standard* indicate, the former complimenting Hunt for the revisions to his poems as improvements on the originals ([Anon.] 1832: 823), and the latter asserting that this volume 'should have a place in the library of every lover of poetry' ([Anon.] 1833: 38).

If the 1832 version of *The Feast of the Poets* found greater favor with a Victorian audience, the earlier versions were bolder and more innovative. The earliest formulation of the original verses is most probably to be found in Hunt's plan, laid out on 22 October 1810, for a poem to be called 'Groundwork of the Planet of Poets, or a Poem describing the *intermediate* State of the most Famous Bards ancient and modern, with the Rewards and Punishments'. The plan of this poem in three cantos evokes in some respects Dante's journey in the *Inferno*: a journey by the poet to the land of the departed (the planet Venus in Hunt's case) and the descriptions of the place of the poet's conversations with great poets from the past, including an account of their views of the state of things on earth and their occupations on Venus. In a similar Dantesque vein, Hunt planned to describe '[t]he reward of those whose works have had a good moral tendency, and *the punishment of those who have prostituted their genius*' (quoted in Landré 1936: II, 468).[4] By 1811 Hunt had evidently decided to write *The Feast of the Poets* instead, although his stance as arbiter and the conversational tone that he adopted in his satirical poem may have found their origins in his earlier plan.

A satire on contemporary poets and dramatic authors evidently fits into an established genre, one which 'looked back to Pope and Churchill as its main exponents,' and which, around the turn of the century, 'enjoyed an increasing vogue, occasioned by conservative reactions to the new movements and fashions' (Rutherford 1961: 20–1). The principal model for Hunt's poem, as he himself acknowledges in the 1815 preface, is John Suckling's 1637 'The Wits',[5] which begins:

> A SESSIONS was held the other day,
> And *Apollo* himself was at it (they say;)
> The Laurel that had been so long reserv'd,
> Was now to be given to him best deserv'd.
> And
> Therefore the wits of the Town came thither,
> 'Twas strange to see how they flocked together;
> Each strongly confident of his own way,
> Thought to carry the Laurel away that day.
>
> (ll. 1–8; Suckling 1971: 71)

Charles L. Squier describes Suckling's poem as being 'of considerable social interest, for it shows something of the complexity and range of the society in which Suckling moved' and also that it is 'admittedly important as a fictional-narrative work of literary criticism' (Squier 1978: 139, 140). One can make the same argument for Hunt's *Feast of the Poets*, as in fact *The Retrospective Review* did in 1824 when it asserted Hunt's *Feast* to be 'incomparably the best' of contemporary poems of a nature similar to Suckling's poem ([Anon.] 1824: 24). *The Feast of the Poets* indicates the popularity of satirical works in the Romantic period, comparable to the success of Byron's *English Bards and Scotch Reviewers* (1809) and Horatio and James Smiths' *Rejected Addresses* (Smith and Smith 1812).

In fact, Byron's *English Bards and Scotch Reviewers* is another important model for Hunt's *Feast of the Poets*, although not one acknowledged directly by Hunt.[6] As Carl Woodring observes, Byron's poem 'had two obvious aims: revenge for personal affronts and the inclusion of all poets and poetasters in vogue. Once included, a poet had to be satirized, but the ruling principle was to include those in vogue' (Woodring 1970: 154). Hunt did not adopt Byron's posture of wide-ranging condemnation, but he certainly surveyed all the popular poets of the time. Among those included are Walter Scott ('Be original, man; study more, scribble less;/Nor mistake present favour for lasting success' [ll. 180–1]); Thomas Moore ('When Moore, coming in, caught the Deity's eye,/Who gave him his hand, and said "Show me a sight/That can give a divinity sounder delight"' [ll.197–9]); Thomas Campbell ('Your versification,—pray give it invention' [l. 191]); as well as Coleridge, Wordsworth, and Robert Southey, whom I will discuss at greater length later. Hunt's inclusion of numerous authors attests to his knowledge of, and independent critical attitude toward, the literary scene of which he is himself part. They also indicate his own un-Byronic self-deprecating attitude *vis-à-vis* his own work, since he does not present himself as a poet worthy to be one of Apollo's guests.

Hunt had briefly discussed Byron's poetry in the last few pages of the notes he added to *The Feast of the Poets* in 1814, concluding that '[t]he characteristics of Lord Byron's poetry are a general vein of melancholy,—a fondness for pithy, suggesting, and passionate modes of speech,—and an intensity of feeling, which appears to seek relief in its own violence' (Hunt 2003: V, 80). Hunt had also indicated in the note his fondness for *Childe Harold's Pilgrimage*, *The Giaour*, and *The Bride of Abydos*. In 1815 Hunt added thirty-four lines devoted to Byron,[7] but he mingles his praise with critical comments on what he now views as an undercurrent of 'misanthropy' in the 'melancholy' that attracted his earlier attention:

> "Pray how came misanthropy into *your* head?
> I suspect (it is true), that in all which you tell us
> Of robbers, and rakes, and such terrible fellows,
> There's something mere scorn could have never devised,
> And a sorrow-wise charity roughly disguised;
> But you must not be always indulging this tone;
> You owe some relief to our hearts and your own;
> For poets, earth's heav'n-linking spirits, were born,
> What they can, to amend,—what they can't, to adorn[."]
> (ll. 229–37; Hunt 1923: 150)

Hunt refers to the oriental tales and voyages that first captivated him when he says of Byron's laurel that it 'with turk's-cap and cypress was mixed' (l. 435). Hunt's anapestic verse lends itself well to the tone here, conveying in his own way the sort of offhand ease Byron himself could affect, as these lines about Byron's nobility show: 'But the fact is, that what with your courts and your purses,/I've never done well with you lords who write verses' (ll. 243–4).[8]

The most substantial change made to the poem published in the *Reflector* as it appeared in the 1814 version was the addition of notes. As Jonathan Wordsworth asserts, '[t]hough more than a hundred lines of verse were added to *The Feast*, they altered the tone very little. It is the hundred pages of additional notes that transform the work' (Wordsworth J. 1996: 145–6). An early review published in the *Champion* underlines the literary value of Hunt's critical prose: 'Of the notes we regret that we have not room to say more than that they display the justest principles of criticism, both as to poetry and versification' ([Anon.] 1814b: 62). Similarly, the *Monthly Review* emphasizes the usefulness of the notes, stating that

> [they] contain a variety of strictures which may be read with profit by those persons who are the subjects of them. They are, however, often too keen to be pleasant: but the most satirical strokes of a man of genius and discernment are of real value, and ought not to be contemptuously

scouted. Mr. Hunt's notes may be considered as lectures for the modern school of poetry.

([Anon.] 1814d: 103)

Hunt's notes testify to his desire to be taken seriously as a literary critic: he elaborates on various lines from the poem and transforms a witty line into a sharp analysis of an author's strengths and weaknesses. Indeed, from the perspective of literary criticism, the notes remain probably the most important section of *The Feast of the Poets* because they anticipate many of the views on prosody, politics, and literature that Hunt would develop at greater length in his literary essays in the *Examiner* in the following years. The notes also indicate Hunt's high regard for most of the writers under consideration, as well as his lofty critical standards; a recurrent theme is that of disappointment with the waste of evident talent. Hunt's annotations to his own poem highlight the symbiotic relationship between prose and poetry in many of his other works as well. His critical voice infiltrates his poetical productions and usually finds expression in the lengthy prefaces he attaches to them, or, in the case of *The Feast of the Poets*, in his notes. At the same time, Hunt may have come to feel that, as more of his views found fuller expression in his prose essays, they were no longer needed as attachments to this poem, and he thus removed them from the 1832 version. However, it was most likely their sharply critical tone that led him to remove the notes, another sign of Hunt's attempt to temper his satire to please his audience.

To provide a proper context for his 'lectures for the modern school of poetry', Hunt refers throughout to illustrious writers such as Milton, Dryden, and Spenser, and argues that the present generation of poets cannot claim to be equally deserving of praise. Pope, perhaps unsurprisingly, is not treated as one of these illustrious predecessors:

But ever since Pope spoil'd the ears of the town
With his cuckoo-song verses, half up and half down,
There has been such a doling and sameness,—by Jove,
I'd soon have gone down to see Kemble in love.[9]

(ll. 17–20; Hunt 2003: V, 33)

Hunt attaches a long note to these lines where he discusses the charge of 'monotonous and cloying versification' against Pope, and he concludes: 'Let the varieties, like all the other beauties of a poet, be perfectly unaffected: but passion and fancy naturally speak a various language; it is monotony and uniformity alone that are out of nature' (Hunt 2003: V, 43, 47). (The issue of poetical language and its relationship to a 'natural' way of expression would come again to the foreground when Hunt published *The Story of Rimini* two years later; Hunt's own attempt at a 'natural' diction incurred attacks upon its innovative incongruities in language.)

Reading the notes of *The Feast of the Poets*, one cannot but agree with the anonymous reviewer for the *Analectic Magazine* who comments that Hunt allows himself to express 'the boldest literary and critical opinions with the most amusing originality and self confidence' ([Anon.] 1814e: 244).[10] Hunt speaks in a self-consciously authoritative fashion in the notes about the writers under consideration in *The Feast of the Poets*, even such popular poets as Thomas Moore, Robert Southey, and Walter Scott. Scott comes in for special criticism, not only for his politics but also for his style ('he wants originality and a language' [Hunt 2003: V, 58]). Sometimes Hunt uses a note to clarify his elliptically brief comments in the poem. For instance, he explains why he chooses to ask Spencer, Montgomery, and Rogers to come back for tea rather than stay for the feast: although he values these three writers, as Apollo's gentle rebuke shows, he wishes them to be more dedicated to their muse (Hunt 2003: V, 50). Or he uses a note to expand his views, as in the case of George Colman the Younger: 'He has been prodigiously overrated in his time, partly perhaps from his real superiority to the Dibdins and Reynoldses as a writer of huge farces, and partly from the applauses of a set of interested actors and gratuitous playwrights, whom he has helped to spoil in return' (Hunt 2003: V, 49). Hunt's comments here are reminiscent of his criticism in the *News* and in the 'Theatrical Examiner' articles faulting the usual reviews of contemporary playwrights for their lack of a critical perspective.

Throughout the work, although there is an undeniable, and understandable, sarcastic element to his view of his contemporaries, Hunt claims in his preface to the first two editions that '[w]hat praise or censure [the author] may have bestowed on any one, has at least the merit of being sincere' (Hunt 2003: V, 31). Yet, as Louis Landré points out, while Hunt demonstrates his critical independence in attacking the major writers of the day, he also exposes himself to retaliation (Landré 1936: I, 131). His sincerity had its costs, and he later came to regret the publication of the early versions of *The Feast of the Poets*. In the 1832 version, Hunt chooses to make his judgments less personal and less passionate (if not less sincere), in the hope of assuaging the various enmities to which the earlier versions gave rise. The new tone is evident in Hunt's preface to the 1832 volume:

> I acknowledge … that a young author was presumptuous in pronouncing judgment upon older men, some of whom made me blush afterwards with a better self-knowledge. I can only offer in excuse, that I had not at the time suffered enough myself, to be aware of the pain to be given in this way; and that I was a young student, full of my favourite writers, and regarding satire as nothing but a pleasant thing in a book.
>
> (Hunt 2003: VI, 91)

In a similar vein, Byron wrote to Coleridge on 31 March 1815, six years after the initial publication of *English Bards and Scotch Reviewers*:

> You mention my 'Satire,' lampoon, or whatever you or others please to call it, I can only say, that it was written when I was very young and very

> angry, and has been a thorn in my side ever since; more particularly as almost all the persons animadverted upon became subsequently my acquaintances, and some of them my friends, which is 'heaping fire upon an enemy's head,' and forgiving me too readily to permit me to forgive myself. The part applied to you is pert, and petulant, and shallow enough; but, although I have long done every thing in my power to suppress the circulation of the whole thing, I shall always regret the wantonness or generality of many of its attempted attacks.
>
> (Byron 1973–94: IV, 286)

Byron did prevent any further reprinting of his poem, to James Cawthorn's great regret.[11] Cawthorn had published with considerable success four editions of the poem between March 1809 and December 1811, as John Cam Hobhouse indicates in a letter to Byron dated 15 August 1810: 'I have no doubt to find Cawthorne preparing another [edition of *English Bards*] when I get home, as I hear the satire is in great Circulation' (Hobhouse 1984: 44). Cawthorn tried unsuccessfully to get Byron's approval for a new edition in 1812, and again 1814.[12] Thus, Cawthorn's motive in publishing Hunt's *Feast of the Poets* may have been the hope of another publishing success with a satirical poem on contemporary literary figures.

Cawthorn first met Hunt in the spring of 1813 when he visited him in Surrey Gaol. At first glance, Cawthorn's visit may have appeared to be simply one among many visits from the world of literary publishing. Yet, in a letter to his wife, Marianne, dated 27 May 1813, Hunt indicates that he believed Cawthorn had some specific purpose for his visit: 'I rather suspect that in addition to what [Cawthorn] knows of me in common with the rest of the public, he has heard something favourable respecting my poetical powers from Lord B' (Hunt 1938: 77). In the same letter, Hunt notes that he showed Cawthorn some lines from *The Story of Rimini*, that Cawthorn expressed some interest in publishing the poem, and that he agreed to advance Hunt some money.[13] On 7 June, Hunt reported another visit from Cawthorn,

> who has kept me some time looking over a catalogue of Italian books, a heap of which he is going to get me, merely for my study for a little while—purchases are not among my dreams at present; but he shows every readiness to help me with my poem, and has already brought me a multitude of authors to which I wished to refer.
>
> (Hunt 1862: I, 90)

Landré wonders whether Hunt was trying to either repay Cawthorn his money or make him wait when he gave him the manuscript of the revised edition of *The Feast of the Poets* on 28 October 1813 (Landré 1936: I, 82). I would suggest that Cawthorn had a genuine interest in *The Feast of the Poets* because of the nature of the poem and the potential publishing success of literary satires, as he had experienced four years earlier when he published Byron's poem. Cawthorn was also very much aware of Hunt's public position at the time, and he probably hoped to take advantage of it. On the title page of his edition of *The Feast of the Poets* the words 'By the Editor of the Examiner' were given, for instance, a prominent place. Since, in the words of Paul Magnuson, 'Title pages are the locations of public signatures' (Magnuson 1998: 138), Hunt's 'public signature' as 'The Editor of the Examiner' underscores his current position of distinction in the literary and political worlds. This technique proved successful to some extent, and the reviews in the *Champion* and the *Monthly Review* mentioned Hunt's political position at the time. the *Champion* reviewer argues that, with the publication of *The Feast of the Poets*, Hunt has shown that

> he can write poetry and criticism, with as much skill as he can treat the drier business of the state. This gentleman has distinguished himself for several years, by the ingenuity, the discrimination, the honesty, and magnanimity of his political writings.
>
> ([Anon.] 1814b: 62)

In addition, the *Monthly Review* comments: 'though his body is in limbo (for he dates from the Surrey Jail,) his mind expatiates with the most unbounded freedom, and his sentiments are expressed with a boldness and energy of which we have few examples' ([Anon.] 1814d: 100). However, the anonymous reviewer for the *Satirist, or Monthly Meteor* evidently did not approve of Hunt's fame, and begins his article: 'We were always of the opinion that Mr. Leigh Hunt, the Editor of the Examiner, was a very silly fellow: in politics, a drivelling man-milliner; and in literature, an empty coxcomb' ([Anon.] 1814c: 327). As Gary Dyer remarks, 'the conservative political bias of many such readers precluded the possibility of fairness' (Dyer 1997: 87). The *Satirist* piece is thus an early instance of the reviewing practice (found in other journals and in regard to other authors as well) that Hunt would experience with more far-reaching consequences after the publication of *The Story of Rimini*: the political opinion of the reviewer sways his judgment of the literary quality of the work under consideration. Thus, whereas the *Champion* had praised Hunt's style and poetical abilities, and the *Monthly Review* had stressed his sound critical judgment, the *Satirist* reviewer sums up his view of the poem in a couple of very acerbic sentences: 'The Feast of the Poets is altogether about as despicable a performance as could well be produced. It is flimsy, it is feeble, unsustained, and impertinent' ([Anon.] 1814c: 337). As for the authors to whom Hunt refers in the poem, some received its publication favorably, particularly Byron and Moore. The former wrote to Hunt on 9 February 1814 to thank him for his note, and added a postscript: 'Since this letter was written I have been at your text which has much *good* humour in every sense of the word' (Byron 1973–94: IV, 51). The latter wrote to his mother in early 1814:

I wish I could send you Hunt's Feast of the Poets, just re-published, where I am one of *the four* admitted to *dine* with Apollo; the other three, Scott, Campbell, and Southey. Rogers, very unfairly, is only 'asked to tea.' I am particularly flattered by praise from Hunt, because he is one of the most honest and candid men I know.

(Moore 1853–6: II, 59)

The anonymous reviewer for the *Satirist* thought nothing of Hunt's honesty, and considered the inclusion of Moore simply based on the fact that he had himself paid a compliment to the Hunts in his *Intercepted Letters* ([Anon.] 1814c: 333–4),[14] a reference that is but one of a number of occasions, as Jeffrey N. Cox notes, where poets 'signalled their alliances in print' (Cox 2003: 64).

An American edition of *The Feast of the Poets* appeared in New York in the summer of 1814 from the publishers Cornelius S. Van Winkle and Charles Wiley.[15] That the edition was published in New York rather than in Philadelphia or Boston was quite unusual at the time, since the latter two cities were the leading centers for republications of British works.[16] John Howard Payne states, in a letter addressed to Hunt on 6 March 1815, that to be published, reviewed, and known in America was to gain some indication of one's larger and more lasting literary appeal:

[T]he ocean, which, with regard to literary fame is like the division between two ages, may afford you the means of comparing your estimation with your cotemporaries [*sic*] on the one side, and posterity on the other; or, in plainer words, prove how much of your fame you may be indebted to localities, and how much to abstract excellence.

(quoted in Hunt 1999: 61)

Although American critical opinions were not often highly regarded in England, Payne has a point when he suggests that a British work published in America would be judged more fairly on its literary merits rather than on the personal and political connections of its author. However fiercely Hunt himself tried to maintain his independence in his own work, Hunt's reviewers, both those favorable and those hostile to his work, were doubtless influenced by his politics. Consequently, the *Analectic Magazine* review of the American edition of *The Feast of the Poets* should offer a reading of the poem free of partisan spirit. Published in the 1814 September issue, this mixed review ends with the statement that

this volume must not be taken with overstrained expectation, or read with the microscopic eye of fastidious criticism. If these conditions are honestly complied with, we do not hesitate to promise the good-humoured reader that he will find *The Feast of the Poets* an elegant repast of literary luxury.

([Anon.] 1814e: 248)

The reviewer sums up adequately a balanced and unprejudiced appraisal of Hunt's poem: it is not written in an elevated style and the poetry is more playful than ponderous; and yet, if approached as a light poem with no exaggerated claims to its own profundity, it reads very well and offers an appraisal of the work of Hunt's contemporaries based on honest and independent judgment.

Whatever critical success *The Feast of the Poets* received in England and in America, the sales of the first edition were not good. Hunt, again pressed for money, had to look for another publisher in an attempt to reissue the poem. In the spring of 1815, he transferred the remaining 250 copies to Gale, Curtis, and Fenner, who reprinted the poem with their names on the title page but in a version otherwise identical to the 1814 imprint.[17] The relationship between Hunt and the publishers Gale and Fenner was evidently good enough for them to give him a large advance for the new edition of *The Feast of the Poets*. It appeared in July 1815, this time with his name on the title page and the words 'Second edition, amended and enlarged'. The 1815 volume still kept some indication of Hunt's political position, with the addition of several poems referring to his imprisonment and his political opinion, including 'To T. M. Alsager, esq. With the Author's Miniature, on Leaving Prison', 'Politics and Poetics', and 'National Song'.

However, this second edition did not sell well either, and Hunt's share of the profit was only £20.12.8 by the end of 1815, in addition to his £250 advance. Gale and Fenner then asked Hunt to reimburse part of their advance. He wrote them on 18 December 1815 that he was unable to do so, but that he hoped to get enough money from the forthcoming sales of *The Story of Rimini* (Landré 1936: I, 87). Though *The Story of Rimini* did not sell well either, by November 1816 Hunt was eventually able to pay the remaining £250 he owed Gale and Fenner, 'those knaves in Paternoster Row' as he would eventually describe them in a letter to Charles Ollier, dated 26 November 1816 (quoted in Landré 1936: I, 88).

Hunt's attempt to make some money with the publication of *The Feast of the Poets* in a revised version, first in 1814 and then in 1815, proved unsuccessful in the end. Instead, it led to more debts and the loss of two potential publishers for his works. Although the poem created a certain amount of personal resentment toward Hunt, it remains an important document for Hunt's critical views on several Romantic writers, especially the so-called Lakers.

Southey and Coleridge

In the first three versions of *The Feast of the Poets*, Hunt writes:

> When all on a sudden, there rose on the stairs
> A noise as of persons with singular airs;
> You'd have thought 'twas the Bishops or Judges a coming,
> Or whole court of Aldermen hawing and humming,

Or Abbot, at least, with his ushers before,
But 'twas only Bob Southey and two or three more.
(ll. 224–29; Hunt 2003: V, 37–8)[18]

The importance accorded to Southey, arriving with Coleridge and Wordsworth (these two not even mentioned by name in the earliest version of these lines) and being addressed by Apollo as the head of the trio, is not unusual for the time. Francis Jeffrey had already grouped Southey with Wordsworth and Coleridge in his October 1802 review of *Thalaba* ([Jeffrey] 1802), and again in his April 1808 review of Crabbe's *Poems*, where he derides the works of 'the Wordsworths, and the Southeys, and Coleridges, and all that misguided fraternity' ([Jeffrey] 1808: 132). Byron had also attacked the Lake poets in *English Bards and Scotch Reviewers*, with Southey at their head, and he famously repeated this attack in *Don Juan*.[19] Hunt follows his contemporaries in treating Southey as linked to Coleridge and Wordsworth, but he demonstrates his independence when he refers favorably to Southey's poetry in the *Reflector* version of *The Feast of the Poets*.[20] Speaking through the voice of the narrator, he declares of Southey: 'As soon as he saw him, Apollo seemed pleased' (l. 169; Hunt 1812a: II, 319). Hunt was indeed pleased enough with Southey's poetry to make him one of the four poets whom Apollo crowns and invites to join his feast. However, Hunt's critical view of Southey's political opinions and acceptance of the laureateship (in 1813) led him to qualify his positive representation of Southey by adding several negative references in the notes attached to *The Feast of the Poets*. For instance, Hunt annotated the second line just quoted in the 1814 version of the poem: 'When this line was written, Mr. Southey had not quite thrown off the mask of independence, nor accepted those meaner laurels which Apollo would have had reason to disdain' (Hunt 2003: V, 62). Hunt's tone in describing Southey grows harshly censorious, not only in this note concerning Southey specifically, but also in other notes throughout the volume. In the note on Thomas Campbell, Hunt declares himself 'disgusted with the puerilities and affectations of Mr. Southey' (Hunt 2003: V, 59). In the note on the Lake poets, Hunt criticizes Southey for having accepted an office under a government which ties up his independence, as well as for being 'one of the pensioned reviewers in the Quarterly' (Hunt 2003: V, 61). And in his note on Byron, Hunt mentions the political allusions to be found in *Joan of Arc* and writes that 'they are such as should make the Laureat and his friends cautious how they resented other people's opinions and dealt about epiphets of indignity' (Hunt 2003: V, 76). Thus Hunt's notes make clear that, however much praise Hunt may have had for some of Southey's poems in 1811, by 1814 he is sharply critical of what he views as Southey's turncoat politics and his desertion of his former republican ideals. In Hunt's eyes, Southey's work with the *Quarterly Review* represents collusion with the Government, and his acceptance of the title Poet Laureate confirmed his new political position.

Southey's laureateship proved to be the subject of Hunt's repeated commentary, both in the pages of the *Examiner* and in his notes to *The Feast of the Poets*.

Apart from his views of Southey, Hunt was already critical of the establishment of the office of Poet Laureate. 'The abolition of the Laureatship could do no violence to any one, not even to the abhorrers of innovation', Hunt declares in the *Examiner* on 15 August 1813. '[I]t would become the character of the country; and is desirable for putting a stop, if on no other account, to the remarks which sensible foreigners as well as natives are inclined to make upon it' (Hunt 1813a: 514). Hunt wrote another article on the same subject containing similar criticism two weeks later (Hunt 1813b).[21] Therefore, when Southey was appointed Poet Laureate in September 1813, Hunt began a mini-campaign against him in the pages of the *Examiner*, criticizing his poetry, and his political views.[22] On 26 September 1813, Hunt announces in the 'Political Examiner': '[A]midst the shouts of men of the world, and the blushes of the honest and the consistent, [the Laureateship crown] is planted on the primitive head of Mr. ROBERT SOUTHEY!' (Hunt 1813c: 609). To explain Southey's appointment, Hunt refers specifically to his allegiance with John Wilson Croker and the *Quarterly Review*, a subject he would take up again in the notes to *The Feast of the Poets*. During the following nine years, several articles and poems mocking Southey and his writings appeared in the *Examiner*, culminating with the publication of Byron's *Vision of Judgment* in the *Liberal* in 1822.[23] Nevertheless, Hunt still includes Southey among the (now) eight poets chosen by Apollo in the 1815 version of *The Feast of the Poets*, even if he is still quite derisive about Southey's laureateship:

> Bob walked at the head with a tattered bay crown,
> And looked such a compound of courtier and clown,
> Such a thing of pure nature that *should* have been true,
> . . .
> When lo, as poor Bob was collecting his wit,
> The thing on his head, as if seized with a fit,
> Began crackling, and splitting, and writhing about,
> And so in a flash and a vapour went out.
>
> (ll. 265–7, 271–4; Hunt 1923: 151)

Hunt mixes humor and politics when he describes Southey's laurels disappearing suddenly in a comically melodramatic display of pyrotechnics after hinting at the King's own role in Southey's appointment, and the poor quality of his choice ('a tattered bay crown/And looked such a compound of courtier and clown'). For Hunt, Southey is a man whose role combines that of fool and royal sycophant.

Notwithstanding his praise for some of Southey's poems, Hunt had serious criticisms against him as a poet and a political man, criticisms that he expressed in *The Feast of the Poets* and elsewhere. In a similar vein, his appraisal of Coleridge and Wordsworth was also mixed. In Hunt's estimation, as George D. Stout remarks, 'they both start from a common point of unjustified deprecation; but … Wordsworth rises very quickly to a peak of admiration, from which he slowly declines through the long later years of his (and Hunt's) life. Coleridge, on the other hand, rises by degrees to a pre-eminence from which he never declines' (Stout 1957: 73).

In the preface to his edition of Coleridge's *Table Talk*, Carl Woodring notes that 'Leigh Hunt was interested in few of Coleridge's subjects outside belles-lettres and the political opinions that Coleridge opposed to his own' (Coleridge S. T. 1990: I, li). Coleridge's politics were associated with Southey's, whose political views Hunt roundly contested. As Paul Magnuson remarks, '[f]rom their early associations as objects of parody and ridicule in the *Anti-Jacobin* to Coleridge's defense of Southey in the *Biographia*, they are intimately linked as the pair of radical poets who turn their coats' (Magnuson 1998: 137). Just as he had openly criticized Southey's change of political opinion from that of his early radical days in the 1790s in the pages of the *Examiner*, Hunt had little respect for Coleridge's political views when he wrote *The Feast of the Poets*.

Coleridge's own opinion of Hunt's politics was not very favorable either during the 1810s, when he associated Hunt with Cobbett and with various other journalistic figures known for their radical politics and anti-religious discourses. One instance of Coleridge's views on the matter appears in a letter to T. G. Street, dated 22 March 1817:

> It is for this reason [i.e. 'The Root of the Evil is *a Public*'], that I entertain toward the Jeffrieses, Cobbetts, Hunts, and all these creatures—and to the Foxites, who have fostered the vipers—a feeling more like Hatred than I ever bore to other Flesh and Blood. So clearly do I see and always have seen, that it must end in the suspension of Freedom of all kind. Hateful under all names these wretches are most hateful to me as Liberticides.
>
> (Coleridge S. T. 1956–71: IV, 714)

The political differences between Coleridge and Hunt extended to a personal hostility when Hunt reprinted Coleridge's early 'Fire, Famine, and Slaughter', and published Hazlitt's hostile reviews of Coleridge's works in 1816.[24] Hazlitt's reviews of *Christabel* and *The Statesman Manual* in the *Examiner*, on 2 June and 29 December 1816 respectively, were the cause of serious irritation for Coleridge, who bitterly complained of Hazlitt's review of *Christabel* in a letter to Hugh J. Rose, dated 17 September 1816:

> There has been a most brutal attack, as unprovoked as it is even to extravagance false, on me both as a man and an author, in the Examiner—written by a man named William Hazlitt, whom I befriended for several years with the most improvident kindness when he was utterly friendless ... Every one particular which he has put down he *knows* to be false. But what can one do?
>
> (Coleridge S. T. 1956–71: IV, 669–70)

Since Hunt was the editor of the *Examiner*, Coleridge assumed that he endorsed Hazlitt's opinions, although Hunt did not in fact always agree with Hazlitt on literary matters or theatrical criticism. Yet, since Hunt himself associated Southey's politics with those of his editor at the *Quarterly Review*, the same association of author with editor could understandably be expected of Coleridge.

Hunt states in his *Autobiography* that he did not have 'the good fortune to know much of [Coleridge] personally' (Hunt 1850: II, 222), but he knew Coleridge's works and views.[25] While discussing what he considers to be a bad stage adaptation by Frederic Reynolds of August von Kotzebue's play *The Virgin of the Sun* in the 'Theatrical Examiner' for 9 February 1812, Hunt makes a tellingly hostile reference to Coleridge, after giving several reasons for his negative view of the play:

> [I]n a word, such cant of every description, that they have no more pretence, or rather just about *as much* pretence, to stand in the same rank with true and triumphant genius, as the ravings of a diseased idleness have to be accounted oracles of wisdom, or the Lectures of Mr. COLERIDGE to render him worthy of the Poets he pretends to analyze.
>
> (Hunt 1812b: 91)

Hunt bases his criticism of Coleridge on the lecture on Shakespeare he attended a few weeks earlier, the only lecture delivered by Coleridge that he would actually attend. An echo of this rather harsh comment on Coleridge's lectures is also present in the *Reflector* version of *The Feast of the Poets*, and, as J. R. de J. Jackson underscores, it 'touches on the discrepancy between the public Coleridge and the private one' (Jackson 1968: 6):

> And Coleridge, they say, is excessively weak;
> Indeed he has fits of the painfulest kind;
> He stares at himself and his friends, till he's blind;
> Then describes his own legs, and claps each a long stilt on;
> And this he calls *lect'ring* on 'Shakspeare and Milton.'
>
> (ll. 244–8; Hunt 1812a: II, 320)

These lines were never reprinted as part of the poem, though Hunt did include them in one of the notes to *The Feast of the Poets* in his 1860 *Poetical Works*, where he added the following comment:

> The lectures alluded to, though not wanting in masterly passages, had been counted failures upon the whole; and the only one which I heard (the first, I think) had been singularly such, being little more than the promise of a better next time. The poet, with his usual dilatoriness, had either not properly prepared himself, or trusted too much to his admirable extemporaneous powers, which may have been daunted by his having to address an audience not entirely presenting familiar faces.
>
> (Hunt 1860: 442)

This is not, however, an unusually harsh judgment on Coleridge's lecturing style, since many of his contemporaries held similar views. The same was said of his series of lectures at the Royal Institution in 1808 where, in Lawrence Wynn's words,

> [Coleridge] might or might not appear; he might or might not be prepared, and he would not be confined by an announced subject, intermixing literary criticism with metaphysics and digressions upon digressions. At his worst he might be rambling and dull; at his best even his apologies were charming, as voice, manner, language, and learning converged in eloquence. Well-known by this time as poet and talker, he was widely enough advertised as lecturer for Leigh Hunt to satirize him as such in his *Feast of the Poets*.
>
> (Wynn 1951: 222)[26]

Earlier in the *Reflector* version of the poem, Hunt describes the arrival of Southey, Wordsworth, and Coleridge. The main thrust here is the criticism of Coleridge, rather than of Southey, when Hunt writes of Apollo:

> But as he had settled it not to be teaz'd
> By all the vain rhymers from bed-room and brook,
> He turn'd from the rest without even a look;
> For Coleridge had vex'd him long since, I suppose,
> By his idling, and gabbling, and muddling in prose[.]
>
> (ll. 170–4; Hunt 1812a: II, 319)

Hunt kept these last two lines in the 1814 and 1815 versions of the poem, but removed them in the friendlier 1832 version, where he describes Coleridge as a 'fine dreamer, with lutes in his rhyme' (Hunt 1923: 708). In the 1860 version, Hunt changed this line to 'And Coleridge, whose poetry's poetry's self' (Hunt 1923: 709), which remains the most succinct positive appreciation of Coleridge's poetry by Hunt. Later in life, Hunt became very familiar with Coleridge's poetry, which he enjoyed enormously, as this comment from *Imagination and Fancy* (1844) illustrates: '[Coleridge's] poetry is so beautiful, and was so quietly content with its beauty, making no call on the critics, and receiving hardly any notice, that people are but now beginning to awake to a full sense of its merits' (Hunt 2003: IV, 92).[27] Hunt was in fact himself amongst those who did not appreciate Coleridge's poems at the time of their first publication, and he actually made quite disparaging comments about him in *The Feast of the Poet*. Nevertheless, Hunt defends his criticism in a note he appended to the poem in 1814:

> Mr Coleridge is a man of great natural talents, as they who most lament his waste of them, are the readiest to acknowledge. Indeed it is their conviction in this respect, which induces them to feel the waste as they do;

> and if Apollo shews him no quarter, it is evidently because he looks upon him as a deserter. Of his poetical defects enough will be said in speaking of those of Mr. Wordsworth; and if as much cannot be said of his kindred beauties, it is rather perhaps because he has written less and is a man of less industry, than because he does not equal the latter in genius. The allusion in the text is to his strange periodical publication, called the Friend.
>
> (Hunt 2003: V, 63)[28]

Hunt makes two main points here: that he considers Coleridge indolent and that he believes that in point of poetic genius there may be no qualitative distinction between Wordsworth and Coleridge, only that Coleridge is poetically less productive and industrious.

Hunt had heard Coleridge recite 'Kubla Khan' at Lord Byron's house on 10 April 1816 (Hunt 1850: II, 228), and was enthusiastic enough, though still quite critical, about his poetry by 24 July 1817 to ask Francis Jeffrey for permission to review *Sibylline Leaves* in the *Edinburgh Review*. 'I dislike [Coleridge's] tergiversation and his subtleties', Hunt writes, but then goes on to expound a more nuanced appreciation of his complex nature:

> I *admire* his genius, but not the manner in which, upon the whole, he has used it; I think him a martyr to indolence, to extremes, to disappointed enthusiasm, to a ready metaphysical faculty of over-refining and talking on any side of any subject; and from all this, perhaps I may say, that I am impartial, and should judge him fairly.
>
> (Hunt 1862: I, 102)

One finds here yet another reference to Coleridge's indolence. One may also observe that, in what is probably the only instance of John Wilson and Hunt sharing an opinion, Wilson also complains of Coleridge's indolence in his review of *Biographia Literaria*: '[Coleridge] rambles from one subject to another in the most wayward and capricious manner; either from indolence, or ignorance, or weakness, he has never in one single instance finished a discussion' ([Wilson] 1817: 5).[29]

Hunt would begin to advocate the superiority of Coleridge's poetical talent over that of Wordsworth only a year later, in 1818 in the preface to *Foliage*. Although Wordsworth is still the dominant presence in the reference to the famous Lake School, this is the first written instance of Hunt's change of mind regarding Coleridge's poetry. Hunt writes about the downfall of the French School of Poetry and puts forward three reasons for its demise. The first reason has to do with 'the political convulsions of the world'; the second is 'the revived inclination for our older and great school of poetry'. 'The third, and not the least', he advances,

> was the accession of a new school of poetry itself, of which Wordsworth has justly the reputation of being the most prominent ornament, but

> whose inner priest of the temple perhaps was Coleridge,—a man who has been the real oracle of the time in more than one respect, and who ought to have been the greatest visible person in it, instead of a hopeless and dreary sophist.
>
> (Hunt 1818a: 10–11)

The 'hopeless and dreary sophist' comment recalls Hunt's remark in his letter to Jeffrey about Coleridge's 'ready metaphysical faculty', and indicates how much he disapproved of that aspect of Coleridge.[30] It is worth noting that Hunt is concerned primarily with Coleridge's poetry here and not with his dramatic works, which he had praised very highly in an article about tragic actors published in 1815, in which he proclaims that 'it may be asserted, not only that Mr. COLERIDGE's *Remorse* has been the only tragedy touched with real poetry for the last fifty years, but that there has been no complete production of the kind since the time of OTWAY' (Hunt 1815b: 89).

After a reference to Coleridge still 'strifl[ing] with his poetical as he has done with his metaphysical talent' in his 1817 review of Keats's *Poems* (Hunt 2003: II, 116), and a brief mention of *The Rime of the Ancient Mariner* in his 1819 *Indicator* essay 'A Tale for Chimney Corner' (Hunt 1819c), Hunt's appreciation of Coleridge's poetry publicly changed for the better in his fourth 'Sketches of the Living Poets', published in the *Examiner* on 21 October 1821, a revised appraisal which Hunt also reprinted in *Lord Byron and Some of His Contemporaries* (1828). His opinion of Coleridge continues to improve with time, particularly with regard to Coleridge's poetry, and several references in Hunt's letters and works published between 1830 and 1850 reflect his amended views.[31]

William Wordsworth

Of all the poets Hunt discusses in *The Feast of the Poets*, in both the original 1811 version and the two extended and revised versions of 1814 and 1815, William Wordsworth is the most relevant for a summary of Hunt's innovative approach toward some of his contemporary writers. Indeed, the three versions of the poem illustrate Hunt's changing opinion of Wordsworth between 1811 and 1815 and demonstrate Hunt's independent attitude as a critic.

It is fair to say that at the beginning of 1811, Wordsworth's reputation was in limbo. As Stephen Gill notes,

> Though to devotees such as Lady Beaumont or Catherine Clarkson his poetic stature was beyond question, to reviewers and the poetry-buying public the author of *Lyrical Ballads* and *Poems, in Two Volumes* was still a figure of fun, fair game for the parodist and satirist, beneath the notice of the cultivated.
>
> (Gill 1989: 289–90)[32]

Hunt at this stage shares the public's view of Wordsworth, and the 1811 version of *The Feast of the Poets* barely recognizes Wordsworth's place among modern poets. However, during the course of his imprisonment at Surrey Gaol, Hunt became more familiar with Wordsworth's poetry. He then started promoting Wordsworth's poetical talent in the notes to the 1814 version of *The Feast*, and, as Lucy Newlyn points out, Hunt's revisions amounted to a significant foregrounding of the scholarly and critical status of the footnote (Newlyn 2000: 179–86).

On 28 May 1815, Leigh Hunt wrote a long letter to William Wordsworth to thank him for his present of the 1815 *Poems*. In the course of this letter, Hunt assures Wordsworth of his sincerity and expresses his new appreciation of Wordsworth's poetry:

> When I send you the book I allude to [i.e. the 1815 second edition of *The Feast of the Poets*], you will also receive the first edition of it, together with a publication in which it had previously appeared in a lesser shape; for you will thus see how you have grown upon me in proportion to my own knowledge & experience; nor should I chuse, in justice to my own feelings, … to disguise from you any thing I have said.
>
> (Hunt 1815c: n. pag.)

This change of opinion in 1815 is quite important when one considers the lines Hunt wrote in the *Reflector* 1811 version of *The Feast of the Poets*: 'And as to that Wordsworth! he'd been so benurst,/Second childhood with him had come close on the first' (ll. 175–6; Hunt 1812a: II, 319). Hunt's earlier brief and dismissive comment on Wordsworth echoes Byron's condescending attitude toward Wordsworth in his *English Bards and Scotch Reviewers*. Addressing Southey in that section of the poem, Byron sharply refers to Wordsworth thus:

> Next comes the dull disciple of thy school,
> That mild apostate from poetic rule,
> The simple WORDSWORTH, framer of a lay
> As soft as evening in his favourite May;
> …
> That all who view the 'idiot in his glory',
> Conceive the Bard the hero of the story.
>
> (ll. 235–8; 253–4; Byron 1980–92: I, 236)

As Muriel J. Mellown comments, Byron regards Wordsworth as 'a simple, but harmless eccentric rather than as a radical setter of dangerous precedents' (Mellown 1981: 85).

It has been argued that Hunt's knowledge of Wordsworth's poetry was practically non-existent when he wrote the lines just quoted for the *Reflector*. In fact, Hunt himself declared at the end of his life,

> I must add, that I knew little at the time of the writings either of Coleridge or Wordsworth, except from extracts in hostile reviews. When I came to read them better for myself, I went to such an extreme the other way, that in subsequent editions of the 'Feast of the Poets,' Wordsworth was extolled as the 'Prince of the bards of his time;' a distinction which I finally could not help thinking, as I still think, belonged properly to Coleridge.
>
> (Hunt 1860: 441)

Wordsworth's reputation in 1811 was based more on the popularity of the *Lyrical Ballads* than on the actual sales of his 1807 *Poems, in Two Volumes*, as Longman still had 230 copies on his hands, nearly a quarter of the edition, in 1814. Furthermore, as Alun R. Jones remarks, '[r]eviews and notices of the collection [1807 *Poems*] were generally hostile, and undoubtedly these affected both the reputation and the sales of the poems' (Jones 1987: xxi). The 1807 *Poems* had indeed been negatively reviewed in the *Critical Review* and the *Edinburgh Review*, and, as he himself notes, it is on these reviews that Hunt based his opinion when he wrote the earliest version of *The Feast of the Poets* (Hunt 1860: 441).

Not surprisingly, Wordsworth did not value Jeffrey's opinion in the years following the publication of his review. In a letter to Robert Gillies, dated 14 February 1815, Wordsworth declares: 'Your opinion of Jeffrey is just—he is a depraved Coxcomb; the greatest Dunce, I believe, in this Island, and assuredly the Man who takes the most pains to prove himself so' (Wordsworth and Wordsworth 1969–70: II, 633).[33] Wordsworth's 1815 'Essay, Supplementary to the Preface' is also particularly critical of Jeffrey in the discussion of contemporary reviews. Wordsworth again attacked Jeffrey as 'a man, self-elected into the office of a public judge of the literature and life of his contemporaries' in his *Letter to a Friend of Robert Burns*, published the following year (Wordsworth 1974: III, 127), a book that Hunt owned himself.[34] Hunt however valued Jeffrey's opinion quite highly in general, and he praised the literary and political principles of the *Edinburgh Review* in a series of 'Political Examiner' articles published in March and April 1810.[35] He declares in the first article published on 18 March that '[n]o man of taste or reflection will quarrel with their admiration of Mr. CAMPBELL's fancy or Mr. DUGALD STEWART's philosophy, and certainly not with their contempt of that maudlin gossip, the Wordsworthian muse' (Hunt 2003: I, 129).[36]

Hunt's knowledge of Wordsworth's poetry improved while in prison, as the following extract from a letter dated 15 April 1817 from Haydon to Wordsworth shows:

> But Leigh Hunt's weathercock estimation of you I cannot account for nor is it worthwhile to attempt it — He first attacks you when he had never read you, then a friend (Mr. Barnes) brought him your Excursion, pointed out your sonnets, and he began to find really that he should have looked

> through a [copy of your] works before he came to a conclusion on the genius displayed in them. He then recanted.
>
> (Haydon 1817: n. pag.)

That Hunt's opinion of Wordsworth improved upon his reading of Wordsworth's sonnets is worth underlining, since sonnets are at once formally conservative, and at the same time illustrative of the poet's gift for writing within the constraint of the form. Hunt's positive appreciation of Wordsworth's sonnets thus indicates his appreciation of Wordsworth's craft as poet. Some of the sonnets, such as 'Milton! thou should'st be living at this hour', also hint at the congenial politics of Wordsworth's youthful radicalism.

When he came to revise *The Feast of the Poets* in 1813, Hunt had also read the fourth edition of the *Lyrical Ballads* (1805), and he had particularly enjoyed 'The Female Vagrant', 'The Nightingale', and 'The Old Cumberland Beggar'. Hunt's charitable spirit and sympathetic nature were most likely pleased to encounter lines such as these in 'The Old Cumberland Beggar':

> And while in that vast solitude to which
> The tide of things has borne him, he appears
> To breathe and live but for himself alone,
> Unblamed, uninjured, let him bear about
> The good which the benignant law of Heaven
> Has hung around him: and, while life is his,
> Still let him prompt the unlettered villagers
> To tender offices and pensive thoughts.
>
> (ll. 163–70; Wordsworth 1984: 76)

It is worth stressing that, in family background and education, both Wordsworth and Hunt are at some remove from the world of peasants and commoners that they evoke and celebrate in their works. Their differences from, as well as their sympathies for, the underclasses give them something of a common ground. Yet, notwithstanding Hunt's improved appreciation of Wordsworth's poetry and his poetical theories, his first views of Wordsworth were marked by reservations.

The first instance of an improved appreciation of Wordsworth appears in a letter addressed to Moore on 20 September 1813:

> By the way, I have taken the opportunity of this re-publication [of *The Feast of the Poets*] to make peace with my conscience and speak much more highly of Wordsworth than at first. I do not pass over his puerilities; they only make me, if possible, still more indignant; but then I do not suffer any indignation to run away with itself; and certainly in the better parts of Wordsworth there appear to me all the elements, not only of a good, but of a great poet,—strong intellect, strong feeling, and dignified consciousness, and a command of the very identical words which he requires.
>
> (quoted in Moore 1853–6: VIII, 157)

It is worth noting here that, although he still denigrates what he considers to be Wordsworth's 'puerilities'—a criticism that echoes Jeffrey's views—Hunt has much hope for his ability to be 'a great poet' in 1813. This hope also appears in the longest note Hunt appended to the 1814 version of *The Feast of the Poets*, a note which accounts for 22 of the 110 pages of annotations he added to the revised version of the poem. In fact, one of the principal reasons behind the project of annotating the poem was Hunt's desire to include his revised opinion of Wordsworth. As the preface to the 1814 version of *The Feast of the Poets* indicates,

> [the author] was anxious to shew that he had at least considered the subjects of which he talked, and was *particularly desirous of doing justice to a great living poet*, of whom, in the first instance, led away by the impatience of seeing him pervert his genius, he had suffered himself to speak with unqualified and therefore unbecoming distaste.
>
> (Hunt 2003: V, 31; my emphasis)

The anonymous reviewer for the *Champion* singles out Hunt's note on Wordsworth because in it 'Mr. Hunt has at once duly appreciated the grand powers of that man's intellect, and has combated with ingenuity and success the extravagant deductions which he would draw from an universally-acknowledged theory' ([Anon.] 1814b: 62). Byron had similarly praised Hunt's note in a letter dated 9 February 1814: '[Y]our notes are of a very high order indeed—particularly on Wordsworth.—' (Byron 1973–94: IV, 51).

However explicit Hunt's insistence that he 'was particularly desirous of doing justice to a great living poet', the lines in *The Feast of the Poets* are still quite derogatory of Wordsworth's poetry. Hunt opens the poem in the same way he did in 1811, with Apollo arriving to celebrate the greatest poets in England and numerous pretenders presenting themselves before the god. After Apollo has rejected several candidates, the narrator describes Southey's arrival with Coleridge and Wordsworth and Apollo's immediate reaction:

> But as [Apollo] had settled it not to be teaz'd
> By all the vain dreamers from bed-room and brook,
> He turn'd from the rest without even a look;
> For Coleridge had vex'd him long since, I suppose,
> By his idling, and gabbling, and muddling in prose;
> And Wordsworth, one day, made his very hairs bristle,
> By going and changing his harp for a whistle.
>
> (ll. 231–7; Hunt 2003: V, 38)

Hunt goes on to complain about one of Wordsworth's poems:

> … some lines he had made on a straw,
> Shewing how he had found it, and what it was for,

And how, when 'twas balanc'd, it stood like a spell!—
And how, when 'twas balanc'd no longer, it fell!
(ll. 244–7; Hunt 2003: V, 38)

This passage evokes the lines from 'The Thorn' ('I measured it from side to side / 'Tis three feet long, and two feet wide') that Coleridge would cite three years later in the *Biographia Literaria* as one of the worst examples of Wordsworth's poetic version of common speech (Coleridge S. T. 1983: II, 52). These lines also suggest Hunt's more serious implication that by its overtly simple subject and style 'The Thorn' is trivializing a topic—the plight of the lower classes—worthy of more serious treatment.

Referring to the Lake School as a group, Hunt then characterizes Wordsworth as 'the very best promise bred up in the school', only to fault him as one who '[m]ust shew himself proudest in playing the fool' (ll. 256–7; Hunt 2003: V, 38).[37] Apollo consequently does not extend an invitation to his feast to Wordsworth, whom he sends home after throwing over the poet 'a cloud that was purple and white,/The same that of old us'd to wrap his own shoulders,/When coming from heaven, he'd spare the beholders' (ll. 277–9; Hunt 2003: V, 39). That Wordsworth leaves the room with Apollo's purple and white cloud hints at Hunt's respect for Wordsworth's powers as a poet, while underscoring Hunt's view that these powers have not, as yet, been employed to the full and proper extent of their potential.

In the 1814 version of *The Feast of the Poets*, this complex mixture of praise and criticism is complicated still further by a more positive view of Wordsworth's poetical ability in the annotations, but even there, his opinion of Wordsworth remains ambivalent. Hunt praises him highly, enumerating his poetic qualities and comparing him favorably with Spenser and Milton: '[Mr. Wordsworth] always thinks when he speaks, has always words at command, feels deeply, fancies richly, and never descends from that pure and elevated morality, which is the native region of the first order of poetical spirits' (Hunt 2003: V, 65). Nevertheless, Hunt declares that Wordsworth has abused his genius by turning away from society in quest for a source of inspiration that might in fact be found in what he has rejected. For Hunt himself, as Nicholas Roe remarks, '"sociality" was a healthy antidote to Wordsworth's rural solitude, and—by implication—to the Tory politics Wordsworth had so emphatically announced in his dedication of *The Excursion* to the "illustrious Peer" the Earl of Lonsdale' (Roe 1997: 118). In Hunt's view, Wordsworth's behavior has something to do with the discrepancy between the poetical theory described in the 'curious and, in many respects, very masterly preface to the Lyrical Ballads' (Hunt 2003: V, 66) and the application of this theory in the poems by Wordsworth included in *Lyrical Ballads*. One might say that Hunt agrees with Wordsworth that

> the taste of society has become so vitiated and so accustomed to gross stimulants, such as 'frantic novels, sickly and stupid German tragedies,

and deluges of *idle* and *extravagant* stories in verse,' as to require the counteraction of some simpler and more primitive food, which should restore to readers their true tone of enjoyment, and enable them to relish once more the beauties of simplicity and nature[.]

(Hunt 2003: V, 66)

In Hunt's view, contemporary taste in literature has been corrupted by an overflow of pointless literature, and only a return to an unadorned language, the famous language of 'a man speaking to men' that Wordsworth advances in the preface to *Lyrical Ballads*, would allow readers to appreciate the surrounding splendor of nature.

Yet Hunt cannot find in Wordsworth's poetry the illustration of these sound principles, at least not in the works he is familiar with at this stage. This does not mean that Hunt considers Wordsworth to be a minor poet. On the contrary, because Hunt values Wordsworth's genius so highly, he still expects much from him in 1814. After all, he calls him 'the greatest poet of the present' in his note to the 1814 version (Hunt 2003: V, 65), as well as in the pages of the *Examiner* in August 1814 (Hunt 1814c: 525). Nevertheless, Hunt publishes Hazlitt's three-part review of *The Excursion* between August and October 1814,[38] a review all the more prominent in the pages of the *Examiner* that year for it was the only literary review of the whole year. No literary notices were published that year either, with the exception of a short piece by Hunt on Southey's 'New Year's Ode' on 16 January (Hunt 2003: I, 309–13), which had more to do with politics than with literature.

Things changed in 1815. Wordsworth sent Hunt a copy of his 1815 *Poems*, probably in the hope of a review in the *Examiner*,[39] and the two of them met during one of Wordsworth's visits to London in 1815. As is well known, Wordsworth did not have a high opinion of Hunt at that time, as his comment in a letter to George Beaumont dated 23 June 1814 makes clear: '[N]either the censure nor the praise of such people [i.e. Hunt] is in *itself* of any value' (Wordsworth and Wordsworth 1993: 145). Wordsworth was nevertheless aware of Hunt's influence as literary critic. His censure or praise, Wordsworth notes in the same letter, 'affects the immediate sale of works, and authors who are tender of their own reputation would be glad to secure Mr Hunt's commendations' (Wordsworth and Wordsworth 1993: 145).

In response to his gift, Hunt wrote to Wordsworth that he was 'known for one of the most ardent of your general admirers' (Hunt 1815c: n. pag.).[40] Hunt's admiration is certainly demonstrated by the revised 1815 edition of *The Feast of the Poets*, which, as Stephen Gill notes, 'reversed most of the poem's earlier judgements and the meeting on 11 June 1815 seems to have been cordial' (Gill 1989: 472). Hunt recalls this meeting in his *Autobiography* with evident pleasure:

It was [in my study] … I had the honour of a visit from Mr. Wordsworth. He came to thank me for the zeal I had shown in advocating the cause of

> his genius. I had the pleasure of shewing him his book [1815 *Poems*] on my shelves by the side of Milton; a sight which must have been the more agreeable, inasmuch as the visit was unexpected.
>
> (Hunt 1850: II, 163)[41]

Haydon also evokes this meeting in a letter to Wordsworth dated 15 April 1817:

> When you were in town you visited him—you remember what he said with an agitated mouth—'The longer I live, and the older I grow, I feel my respect for your Genius increase, Sir.' These were *his words*—
>
> (Haydon 1817: n. pag.)

Now familiar with *The Excursion*, 1815 *Poems*, and *The White Doe of Rylstone*, Hunt writes in the preface to the revised edition of *The Feast of the Poets*:

> As to the principal poet alluded to, the Author does not scruple to confess, that his admiration of him has become greater and greater between every publication of 'The Feast of the Poets.' He has become a convert, not indeed to what he still considers as his faults, but, to use a favourite phrase of these times, to the 'immense majority' of his beauties[.]
>
> (Hunt 1815a: ix)

Hunt also adds some new lines to the poem:

> Yet the bard was no sooner obeying his king,
> And gliding away like a shadow of spring,
> Than the latter, who felt himself touched more and more
> Tow'rds a writer whose faults were as one to five score,
> And who found that he shouldn't well know whit to say,
> If he sent, after all, his best poet away,
> Said, 'Come, my dear Will,—imperfections apart,—
> Let us have a true taste of our exquisite art;
> You know very well you've the key to my heart.'
>
> (ll. 329–37; Hunt 1923: 153)

He wittily refers to Wordsworth's apostasy and his allegiance to George III ('obeying his king'), and declares that, even if the radical Wordsworth no longer finds expression in his poetry, Hunt still values his poetical power and publicly acknowledges it. These lines are followed by the chorus of Scott, Campbell, Southey, Byron, and Moore crying 'at last, with a passion sublime/"This, this is the Prince of the Bards of his Time!"' (ll. 362–3; Hunt 1923: 154).

Hunt's opinion of Wordsworth improved with the publication of the 1815 *Poems*. He became better acquainted with Wordsworth's poetry, and he also responded positively to Wordsworth's poetical theory as articulated in the preface and in the 'Essay, Supplementary to the Preface' included in this volume, two pieces of writing that Hunt later publicly promoted in a footnote to his 1832 preface: 'Every lover of poetry, and especially every critical reader of it, ought to make himself intimate with them' (Hunt 2003: VI, 95). In a note to the 1815 *Feast of the Poets*, Hunt specifically points to Wordsworth's new attitude regarding the question of whether poetry can exist independently from verse in the 'Essay' (Hunt 1815a: 92). Knowing Hunt's poor estimation of Pope, one can argue that Hunt would also have been pleased to read in the 'Essay' that Wordsworth was not an ardent admirer of Pope, even though the latter's poems, in Wordsworth's words, 'still retain their hold upon public estimation,—nay, there is not a passage of descriptive poetry, which at this day finds so many and such ardent admirers' (Wordsworth 1974: III, 73–4).[42] More knowledgeable of Wordsworth's poetical theory and of his poems, Hunt comes to appreciate Wordsworth more fully when he publishes the revised version of *The Feast of the Poets*. The revisions also indicate Hunt's continuing reassessment of his contemporaries and of his own views.

The reviews of *The Excursion* that appeared in 1815 attest to Hunt's distinctive stance on Wordsworth. For instance, if James Montgomery's review in the *Eclectic Review* was positive overall (Montgomery 1815), the review published in the May 1815 issue of the *British Critic* judged the poem too obscure ([Anon.] 1815a: 450). Although Hunt would hint at the difficulty of the piece, he was clearly impressed by Wordsworth's achievement when the 1815 edition of *The Feast of the Poets* appeared, with its assertion that Wordsworth is 'the Prince of the Bards of his Time!' (l. 363; Hunt 1923: 154).

The publication of Wordsworth's 1815 *Poems* however did not improve public opinion of the poet. Wordsworth's preface and 'Essay, Supplementary to the Preface' were the primary targets of criticism. James Hogg told John Murray, in a letter dated 7 May 1815, that he had heard the literary world 'was laughing immoderately at Mr Wordsworth's new prefaces which certainly excel all that ever was written in this world in egotism, vanity and absurdity' (quoted in Strout 1946: 103). In addition, Jeffrey cleverly responded to Wordsworth's thinly disguised attack on his character in the review of John Wilson's *The City of the Plague, and Other Poems*. In this review, Jeffrey declares himself to be distressed when he sees in true poets traces of 'party profligacy or personal spite or rancour' ([Jeffrey] 1815a: 460).[43] Other reviewers would specifically target Wordsworth's prefaces in their reviews. Yet, although the anonymous reviewer for the *Monthly Review* declares Wordsworth's preface to be neither 'remarkable for clearness of idea nor for humility of tone' ([Anon.] 1815b: 225), Hunt praised it highly in his notes to *The Feast of the Poets*. Furthermore, Hunt's own poetical theory involved increasingly Wordsworthian ideas, as is reflected in *The Story of Rimini* and the claim for a natural language in poetry.

Of course, Hunt's was not the only positive voice to emerge from the public debate concerning Wordsworth's poetry. Thomas Noon Talfourd's essay

'An Attempt to Estimate the Poetical Talent of the Present Age' is unequivocal in its praise of Wordsworth's character and his poetry, and it attacks the *Edinburgh Review* (Talfourd 1815: 462). However, the *Pamphleteer* did not have the same level of circulation as other major periodicals of the time, and the overall picture of Wordsworth's public reputation at the end of 1815 is still rather negative. Although several friends of Wordsworth's spoke out in favor of his poetry, Wordsworth was not a popular writer. As Gill remarks, '[s]eriously questioned when not actually ridiculed, his poetry was not selling' (Gill 1989: 311).[44] Thus, while Wordsworth aspired to be as popular as Scott and Byron, the sales of his poetry volumes were certainly disappointing to him. Hunt's praise of Wordsworth in the 1815 edition of *The Feast of the Poets* sets Hunt's work apart from the majority of the published criticism available at the time.

Wordsworth's wider reputation in 1814 and 1815 continued to ebb, while Hunt's personal appreciation of the poet, and particularly his praise for Wordsworth's poetry in the extended notes to the 1814 and 1815 versions of *The Feast*, set him apart from the majority of critics. Hazlitt's three-part review of *The Excursion* in the *Examiner*[45] did not contribute to the popularity of the poem, but it was surely Francis Jeffrey's review—'the most devastating critique Wordsworth was ever to suffer' (Gill 1989: 305)—in the November issue of the *Edinburgh Review* that set the tone for the reception of Wordsworth's poems in 1815. Given the widespread disregard of the poet, Hunt's improved opinion of Wordsworth, apparent in the 1815 version of *The Feast of the Poets*, thus demonstrates his independence as a critic. That Hunt should change his mind about Wordsworth, and in public, is evidence not of critical incapacity, I argue, but of an acute and responsive critical intelligence that was reluctant to conform to the literary prejudice of the time.

By praising Wordsworth so highly in 1815, Hunt was now aligning himself with a growing number of Wordsworth's admirers, while distancing himself somewhat from those who did not share this admiration. For instance, Byron repeatedly complained about Wordsworth and the Lakers, as well as about Hunt's increasing infatuation with Wordsworth, questioning his calling Wordsworth the 'prince of the bards of his time' in a letter to Hunt dated 7 October 1815 (Byron 1973–94: IV, 317), and declaring in another letter sent on 30 October 1815: 'I take leave to differ from you on Wordsworth as freely as I once agreed with you—at that time I gave him credit for promise which is unfulfilled—I still think his capacity warrants all you say of *it* only—but that his performances since "Lyrical Ballads"—are miserably inadequate to the ability which lurks within him' (Byron 1973–94: IV, 324). Francis Jeffrey had also published numerous negative comments about Wordsworth's works over the previous fifteen years, in particular in his reviews of Southey's *Thalaba* in 1802, of *The Excursion* in 1814, and of *The White Doe of Rylstone* in October 1815 ([Jeffrey] 1802; [Jeffrey] 1814; [Jeffrey] 1815b). The latter's opening sentence is quite revealing: 'This, we think, has the merit of being the very worst poem we ever saw imprinted in a quarto volume' ([Jeffrey 1815b]: 419). Hunt's opinion of *The White Doe of Rylstone*, if quite mixed, is still far more positive than Jeffrey's:

> The White Doe, it is true, which seems to have been written some time back, does not appear to be among his happiest performances, though containing, as almost all his performances do, touches of exquisite beauty. It is a narrative poem; and there is something in this kind of writing too much *out in the world* for the author's habitual powers.
>
> (Hunt 1815a: 109)

Hunt reprinted four of Wordsworth's sonnets in the *Examiner* between January and March 1816,[46] possibly, as James Chandler suggests, by way of compensation for the personal attack in Hazlitt's *Comus* article the previous year (Chandler 1987: 352). Hunt nevertheless criticized Wordsworth's political views in February 1816, especially following Napoleon's defeat and Wordsworth's claim that this was a divine punishment.[47] In the first part of his review of Keats's *Poems* which appeared on 1 June 1817, Hunt commends Wordsworth as the person who 'has advanced [the Lake School] the most, and who in spite of some morbidities as well as mistaken theories in other respects, has opened upon us a fund of thinking and imagination that ranks him as the successor of the true and abundant poets of the older times' (Hunt 2003: II, 116). However, from 1818 onward, Hunt's praise of Wordsworth as a great poet would always be framed within the context of predominantly negative comments, as in his review of *Peter Bell*, published in the *Examiner* on 2 May 1819. Hunt commends some 'masterly descriptions' in the poem, but complains of the moralistic overtone of the story: 'We are really and most unaffectedly sorry to see an excellent poet like Mr. Wordsworth returning, in vulgar despair, to such half-witted prejudices' (Hunt 2003: II, 187). Hunt criticizes Wordsworth's pedantic attitude in the story, as well as the subject matter of fear and bigotry itself. Similar mixed references to Wordsworth and the Lakers are found in Hunt's reviews of P. B. Shelley's works in 1818 and 1819. In his review of *The Revolt of Islam*, Hunt declares:

> If the Lake School, as they are called, were not as dogmatic in their despair as they used to be in their hope, we should earnestly recommend the passage [on 'moral ruin'] to their attention. They might see in it, at any rate, how it becomes an antagonist to talk; and how charitable and consistent the mind can be, that really inquires into the philosophical causes of things.
>
> (Hunt 2003: II, 155)

A year later, Hunt writes in his review of *Rosalind and Helen*: 'The object of Mr. Wordsworth's administrations of melancholy is to make men timid, servile, and (considering his religion) selfish;—that of Mr. Shelley's, to render them fearless, independent, affectionate, infinitely social' (Hunt 2003: II, 192).

It is therefore quite telling that Hunt did not include a section on Wordsworth in *Lord Byron and Some of his Contemporaries*, which was in many ways the equivalent of Hazlitt's *The Spirit of the Age*, a list of those Hunt considered to be the important literary figures of the previous two decades. Yet Hunt did praise Wordsworth again in his review of several of Moxon's publications, published in the *Tatler* in June 1831: 'We have said that [Wordsworth] is the best poet of his time. It is an old opinion of ours, and we are proud to say that it remains just what it was' (Hunt 2003: III, 182).[48] However, even this complimentary reference still contained a negative comment on Wordsworth's social and political opinions:

> [Wordsworth] has chosen to live like a hermit, and prefer a Government salary and the luxuries of poetical meditation, and yet fancies that the world ought to receive his reveries as oracular in all their parts, instead of liking them for what they are—the effusions of a mind so highly poetical, saddened and narrowed by education, discoloured perhaps by the insensible indulgences of the temperament naturally belonging to it, all events grudging that cheerful advancement of mankind which it ought to have been among the first to lead.
>
> (Hunt 2003: III, 183)[49]

Hunt's reference to Wordsworth's job as controller of stamps is reminiscent of his criticisms of Southey's laureateship and his enslavement to the Government's purse at the price of his independence. Hunt thus thinks that both poets are no longer in touch with the contemporary issues that, in his mind, really matter.

Ultimately, as Jeffrey N. Cox notes, the differences between Hunt and the Lakers, as exemplified by Wordsworth, arose over the issue of social awareness and their 'rejection of collective cultural and social action' (Cox 1999: n. pag.), a collective action espoused by Hunt and his circle in the years following Napoleon's defeat. Because of the Lakers' views of the Government's actions in the late 1810s and early 1820s, Hunt was unable to sustain a positive opinion of their works at that time, hence his repeated attacks on Southey, his slow acknowledgement of Coleridge's powers, and his mixed feelings *vis-à-vis* Wordsworth's poetry. Hunt would eventually bestow more ardent praise on Coleridge and Wordsworth, but he remained much more a devoted defender of Keats and Shelley, whose poetry embodied the aesthetic and political views he most admired. Hunt found in the poetry of Keats the combination of style and subject matter that he sometimes lamented as lacking in Wordsworth. He also strongly recommended Shelley's poems for their contributions to, and attempts to improve on, the social and political climate in the late 1810s, a time when the Lakers' poetry appeared to have turned away from their earlier radical politics. Politics remain a constant aspect not only of the poetic production in the middle of the second decade of the nineteenth century, but also of the reception of poetry, as Hunt's own work, *The Story of Rimini*, illustrates.

3 1816–1821

> Mr. Hunt ought to have been a gentleman born, and to have patronised men of letters. He might then have played, and sung, and laughed, and talked his life away; have written manly prose, elegant verse; and his *Story of Rimini* would have been praised by Mr. Blackwood.
>
> William Hazlitt, *The Spirit of the Age* (Hazlitt 1930–4: XI, 177)

1816 was arguably the most significant year in Leigh Hunt's career as a Romantic poet. After a two-year imprisonment, he had spent much of 1815 going back to the theater and seeing Edmund Kean, the actor whom Hazlitt had praised so highly in the pages of the *Examiner*. Hunt had also begun the 'Round Table' series with Hazlitt in January 1815, and published the second edition of *The Feast of the Poets* and *The Descent of Liberty*. However, Hunt's most concerted efforts in 1815 were devoted to revising and finishing one of his most important poems: *The Story of Rimini*. The publication of the poem in duodecimo format[1] at the end of January 1816, as Ann Blainey remarks, 'proclaimed [Hunt's] poetic ambitions to the public and, despite censure for obscurity and quaintness, it won a generous measure of favour' (Blainey 1985: 88). The poem marked a turning point in Hunt's life and would have historical repercussions for the whole second generation of Romantic poets in ways that the author of *The Story of Rimini* did not foresee at the time.

Dante and the politics of language

Hunt wrote most of *The Story of Rimini*, a narrative poem based on Dante's story of Paolo and Francesca (*Inferno*, Canto V, ll. 127–38), during his imprisonment at Surrey Gaol from 1813 to 1815.[2] As he recalls in his *Autobiography*:

> [L]ooking among my books for some melancholy theme of verse, by which I could steady my felicity, I unfortunately chose the subject of Dante's famous episode. I did not consider, indeed at the time was not critically aware, that to enlarge upon a subject which had been treated with exquisite sufficiency, and to his immortal renown, by a great master, was not likely, by any merit of detail, to save a tyro in the art from the

> charge of presumption, especially one who had not yet even studied poetical mastery itself, except in a subordinate shape.
>
> (Hunt 1850: II, 170)[3]

Hunt's contemporaries much appreciated Dante's story, although in 1816 the *Divine Comedy* had not yet reached the peak of its popularity during the Romantic period.[4] It was Dante's concise style in this episode—Hunt himself described it as 'a long tragedy in half-a-dozen lines' (Hunt 1846: I, 67)—that typically attracted critical praise. The anonymous reviewer of Biagioli's edition of *The Divina Commedia* and Cary's *Vision of Dante* thus commends Dante's conciseness, especially the Francesca episode, in his review for the *Edinburgh Review* in 1818:

> Dante … will be found never to employ more than a stroke or two of his pencil, which he aims at imprinting almost insensibly on the hearts of his readers. Virgil has related the story of Eurydice in two hundred verses; Dante, in sixty verses, has finished his masterpiece—the Tale of Francesca da Rimini.
>
> ([Anon.] 1818a: 454)

The passage from the *Inferno*, with Francesca narrating her story to Virgil and Dante the Pilgrim, runs as follows in Henry Francis Cary's translation:

> One day,
> For our delight we read of Lancelot,
> How him love thrall'd. Alone we were, and no
> Suspicion near us. Oft-times by that reading
> Our eyes were drawn together, and the hue
> Fled from our altered cheek. But at one point
> Alone we fell. When of that smile we read,
> The wished smile so rapturously kiss'd
> By one so deep in love, then he, who ne'er
> From me shall separate, at once my lips
> All trembling kiss'd. The book and writer both
> Were love's purveyors. In its leaves that day
> We read no more.
>
> (Canto V, ll. 123–35; Alighieri 1844: 76)

As Cary notes in his edition, 'Mr. Leigh Hunt has expanded the present episode into a beautiful poem, in his "Story of Rimini"' (Alighieri 1844: 75). These specific lines formed the basis for the third canto of *The Story of Rimini*; the rest of the poem describes the first meeting of Paolo and Francesca, their journey to Rimini, and the fatal duel between Giovanni and Paolo.[5]

It is worth noting that Dante puts the abridged version of the story in the mouth of Francesca herself, and then allows Virgil and Dante the Pilgrim to offer their rather different comments. In his retelling of Dante's story, Hunt, by contrast, speaks more in his own voice and offers more in the way of his own interpretative commentary. Hunt's presumption in giving such prominence to his own poetic voice, and his use of colloquial language in treating these great historical and literary figures, must have offended many readers. Also offensive must have been his portrayal of the two lovers acting out of natural human feelings, in contrast to Dante's *amor*, an almost supernatural force that invades Paolo and Francesca and compels them into action.

At the same time, by expanding and elaborating the background behind the famous story in the first two cantos of *The Story of Rimini*, Hunt also made the motivation of the characters more comprehensible and hence sympathetic to his audience. Dante tells the reader nothing of Francesca's feelings before the famous kiss and nothing about her arranged marriage to the older brother. He does sketch some of the socio-political background of the story of Paolo and Francesca in canto XXVII of *Inferno*, where he portrays the father of Francesca's husband as a cruel and aggressive ruler, '[t]he old mastiff of Verruchio .../That tore Montagna in [his] wrath' (Canto XXVII, ll. 43–4; Alighieri 1844: 188). The compassion Francesca seems to inspire in Dante's poem is for some readers undermined by her speech, with its superficial glamour and intrinsic incoherence.[6] Furthermore, although Dante's poetic treatment shows some consideration for the lovers, his consignment of both of them to the Inferno does suggest his view that God condemned their illicit passion. Hunt's treatment of the story moves in the other direction by enlisting the reader's feelings on the side of the lovers. It also implies a common cause between the right to self-determination—a politico-legal issue of much importance in the wake of the French and American revolutions and during the time leading up to the first Reform Bill of 1832—and the right to romantic love, presented as a fundamental human universal. Hunt, who had himself been imprisoned unjustly (as he must have believed since, in his eyes, his attack on the Prince Regent was justified), was naturally disposed to take a sympathetic view of the story. In his version, Francesca serves to illustrate the absence of freedom experienced by wives, as well as non-conformist liberal writers. She is first described as

> ... Ravenna's pride,
> The daughter of their prince, [who] becomes a bride,
> A bride, to crown the comfort of the land:
> And he, whose victories have obtained her hand,
> Has taken with the dawn, so flies report,
> His promised journey to the expecting court
> With hasting pomp, and squires of high degree,
> The bold Giovanni, lord of Rimini.
>
> (Canto I, ll. 29–36; Hunt 2003: V, 169)

Hunt chooses to characterize her status as a commodity with the line, 'A bride to crown the comfort of the land'. Francesca is an object, a crown, to be used for the benefit of the country, but Hunt also subverts the symbolic dimension of the crown and its royal associations by emphasizing what the role of kings should be: to serve their people. Hunt reinforces his observation a few dozen lines later when he writes:

> Till, as she views the countless gaze below,
> And faces that with grateful homage glow,
> A home to leave, and husband yet to see,
> Fade in the warmth of that great charity;
> And hard it is, she thinks, to have no will;
> But not to bless these thousands, harder still.
>
> (Canto I, ll. 111–16; Hunt 2003: V, 171)

Lacking control over her destiny ('And hard it is, she thinks, to have no will'), Francesca upholds her responsibility to 'these thousands', 'the countless gaze'. Hunt thus cunningly comments on the monarchy and its patriarchal principle (Francesca is after all given to Giovanni by her father Guido, 'fond from habit of intrigue and art,/And little formed for sentiments' [Canto II, ll. 32–33; Hunt 2003: V, 177]). In fact, as Greg Kucich argues, the puns, jaunty rhymes, spry neologisms, and loosened couplets of *The Story of Rimini* 'intrude upon the stateliness of the poem's formal measure, the heroic couplet, while forwarding various critiques of aristocratic hierarchy and established moral propriety' (Kucich 1999: n. pag.).

Thus, one of the major differences between the story of Paolo and Francesca in the *Inferno* and in Hunt's poem lies in the fact that, in Nicholas Roe's words, 'the emphasis has shifted from sin and damnation to a sympathetic understanding' (Roe 1997: 120). Vincent Newey notes further that '[t]he poem … was intended to inculcate a sense not only of true justice but also of possible improvement in human affairs' (Newey 1995: 169). Hunt's *Examiner* articles published from 1808 to 1816 demonstrate the very personal interest he had in the general improvement of his contemporary society. Yet his poetry is often viewed primarily as an exercise in imaginative escapism: this view is especially common in the case of a poem such as *The Story of Rimini*, with its descriptions of processions, forests, and other natural settings. However, a close reading of the language of the opening scene of *The Story of Rimini* suggests another possible approach:

> The sun is up, and 'tis a morn of May
> Round old Ravenna's clear-shewn towers and bay,
> A morn, the loveliest which the year has seen,
> Last of the spring, yet fresh with all its green;
> …
> 'Tis nature, full of spirits, waked and springing:—
> The birds to the delicious time are singing,
> Darting with freaks and snatches up and down,

Where the light woods go seaward from the town;
While happy faces, striking through the green
Of leafy roads, at every turn are seen[.]
(Canto I, ll. 1–4, 15–20; Hunt 2003: V, 169)

The nature described so beautifully here is not the passive object of the escapist's gaze but a site of much activity ('full of spirits'), of many creatures with 'happy faces', who live in a world of their own and not merely to give pleasure to those who view them. Hunt's presentation of nature is not as a contrast or alternative to human society but the site of a busy social environment of a similar kind.

In 1847 William Howitt reported, in his recollection of famous British poets, how he came to read *The Story of Rimini* in the company of two friends in Sherwood Forest: 'A hasty peep into it had led [us] to believe it would blend well in the perusal with the spirit of the region of Robin Hood and Maid Marian' (Howitt 1847: II, 346). The setting of *The Story of Rimini* could easily bring to mind Sherwood Forest, but it is also the political dimension of the poem that evokes Robin Hood and the political connotations associated with the myth of Robin Hood. As Roe argues, by the end of the eighteenth century Robin Hood 'had been transformed into a revolutionary, a proto-Jacobin opposed to the social and political establishment' (Roe 1997: 145).[7] Several poems were written during the Romantic period in which Robin Hood embodied the authors' political views. Roe further argues that several sonnets written by John Hamilton Reynolds, Keats, and Hunt in 1818 contain the same political subtext in their evocation of the myth of Robin Hood. And *The Story of Rimini*, although published two years before, invites such a reading. In fact, contemporary reviews of Hunt's poem show 'how poetry of retirement and the natural world which may seem bland and uncontroversial to modern readers was perceived as immoral, seditious, and traitorous by some of its first readers' (Roe 1997: 132). Hunt's poem was thus attacked not only because of its author and his political creed, but also because it depicted a dangerous story of rebellion against authority within a world that embodied the ideals of revolution.

Although it permeates the poem in many ways, Hunt's political outlook is not as forcibly expressed in the published poem as in some cancelled lines. The manuscript version of *The Story of Rimini* includes the following stanza, which would have appeared at the beginning of the poem:

For not [merely] by contrast lov'd was Guido's heir
Nor the mere dotage of a realm's despair,
No pamper'd prodigal, unshamed in waste,
Whose childishness remains when youth is past,
No smirking ~~idler~~ ideot, trusting for its throne
To custom and a worn out race alone,
Nor aught that makes an old head shake to see

~~Sure signs of an expiring royalty~~
~~smitten~~
~~The driv'lling mirth of dying royalty~~
~~The sapless sheets of fading royalty~~
~~The dancing death of sinking royalty~~
The fond neglect of sinking royalty[.]

(quoted in Short 1972–3: 209)

Clarice Short rightly reads this passage as containing a strong political message, as it could easily be seen as a commentary on George III or, more likely in light of Hunt's imprisonment, the Prince Regent. Consequently, as Short suggests, '[d]iscretion may have deterred him from running the risk of jeopardizing the poem's success by beginning it with an attack on inadequate rulers' (Short 1972–3: 209, 211). Hunt decided to delete these lines after his release from prison, and he may have been motivated by a desire to avoid another direct legal confrontation with supporters of the royal family.[8]

Hunt's time in prison may have influenced the poem in other ways as well. Spending what he calls 'long/And caged hours' while rains '[w]ash[ed] the dull bars', Hunt certainly found some comfort in reading and writing about Italy.[9] James R. Thompson asserts that Hunt 'wrote poetry, even his satires, as a kind of therapy; the poem's primary significance lay in the act of creation itself' (Thompson 1984: 23). Yet, even the touching lines that open the third canto suggest that more than poetic self-therapy is at work, and the consolations offered by poetic imagination are not merely escapist:

Now why must I disturb a dream of bliss,
Or bring cold sorrow 'twixt the wedded kiss?
Sad is the strain, with which I cheer my long
And caged hours, and try my native tongue;
Now too, while rains autumnal, as I sing,
Wash the dull bars, chilling my sicklied wing,
And all the climate presses on my sense;
But thoughts it furnishes of things far hence,
And leafy dreams affords me, and a feeling
Which I should else disdain, tear-dipped and healing;
And shews me,—more than what it first designed,—
How little upon earth our home we find,
Or close the intended course of erring human-kind.

(Canto III, ll. 1–13; Hunt 2003: V, 182)

Though most of Hunt's contemporaries appreciated his version of this famous story, modern critics tend to neglect *The Story of Rimini*. In critical studies of John Keats, Hunt's poem is discussed primarily as an illustration of his influence on the early Keats in terms of style and content, as in the case of Walter Jackson Bate's biography *John Keats* (Bate W. J. 1963) or in Richard Cronin's article 'Keats and the Politics of Cockney Style' (Cronin 1996a).[10] The only notable exceptions are John O. Hayden's article 'Leigh Hunt's *Story of Rimini*: Reloading the Romantic Canon', which argues persuasively and in detail for a new appreciation of the poem (Hayden 1987), Jane Stabler's discussion of Hunt's aesthetics of intimacy (Stabler 2003), and Greg Kucich's investigation of Cockney poetic style (Kucich 2003). These critics' reading differs from the earlier view of Oscar Kuhns, who severely criticizes Hunt's poem, protesting specifically against

> the infinite distance there is between the extraordinary conciseness, the heart-piercing pathos, and the refined reticence of Dante and all this long-drawn-out mawkish sentimentality. In the whole four cantos there are but few reminiscences of the language and figures of Dante; there is none of his atmosphere. Hunt tells us but little more than he found in the *Inferno*[.]
>
> (Kuhns 1904: 148–9)

However, as T. S. Eliot once remarked, 'the important debt to Dante does not lie in a poet's borrowings, or adaptations from Dante' (Eliot 1965: 132). Kuhns misses the point of *The Story of Rimini* when he condemns Hunt for imitating Dante badly. In fact, Hunt uses Dante's story as a point of departure for a poem of his own. The verse form of *The Story of Rimini* makes a similar departure from tradition with Hunt's distinctive use of the rhyming couplet, a move away from Pope's style in order to have a freer use of the heroic couplet and of feminine endings.

As Wordsworth observes in his 'Essay, Supplementary to the Preface [of 1815 *Poems*]', 'every author, as far as he is great and at the same time *original*, has had the task of *creating* the taste by which he is to be enjoyed' (Wordsworth 1974: III, 80), and Hunt's linguistic innovations were not readily accepted by his immediate contemporaries. An instructive comparison can be made between Hunt's poetic language in *The Story of Rimini* and Dante's account of his own attempt to create a new language for poetry in his unfinished treatise *De Vulgari Eloquentia* (written in 1303–04). As Blunden remarks, '[*The Story of Rimini*] pointed the way to a flexibility of style in verse, and the necessity for the poets of a strongly advancing race to acquire expression through the medium of significant daily speech' (Blunden 1930: 103). Jeffrey N. Cox also notes that '[Hunt's] *Story of Rimini*, with its assault upon established poetic convention in the stronghold of the heroic couplet, not only pushed further Wordsworth's innovations in prosody but also paved the way for *Endymion* and *Epipsychidion*' (Cox 1998: 41). Dante was the first defender of the (embellished) vernacular language, rather than Latin, for poetry. For Dante, the vernacular is 'the language which children gather from those around them when they first begin to articulate words; or more briefly, that which we learn without any rules at all by imitating our nurses' (Alighieri 1990: 47). In the second book of *De Vulgari Eloquentia*, Dante goes on to restrict the thrust of his argument by specifically advocating 'the illustrious vernacular', which does not include 'words that are childish because of their simplicity, … nor those that are feminine because of their softness, … nor those that are rustic on account of their hardness, … nor those urbane words that are glossy or bristly' (Alighieri 1990: 79). Although Hunt's earliest published poems self-consciously evoked a classical education, composing in Latin was not really an option for poets of his time. In using colloquial language in *The Story of Rimini*, however, Hunt was announcing a departure from the ostentatiously learned Latinate poetry of Dryden and Pope. Thus, he goes further than Dante in his advocacy of 'vernacular' language by using colloquial language in *The Story of Rimini*, as well as simple, feminine, and urbane words. Hunt's urbane sense of language implies an espousal of lower-class values as opposed to the elevated, higher-class values associated with classical language. Hunt would be censured chiefly for this urbane sense of language in *Blackwood's Edinburgh Magazine* and in the *Quarterly Review*. Interestingly, Dante himself did not actually follow the 'refined and selective language of his treatise' when he began writing the *Divine Comedy* a few years later. He preferred to use 'his more varied and vigorous native Florentine mingled with other external elements' (Grayson 1962: 70–1). Therefore, in its use of the vernacular, Hunt's poem continues a project begun by Dante, that of bringing the language of the poet even closer to the language spoken by the readers.

In the preface to *The Story of Rimini*, Hunt updates the prefaces of *Lyrical Ballads* in a poetical theory that underscores the need to use an 'actual, existing language' in poetry (Hunt 2003: V, 168). Eschewing the artifice of French neo-classical poetry, Hunt defends the poet's natural faculties to interpret the world around him, and to express himself in what he describes as 'a free and idiomatic cast of language' (Hunt 2003: V, 167). *The Story of Rimini* exhibits throughout what Hunt would describe a few years later in the preface to *Foliage* as the hallmarks of real poetry: 'A sensativeness [*sic*] to the beauty of the external world, to the unsophisticated impulses of our nature, and above all, imagination, or the power to see, with verisimilitude, what others do not' (Hunt 1818a: 13). Hunt implements his innovative approach to poetry in *The Story of Rimini* by coining new words, and by breaking away from the practice of closed couplets.[11] Hunt repeatedly uses overflowing heroic couplets to imbue his poem with a feeling of sensuousness, as in these lines:

> What need I tell of lovely lips and eyes,
> A clipsome waist, and bosom's balmy rise,
> The dress of bridal white, and dark curls
> Bedding an airy coronet of pearls?
>
> (Canto I, ll. 121–4; Hunt 2003: V, 171)

> Enough of this. Yet how shall I disclose
> The weeping days that with the morning rose,

How bring the bitter disappointment in,—
The holy cheat, the virtue-blinding sin,—
(Canto III, ll. 14–17; Hunt 2003: V, 182)

Then at the tournament,—who there but she
Made him more gallant still than formerly[.]
(Canto III, ll. 300–1; Hunt 2003: V, 188)[12]

Hunt's frequent use of present participles, of adjectives ending in 'y', and of adjectives and adverbs ending in 'ly' throughout the four cantos of the poem creates what Claude Lee Finney appropriately calls Hunt's 'sprightly, jaunty, lively, and flowing effects' (Finney 1963: I, 86). The following stanza serves as an example:

There's not in all that crowd one gallant being,
Whom if his heart were whole, and rank agreeing,
It would not fire to twice of what he is,
To clasp her to his heart, and call her his.
(Canto I, ll. 125–8; Hunt 2003: V, 171)

Moreover, his choice of words such as 'Darting' (I, 17), 'swarming' (II, 270), 'trampling' (IV, 495), 'scattery' (I, 22), 'shadowy' (II, 187), and 'lightsomely' (III, 46) illustrate his attempt to bring simple, colloquial words into poetic use. Hunt persisted in these efforts even though most contemporary reviewers objected to this distinctive use of colloquial language,[13] and to his attempt to break away from the classical language associated with poetry. Because of his own interest in landscape and nature (with all their political connotations), Hunt also provides the reader with quite original descriptions of natural scenes, as in the opening of the poem (Canto I, ll. 1–24; Hunt 2003: V, 169) or in the description of Francesca's garden (Canto III, ll. 382–485; Hunt 2003: V, 190–2).

Hunt's linguistic and stylistic initiatives in *The Story of Rimini* follow Wordsworth's injunction to use the 'real language of men' in poetry (what Hunt terms the 'actual, existing language' of men). However, Hunt updates Wordsworth's theory and puts it to work in his own theory and poetic practice. In *The Story of Rimini*, Hunt offers his readers a new approach to poetic language, and he creates a distinct verbal identity, a unique 'verbal fingerprint' (to adopt Seamus Heaney's term).[14] This distinctive identity finds expression in new vocabulary and linguistic inventions, as illustrated in the examples mentioned above. Hunt's strong poetic personality was also powerful enough to surprise most readers, as well as to provoke a vehement reaction from some of the reviewers. Because of his political views, Hunt was open to attack and ridicule based on his unconventional verses. A closer look at this founding document of the Cockney School offers a clearer focus on, and as a result a greater insight into, how Hunt implemented the poetical theory he outlines in his preface. *The Story of Rimini* also illustrates how Hunt's linguistic innovations, inspired by his model, Dante, had a direct impact on Romantic poetry in general, and on Keats in particular.

Notwithstanding the potentially controversial nature of Hunt's commentaries on society and the political content of *The Story of Rimini*, reviewers focused their attacks principally on the use of colloquial language and on the incestuous implications of the content.[15] Hunt did ultimately achieve his goal of 'unsettl[ing] the "authorized" complacencies of Regency life' (Roe 1997: 122), but the consequences were more far-reaching than Hunt and his circle had anticipated. For their part, his friends predicted that the poem would be a success, and they welcomed its publication with high praise.

The Story of Rimini and Lord Byron

On 25 September 1815, Benjamin Robert Haydon writes to Hunt: 'I think you have exquisite poetical feeling and I think that your present *Story of Rimini* will stamp you on the heart of the World' (quoted in Hunt 1938: 97). On 15 February 1816, William Hazlitt declared:

> I have read the story of Rimini with extreme satisfaction. It is full of beautiful and affecting passages. You have I think perfectly succeeded. I like the description of the death of Francesca better than any. *This will do*. You are very metaphysical in the character and passion, but we will not say a word of this to the ladies.
>
> (Hazlitt 1978: 153)[16]

In referring to Jeffrey's famous negative review of Wordsworth's *The Excursion* ('*This will never do*' [Jeffrey 1814: 1]), Hazlitt suggests a comparison between Wordsworth and Hunt, a comparison the latter in fact invited himself. In his preface to *The Story of Rimini*, Hunt adopts Wordsworth's discourse on the language of men as suited for poetry. Hazlitt's allusion to Jeffrey's response to *The Story of Rimini* was also prophetic. Jeffrey would prove to be quite positive in his assessment of the poem, writing to Moore on 28 May 1816 that '[*The Story of Rimini* is] very sweet and very lively in many places, and is altogether piquant, as being by far the best imitation of Chaucer [*sic*] and some of his Italian contemporaries that modern times have produced' (quoted in Moore 1853–6: II, 100). Hunt's lifetime friends Charles and Mary Lamb also express their happiness at seeing the poem in print in a letter dated 23 March 1816:

> We were much gratified by the token of your remembrance, though we had read Rimini previously with great delight, & agree in thinking it superior to your former poems. The third Canto is in particular my favourite. We congratulate you most sincerely on the fruit of your prison hours.
>
> (Lamb and Lamb 1975–8: III, 209–10)

On 8 December 1816, P. B. Shelley declares himself 'exceedingly delighted' by *The Story of Rimini*, and asserts that '[t]he *story* of the poem has an interest of a very uncommon & irresistible character' (Shelley P. B. 1964: I, 518). Earlier that year, Thomas Mitchell had offered Hunt one of the most thought-provoking praises, along with some reservation that anticipated some of the reviews:

> You know my idolatry for Lord Byron, who touches me more than any man except Shakespeare; nothing of his, in my opinion, ever showed more power than Rimini. There are passages however which wanted a friend's eye, before they went into the world—You belong to posterity or I would not talk to you thus.
>
> (Mitchell 1816: n. pag.)

Around March to April 1816, Byron wrote to Hunt that Sir Henry Englefield had praised *The Story of Rimini* to John Murray, and that '[J. H.] Frere—and all the Arch-literati—I hear—are also very unanimous in a high opinion of the poem' (Byron 1973–94: V, 58–9). Byron's own opinion of *The Story of Rimini* is probably the most important. He had offered Hunt ongoing help and encouragement during the composition of the poem, and Hunt acknowledges his support in his famous dedication of the poem to Byron. From May 1813 onwards, Byron frequently visits Hunt in prison, often with books useful for Hunt's poem (Byron 1973–94: II, 281). Hunt writes to Marianne on 25 May 1813: '[Byron] came on Sunday … and knowing what I wanted for my poem, brought me the last new Travels in Italy, in two quarto volumes' (Hunt 1862: I, 88). He also fondly recalls Byron's visits in his *Autobiography*:

> He used to bring books for the *Story of Rimini*, which I was then writing. He would not let the footman bring them in. He would enter with a couple of quartos under his arm; and give you to understand that he was prouder of being a friend and a man of letters, than a lord.
>
> (Hunt 1850: II, 310)

Byron and Hunt corresponded regularly between 1813 and 1815, and the tone of Byron's letters from this period is generally informal and friendly. Byron writes in his first surviving letter to Hunt dated 2 December 1813: 'It is my wish that our acquaintance or—If you please to accept it—friendship may be permanent' (Byron 1973–94: III, 189). Of the twenty-six surviving letters Byron wrote to Hunt, he addresses him as 'Dear Sir' in the first three (2 December 1813, 22 December 1813, and 9 February 1814), and from May to 1 June 1815 he writes 'My dear Hunt' or 'Dear H.', which he would use for the rest of their correspondence, with the exception of a letter dated 29 October 1822 where Byron addresses Hunt as 'My dear Leigh'. It might not be surprising therefore to find Hunt writing on a piece of paper 'Dear Byron, Shall I keep this couplet?' around June 1815 (Byron 1973–94: IV, 295).

Hunt also publicly praised Byron in the 1815 version of *The Feast of the Poets*, admitting him to Apollo's table and declaring him to be amongst the eight major poets of the time, as well as in an article in the *Examiner* when *The Story of Rimini* was published.[17] As early as 28 May 1813, Hunt had written to his wife:

> You must know I have got a fancy into my head that I can be of some use to his Lordship. … Perhaps a friend, if we grow intimate, of a taste like his own and full of quite as much excitability, but luckily induced to more philosophical habits by the nature of circumstances, may be able to render his heart and his understanding a service, and help to lead him off into enjoyments more congenial with both.
>
> (quoted in Landré 1936: I, 77)

Hunt's relationship with Byron, however, had some less positive consequences. On 26 February 1816, Byron warns Hunt that his association with *The Story of Rimini* might not contribute to the poem's success:

> Your prefatory letter to 'Rimini' I accepted as it was meant as a public compliment & a private kindness—I am only sorry that it may perhaps operate against you—as an inducement & with some a pretext—for attack—on the part of the political & personal enemies of both.
>
> (Byron 1973–94: V, 32)[18]

Ultimately, Hunt's confident expression of friendship in his dedication of *The Story of Rimini* to Byron did lead him to be attacked by several reviewers.[19] Despite the attacks on both the dedication to Byron itself and on the familiar tone Hunt adopted in his address to a lord, Hunt published a defense of Byron in the *Examiner* on 21 April 1816 ('Distressing Circumstances in High Life'), and his 'Epistle to the Right Honourable Lord Byron on his Departure for Italy and Greece' the following week. The opening lines gave further grounds for attack to critics:

> SINCE you resolve, *dear Byron*, once again
> To taste the far-eyed freedom of the main,
> And as the coolness lessens in the breeze,
> Strike for warm shores that bathe in classic seas[.]
>
> (ll. 1–4; Hunt 2003: V, 129; my emphasis)

Hunt reprinted the poem in *Foliage* two years later, reasserting publicly his warm personal feelings for Byron. In addition, he wrote of Byron as 'my noble friend' in the preface to *Foliage* (Hunt 1818a: 14), and again in the *Examiner* on 29 April 1821.[20]

Byron showed his ongoing interest in *The Story of Rimini* as well as his friendly feelings towards Hunt at that time with his comments on the manuscript version of the poem throughout the year 1815, when Hunt was busily engaged in completing it. As Blunden points out, Byron's notes 'were in the most soothing tones of approval, with some interjections of discord, and hints for revision' (Blunden 1930: 79).[21] These notes, as well as several letters written to Hunt and others in October and November 1815, show Byron's admiration for Hunt's poem, and again particularly for the third canto. Thus, on 22 October 1815, Byron writes to Hunt:

> My dear Hunt—You have excelled yourself—if not all your Contemporaries in the Canto which I have just finished—I think it above the former books—but that is as it should be—it rises with the subject—the conception appears to me perfect—and the execution perhaps as nearly so—as verse will admit.——There is more originality than I recollect to have seen elsewhere within the same compass—and frequent & great happiness of expression—in short—I must turn to the faults—or what appears such to me—there are not many—nor such as may not be easily altered being almost all *verbal*:—and of the same kind of those I pretended to point out in the former cantos—viz—occasional quaintness—& obscurity—& a kind of harsh & yet colloquial compounding of epithets—as if to avoid saying common things in the common way—'difficile est proprié communia dicere' seems at times to have met with in you a literal translator.—I have made a few & but a few pencil marks in the M.S.—which you can follow or not as you please.——The poem as a whole will give you a very high station—
>
> (Byron 1973–94: IV, 319–20)[22]

Praises for Hunt's originality and his achievement in expanding on Dante's story would also appear in several reviews of the poem. Some also included, however, similar remarks about Hunt's diction, his 'occasional quaintness—& obscurity—& a kind of harsh & yet colloquial compounding of epithets'. Yet, although Byron had some reservations about the poem, he wholeheartedly recommended it to John Murray. 'I think it the *safest* thing you ever engaged in', Byron writes to Murray on 4 November 1815. 'I speak to you—as a man of business—were I to talk as a reader or a Critic—I should say it was a very wonderful & beautiful performance—with just enough of fault to make its beauties more remarked & remarkable' (Byron 1973–94: IV, 331).[23] Thanks to Byron's recommendation, Murray became the publisher of the first edition of *The Story of Rimini*. However, Hunt's relationship with Murray later became strained when they disagreed over financial arrangements (Landré 1936: I, 87–8). Donald H. Reiman suggests that Murray's antagonism toward Hunt might come from the publication of *The Story of Rimini*:

> John Murray had agreed to print the first edition of 500 to 750 copies at his own risk, Hunt to receive half the profits and retain his copyright. When the edition seemed to be selling well, Murray sent Hunt £50—

> slightly more than half the net profits. Hunt then (April 9, 1816) offered to negotiate with Murray for the copyright, asking him for a loan of £450 on security, to be reduced by the amount Murray might finally offer him for the copyright. Murray interpreted this as an appeal for charity [and] Hunt felt insulted[.]
>
> (Reiman 1973–86: V, 222)[24]

A letter written to the bookseller John Booth on 17 September 1816 clearly indicates Hunt's opinion of Murray:

> I have not yet parted with Rimini, & perhaps shall not at all during these times, unless the publisher ^of the first edition^ who treated me in a very singular manner & with whom I have had no intercourse since, should take it into his head ~~of~~ to act a little handsomely, as there are some symptoms perhaps of his doing.
>
> (Reiman 1973–86: VII, 69)

Hunt eventually disposed of the copyright of *Rimini* to another publisher. But the result was that, according to Reiman, 'Hunt became more and more antagonistic toward Murray personally, permitting derogatory mention of him [by Hazlitt] to appear in the *Examiner* in May 1817' (Reiman 1973–86: V, 222).

Contemporary reviews

The reception of *The Story of Rimini* in the contemporary periodical press clearly indicates that it was without any doubt Hunt's best-known poem of the Romantic period. The British edition received no less than ten reviews between March and September 1816. These were followed a year later by the first two articles on the Cockney School written by 'Z', i.e. John Gibson Lockhart, and published in the October and November 1817 issues of *Blackwood's Edinburgh Magazine*. The American edition of *The Story of Rimini*, also printed in 1816, was reviewed in July of the same year in the *North American Review*, one of the four major American literary magazines in the 1810s, and one considered to be '[t]he chief organ of New England opinion for the first half of the nineteenth century' (Power 1964: 53).

The ongoing reception of the poem was somewhat mixed, although with all this attention in the periodicals, it might not seem surprising that the poem went through a second edition in late June 1817, and a third one in 1819.[25] Yet, repeated publication did not mitigate the attacks in the press from Hunt's political enemies. Writing about *The Story of Rimini*, Edmund Blunden notes that

> [w]hile this spirited, sensuous, uncertain and extravagant narrative was hailed in the highest terms by such friends as Hazlitt and Byron … its

> public effect was perhaps unfortunate for its author. It gave him a definite rank, but it exposed him through its mannerism of indifferent ease and tropical colour to the savagery of the opposite faction in politics and poetics.
>
> (Blunden 1922: 733–4)

Hunt himself describes the 'savagery of the opposite faction in politics and poetics' in his *Autobiography* when he writes of 'the wrath of the Tory Critics':

> [*The Story of Rimini*] would have met with no such hostility, or indeed any hostility at all, if politics had not judged it. Critics might have differed about it, of course, and reasonably have found fault; but had it emanated from the circles, or had been written by any persons not obnoxious to political objection, I believe there is nobody at this time of day, who will not allow, that the criticism in all quarters would have been very goodnatured, and willing to hail whatever merit it possessed.
>
> (Hunt 1850: II, 172–3)

Indeed, even though the contemporary reviews were on the whole positive, the impact of the reviews published in the *Quarterly Review* and *Blackwood's Edinburgh Magazine* did not earn Hunt any poetical credentials during the Romantic period, but rather a negative public image that would take years to alleviate. In a letter to Byron dated 26 May 1816, John Cam Hobhouse neatly summed up the treatment of the poem in the January issue *Quarterly Review*, actually published in May of that year: '*Rimini* is bedevilled' (Hobhouse 1984: 222).

Under the editorship of Dr Watkins, the *New Monthly Magazine* published a short review of *The Story of Rimini* on 1 March 1816. The anonymous reviewer had no real interest in the poem itself, which he summarily dismisses with the following sentence: 'Of the book itself we shall only say, that the subject is taken from an episode in Dante; but most miserably expanded in the present version' ([Anon.] 1816a: 149). Besides the two reviews previously mentioned, this is the only review that makes no positive comment on the poem, not even on the opening lines often praised by other reviewers. In fact, the main part of the review is concerned with the dedication to Byron, or, to quote from the review, the 'very pleasant piece of chit-chat, the object of which is, to shew on what a footing [the author] stands with some of the nobility' ([Anon.] 1816a: 149). The reviewer quotes the beginning of Hunt's well-known dedication:

> My Dear Byron, You see what you have brought yourself to by liking my verse. It is taking you unawares, I allow; but you yourself have set example now-a-days of poet's dedicating to poet; and it is under that nobler title, as well as the still nobler one of friend, that I now address you.

The reviewer comments strongly: 'The easy impudence of this address, and the ungrammatical vulgarity of language, cannot but bring to our recollection the polished manner of Tom Shuffleton in the comedy' ([Anon.] 1816a: 149).[26] In one sentence this reviewer encapsulates two of the main subjects of all the reviews of *The Story of Rimini*: the daring social equality implied in his dedication of the poem to a peer of the realm, and the presumptuous use of colloquial language throughout the poem.

Actually, reviewers more often praised than attacked the language and style of Hunt's poem. Josiah Conder, in his review for the *Eclectic Review*, published in April 1816, opens his article with references to 'the easy grateful style of familiar narrative' one finds in *The Story of Rimini*, as well as 'the fresh diction of Mr. Hunt' ([Conder] 1816: 380, 381). He goes on to quote the opening lines of the poem, and he is in fact so enthusiastic about Hunt's work that he continues quoting extensively from it, interspersing comments such as 'The following are but touches, but they are exquisite ones' or 'The description of the bride is, we think, very touching' ([Conder] 1816: 382, 383).[27] The incest theme of the poem is described as 'a criminal passion' but Hunt is given 'full credit for the decency of his representations, [and] for the absence of every thing that can disgust, or seduce, or inflame' ([Conder] 1816: 381). Conder, an evangelical nonconformist writing in a periodical with a strong religious background, cannot but note that 'we doubt whether such stories are not likely to do some hurt to the cause of morality' ([Conder] 1816: 381). He makes his strongest criticism at the end of the review when he attacks Hunt's 'flippant and infidel remark which disfigures [the description of the death of Francesca]' ([Conder] 1816: 385). That a clergyman would attack lines that throw some doubt on the notion of eternal damnation such as 'The gentle sufferer was at peace in death' (Canto IV, l. 412; Hunt 2003: V, 204) is not really surprising, as an American reviewer of the poem pointed out in a note a few months later ([Tudor] 1816: 283).

The theme of incest was hardly an original subject in itself when Hunt published *The Story of Rimini*,[28] and in fact, the incest in question in the poem is technical, or conventional, rather than 'natural', since Paolo is the brother of Francesca's husband. Yet, reviewers at the time could not be seen to condone such a theme, and thus praise for any poem dealing with such a subject was by nature precarious. An anonymous reviewer for the London monthly, the *British Lady's Magazine*, succeeds in this delicate task:

> in our opinion, [Hunt] could not have set himself a task of greater difficulty and delicacy to execute, than to pourtray [sic] the progress of such a fatal passion with the truth which is due to nature, and the moral justice which the laws of society demands. It is by no means in the spirit of flattery that we pronounce our judgment on this performance; but we are absolutely constrained to applaud the execution of a master, though we have some repugnance to approve the subject which calls forth his powers.
> ([Anon.] 1816b: 239)

The reviewer further asserts:

> In his descriptions of inanimate nature, as well as in his delineation of human passions, the author of 'Rimini' is at once original and correct: neither his scenes nor his characters can be mistaken for copies of former artists, but are evidently new creations of mind, bearing the genuine stamp of sovereign genius!
>
> ([Anon.] 1816b: 239)

To support this point, the following two double-column pages consist of a long extract from the first canto (the procession of Paolo into Ravenna) and another one from the closing of the second canto (Francesca's arrival in Rimini).

Another significant review was one by William Roberts,[29] which combined an account of Byron's *The Siege of Corinth* and *Parisina* with Hunt's *The Story of Rimini*. Between the dedication to Byron and the shared theme of incest in two of the poems under review, these works seemed appropriate for a common appraisal. In fact, as Richard Cronin argues, Byron's *Parisina* may have actually been indebted to Hunt's poem, as '[i]n both poems the husband detects the crime when the wife speaks endearments to her lover in her sleep' (Cronin 1996a: 804). Frederick L. Beaty makes a similar case, arguing that '[s]ince Byron had carefully proofread *The Story of Rimini* in 1815, it is not surprising that Hunt's poem should have influenced *Parisina*, written at approximately the same time' (Beaty 1960: 399).[30]

Although only the last five pages of the review are devoted to Hunt's poem, Roberts had already discussed the incest theme in Byron's *Parisina* before turning to *The Story of Rimini*. An evangelical periodical would naturally attack this theme, but it is worth noting that, again, the reviewer praises Hunt for his handling of such a delicate subject:

> [I]t must be admitted, to [Hunt's] honour, that the superstructure which he has raised upon it is not a temple to licentious love, and that he has touched with as much decency, as the conduct of the story would admit, the crime which he has painted the consequences in the language of virtue.
>
> ([Roberts] 1816: 466)

The section of the review dealing with Byron's *Parisina* is not so positive.[31] Overall, the review is not very favorable toward Hunt either, especially in what Roberts considers 'the favourite idiom of this writer, [which] degenerates almost into gossip' and the 'silly scheme of poetical reform of which he vainly aspires to be the founder' ([Roberts] 1816: 466, 469). Hunt's language and his Wordsworthian attempt at using the 'proper language of poetry', the language that he describes in the preface as being 'nothing different from that of real life, and [that] depends for its dignity upon the strength and sentiment of what it speaks' (Hunt 2003: V, 167), is once again under attack. Most reviewers took exception to Hunt's colloquial usage and his attempt to describe 'natural things in a language becoming of them' (Hunt 2003: V, 168). They also complained about Hunt's claim to a new poetical system, namely, his wish to use colloquial language and everyday subject matter, a system that Byron himself later disapproved of as a 'strange style', and in fact a departure from natural language.[32]

If the theme of *The Story of Rimini* was to varying degrees criticized by most reviewers, the anonymous reviewer for the *Augustan Review*, a London monthly claiming no political creed but with a liberal bias in its literary review (Hayden 1969: 261), stands apart. This review's distinctive response does not consist in an ardent praise of Hunt's poem, but rather in the unusual way in which he handles, or to be more precise ignores, the incest theme. Indeed, the reviewer offers the following description of the poem:

> We seem to feel a sort of property in an idea which is familiar to our own minds, but which we never heard breathed by the voice, nor saw traced by the pen of another; and such passages combine with the charm of novelty in the expression, the interest of old acquaintanceship with the image suggested.
>
> ([Anon.] 1816c: 478)

The reviewer never mentions the word *incest*, nor condemns the love between Francesca and Paolo—a unique instance amongst the reviews under consideration. Even the dedication escapes criticism, as the reviewer ends the article: 'The dedication is to Lord Byron. We could not help thinking it rather arrogant, till we had read the poem' ([Anon.] 1816c: 479).

Again, Hunt's language receives most attention in the anonymous review published in the *Monthly Review; or Literary Journal* in June 1816. Several passages are praised for their descriptions of life and nature, in particular the opening lines of the poem. The reviewer concludes: 'We cannot dismiss this publication without our repeated tribute of applause to the strong interest excited by the author in the fate of his characters, and to his natural and original style of poetic composition' ([Anon.] 1816d: 142). On the other hand, Hunt's 'inadmissible freedom in rhythm and phraseology' ([Anon.] 1816d: 142) is denounced with a lengthy reference to the preface in which he discusses poetic language as reflecting the language of real life. The reviewer goes on to enumerate a long list of Hudibrastic heroic couplets used by Hunt throughout the poem, and points out some other lines that, in his opinion, do not make sense or are too irregular.

Hunt's poetical experiment in *The Story of Rimini* is also the focus of the anonymous review published in the *Dublin Examiner* in June 1816. The poem, according to the reviewer, 'contains a good many harsh and unmusical lines, and the expression sometimes borders upon vulgarity' ([Anon.] 1816e: 143). The reviewer also complains of the treatment of incest in *The Story of*

Rimini, 'one of the blackest crimes under which human nature can sink', and the way Hunt describes it 'in colour so alluring as scarcely to shock the purest and most delicate mind' ([Anon.] 1816e: 131). Nevertheless, the tone of the review is overall very positive, with Hunt's 'half-antiquated, but expressive phraseology' ([Anon.] 1816e: 130) praised alongside his 'language perfectly true to nature, and benefiting the condition of human creatures' ([Anon.] 1816e: 131). After numerous quotations from each canto, the reviewer asserts that if readers 'consider [the poem] upon its own merits, we have not much doubt but it will acquire a deserved popularity' ([Anon.] 1816e: 143).

A friend of Thomas Moore and employer of William Hazlitt, Francis Jeffrey was true to his personal opinion when he published the review of *The Story of Rimini* in June 1816.[33] At the end of May 1816, Moore wrote to Jeffrey, 'I hope you mean to praise Rimini—I would do it *for spite*' (Moore 1964: I, 395). Moore was implying that Jeffrey should publish a positive review of the poem in order to annoy some of his competitors rather than to please Hunt. After all, Byron had written to Moore two months before about the possibility of Moore writing a review for the *Edinburgh Review*:

> Leigh Hunt's poem is a devilish good one—quaint, here and there, but with the substratum of originality, and with poetry about it, that will stand the test. I do not say this because he has inscribed it to me, which I am sorry for, as I should have otherwise begged you to review it in the Edinburgh. It is really deserving of much praise, and a favourable critique in the E[dinburgh] R[eview] would but do it justice, and set it up before the public eye where it ought to be.
>
> (Byron 1973–94: V, 35)

In his *Life of Lord Byron*, Moore indicates that his response was: 'With respect to Hunt's poem, though it is, I own, full of beauties, and though I like himself sincerely, I really could not undertake to praise it *seriously*. There is so much of the *quizzible* in all he writes, that I never can put on the proper pathetic face in reading him' (Moore 1854: III, 201). Not surprisingly, Moore's opinion of the poem was slightly different, though still frank in his criticism, in his letter to the author, dated 7 March 1816:

> Your Rimini is beautiful—and its only faults such as I know you are aware of & prepared to justify—there is a maiden charm of originality about it— … in short, it is Poetry—and notwithstanding the quaintnesses, the coinages and even affectations, with which, *here* and *there* … I have only time to say again that your Poem is beautiful—and that, if I not exactly agree with [*sic*] *some* of your notions about versification & language the general spirit of the work has more than satisfied my utmost expectations of you—
>
> (Moore 1964: I, 389)

Again, the main negative criticism of the poem turns on Hunt's language. Hunt's innovative approach to poetry, as outlined in the preface of *The Story of Rimini*, is something that Moore could not agree with; Moore's own poems of that period reveal the extent of his own opinions concerning poetical language, particularly as seen in *Lallah Rook* and *Legendary Ballads*.[34] Moore preferred the poetry and subject of *The Feast of the Poets*, a witty and satirical style that he would himself develop further in his very popular poems *The Fudge Family in Paris* and its 'sequel' *The Fudges in England*.

Jeffrey's review presents a refreshing contrast to the various publications related to *The Story of Rimini*. He finds faults in the poem but is generally positive,[35] and makes a good case for the compliments he pays to Hunt: 'THERE is a good deal of genuine poetry in this little volume; and poetry, too, of a very peculiar and original character' ([Jeffrey] 1816a: 476). His second paragraph, in particular, illustrates the balanced tone of the review:

> Though [Hunt] has chosen, however, to write in this style [i.e. a style resembling Chaucer's], and has done so very successfully, we are not by any means of opinion, that he either writes or appears to write it as naturally as those by whom it was first adopted; on the contrary, we think there is a good deal of affectation in his homeliness, directness, and rambling descriptions. He visibly gives himself airs of familiarity, and mixes up flippant, and even cant phrases, with passages that bear, upon the whole, the marks of considerable labour and study. In general, however, he is very successful in his attempts at facility, and has unquestionably produced a little poem of great grace and spirit, and, in many passages and many particulars, of infinite beauty and delicacy.
>
> ([Jeffrey] 1816a: 477)

Like Byron, Jeffrey specifically praises the third canto of *The Story of Rimini*, 'the most interesting part of the poem' ([Jeffrey] 1816a: 482), and he quotes from it extensively. Jeffrey is also particularly persuasive in summarizing the pros and cons of Hunt's poetic language. He notes that

> [t]he diction of this little poem is among its chief beauties—and yet its greatest blemishes are faults in diction.—It is very English throughout—but often very affectedly negligent, and so extremely familiar as to be absolutely low and vulgar.
>
> ([Jeffrey] 1816a: 491)

He then quotes phrases such as 'a clipsome waist' or 'a scattery light', and lines such as 'She had stout notions on the marrying score' to illustrate his point.[36]

The passages cited by Jeffrey represent Hunt's implicit claim that the conversational language of those who are *not* gentry represents 'natural' language, and thus the more 'elevated' language is construed as 'artificial'. Conservative political opponents might justly object to the attempt by 'Cockneys' to use their accents to promote their own socio-politico-linguistic status, especially since Hunt is not writing about a leech gatherer or an 'Idiot boy' but about members of the historical ruling class of medieval Ravenna. Hunt's underlying argument in giving a sympathetic reading, and often colloquially phrased version, of their story is that the romantic experience of the high born is not essentially different from that of ordinary folk. Hunt reinforces this claim through the familiar tone of his address to Byron in the dedication. Hunt's point is that all human beings share a common 'nature' that even 'Cockneys' can understand and express. Behind the theme and language of *The Story of Rimini* lies a potentially radical politics, an element largely absent from Dante's version of the story.

It is ironic that Jeffrey praised a poem with Wordsworthian diction, a diction he so vehemently protested against in his 1802 review of Southey's *Thalaba* ([Jeffrey] 1802). In any case, Jeffrey's review is most significant as a fair assessment of the contemporary reception of *The Story of Rimini* and of Hunt as a poet. Halfway through the review, Jeffrey makes the following statement:

> Mr Hunt ... does not belong to any of the modern schools of poetry; and therefore we cannot convey our idea of his manner of writing, by reference to any of the more conspicuous models. His poetry is not like Mr Wordsworth's, which is metaphysical; nor like Mr Coleridge's, which is fantastical; nor like Mr Southey's, which is monastical.
>
> ([Jeffrey] 1816a: 487)

In June 1816, Hunt was officially of no school of poetry, although his diction evoked the Lakers. Repeatedly labeled as 'original' in his attempt at expanding Dante's famous episode, Hunt found himself on the verge of poetical success, with a second edition in 1817.[37] However, by October 1817 Hunt would be better known as the 'chief Doctor and Professor' of the Cockney School of Poetry ([Lockhart] 1817: 38). From then on, his place in the poetical world of the late 1810s and 1820s would not be as an innovative and respected poet, but, to borrow the title of Lockhart's second letter to Hunt, as the 'King of the Cockneys' ([Lockhart] 1818a: 196).[38]

Although not published in an important or influential magazine, the review that appeared in the September issue of the *Literary Panorama* confirms an appreciation of Hunt's poem as containing numerous beautiful descriptions, beginning with the opening of *Rimini*: 'Perhaps there never was a more splendid opening than that of the present poem' ([Anon.] 1816g: 939). It also praises an originality that distinguishes Hunt from most of his peers—a compliment regularly bestowed on Hunt by his contemporaries, from Byron to anonymous reviewers. Except for a few remarks on the poem's occasional carelessness in versification, the only negative comment has to do with the morality of the poem:

> [W]e desire earnestly that a man of such talents would consider whether it were not infinitely to his advantage in every respect, not to awake the mind to poetry only, but to virtue also, not merely to delight the world, but to improve it.
>
> ([Anon.] 1816g: 944)

The reviewer applauds Hunt's talent and ideas, but concludes the article with his injunction that poetry could, and in fact should, contain a moral dimension found wanting in Hunt's work.

The reviews of *The Story of Rimini* published in the *Quarterly Review* and *Blackwood's Edinburgh Magazine* are among the best known articles published during the Romantic period, together with Jeffrey's review of Wordsworth's *The Excursion*, and John Taylor Coleridge's review of Shelley's *The Revolt of Islam*. The reviews in *Blackwood's* and the *Quarterly Review* reveal strong poetical and political biases against Hunt, and in fact against everything he represented as the perceived head of a new poetical school.[39] As Alan Lang Strout observes, 'Perhaps there exists no better example of political malignity in the periodical criticism of the early nineteenth century than the reviews in these Tory publications of Hunt's *The Story of Rimini*' (Strout 1937: 151). An atmosphere of political malignity is certainly present in these reviews; but their aggressive stance also stems, in the case of *Blackwood's*, from the desire to establish a new publication.[40] Several scholars, including Roe 1997, Cox 1998, Kucich 1999, Wheatley 1992, and de Montluzin 1998, have analyzed these reviews in depth.[41] My concern here is with Hunt's reaction to them, as well as with the other comments of his contemporaries.

Leigh Hunt and his brother John responded publicly to these reviews in the *Examiner*, as Hunt explained to Moore in a letter dated 24 March 1818:

> You have seen or heard, perhaps, of this anonymous raf who attacked me in a Scotch magazine. My brother, in his over-zealousness for me, unfortunately inserted a paragraph about me in the paper, and then I was obliged to notice [the anonymous reviewer] in the same way. We have not succeeded in dragging or provoking him forth; and he has since, after a certain glowling [*sic*] but always mean fashion, recanted, pretending he did not mean to attack me privately.
>
> (quoted in Moore 1853–6: VIII, 236)

Despite three requests published in the *Examiner* on 2 November, 16 November, and 14 December, the Hunts were unsuccessful in their attempts to challenge Z, the anonymous reviewer, to 'avow himself; which he cannot fail to do, unless to an utter disregard of all *Truth* and Decency, he adds the height of Meanness and COWARDICE' (Hunt 1817c: 729).[42] Hazlitt also responded to these reviews in two publications, and Keats wrote to Benjamin Bailey on 3 November 1817:

> There has been a flaming attack upon Hunt in the Endinburgh [*sic*] Magazine—I never read any thing so virulent—accusing him of the greatest Crimes—dep[r]eciating his Wife his Poetry—his Habits—his company, his Conversation—
>
> (Keats 1958: I, 179–80)

It is unambiguous from these reviews that Hunt's personal and political life were throwing a shadow over his poetry. It is also clear that 'Z was only too ready to yoke the sexual politics of *The Story of Rimini* to the radical programme of the *Examiner*, by way of denouncing both' (Roe 1997: 121).

What is less known is that these reviews stimulated the publication of two anonymous pamphlets defending Hunt against the harsh criticism he received. The first was published in 1816, entitled *An Address to that Quarterly Reviewer who touched upon Mr. Leigh Hunt's 'The Story of Rimini'*.[43] The writer, now identified by John Barnard as Hunt's friend Charles Cowden Clarke (Barnard 1997), is virulent in his attack on John Wilson Croker and William Gifford's review:

> I BELIEVE it is unlikely that any one of ordinary experience and discernment, could read the first twelve or fourteen lines of your article on Mr. Hunt's 'The Story of Rimini,' without thinking them a tissue of falsehood—ill woven to be sure!—but full as malicious as inconsequent.
>
> ([Clarke] 1816: 3)[44]

Clarke is referring here to the reviewers' claim at the beginning of the article that

> A CONSIDERABLE part of this poem was written in Newgate, where the author was some time confined, we believe for a libel which appeared in a newspaper, of which he is said to be the conductor. … [W]e have never seen Mr. Hunt's newspaper; we have never heard any particulars of his offence; nor should we have known that he had been imprisoned but for his own confession. We have not, indeed, ever read one line that he has written, and are alike remote from the knowledge of his errors or the influence of his private character.
>
> ([Croker and Gifford] 1816: 473)

These introductory sentences are indeed hard to believe since the sole reference to Hunt's imprisonment is 'my long/And caged hours' (Canto III, ll. 3–4; Hunt 2003: V, 182),[45] and no mention is made of the cause of his imprisonment. Furthermore, as Clarke notes, the reviewers' claim that they have not 'read one line' of the *Examiner* suggests that they must have been out of the country for the preceding nine years. The author of another anonymous pamphlet also points out that Z failed in his attempt to minimize the public's knowledge of Hunt: 'Is it credible that such an insignificant trifler as [Hunt] is represented, would have caused so much spleen? Mr. Z betrays himself; he shows that he thought, that he well knew, the contrary' ([Anon.] 1817c: 17).

In fact, Hazlitt accurately describes the reviewers' point for such a claim in *A Letter to William Gifford, Esq.*, published in March 1819:

> In order to give as favourable an impression of that poem as you could, you began your account of it by saying that it had been composed in Newgate, though you knew that it had not; but you also knew that the name of Newgate would sound more grateful to certain ears, to pour flattering poison into which is the height of your abject ambition.
>
> (Hazlitt 1930–4: IX, 26)

Hazlitt's description of the reviewer's attack on Hunt is curiously reminiscent of the murder of the King in the garden in *Hamlet*, which is rather appropriate for an essay on the 'King of the Cockneys'. Seven years later, in his essay 'The Periodical Press', Hazlitt would come back to this attack on Hunt:

> The first announcement of the work [*The Story of Rimini*], in a Ministerial publication, sets out with a statement, that the author has lately been relieved from Newgate—which gives a felon-like air to the production, and makes it necessary for the fashionable reader to perform a sort of quarantine against it, as if it had the gaol-infection. It is declared by another critic ['Z'], in the same pay, to be unreadable from its insipidity, and afterwards, by the same critic, to be highly pernicious and inflammatory—a slight contradiction, but no matter!
>
> (Hazlitt 1930–4: XVI, 236–7)

The reviews published in the *Quarterly Review* and *Blackwood's Edinburgh Magazine* contain numerous instances of thinly disguised personal attacks on Hunt and his political stance as editor of the *Examiner*.[46] Lockhart thus writes:

> The poetry of Mr Hunt is such as might be expected from the personal character and habits of its author. As a vulgar man is perpetually labouring to be genteel—in like manner, the poetry of this man is always on the stretch to be grand.
>
> ([Lockhart] 1817: 39)

The personal nature of this attack, and the possibility of a libel case, led Baldwin and Cradock, the London booksellers listed as William Blackwood's correspondents for the magazine, to discontinue their association with *Blackwood's* (their names do not appear on the second issue). Although Baldwin and Cradock were shocked by the virulence of Z's attack, they did comment in a letter to William Blackwood dated 3 November 1817 that '[b]eing a convicted libeller himself, Mr Leigh Hunt has little right to complain of such attacks' (quoted in Oliphant 1897: I, 134–5). John Richardson, a solicitor from Edinburgh, held a higher opinion of Hunt, but nevertheless condemned *The Story of Rimini* in a letter to William Blackwood, dated 20 November 1817:

> [W]ith all his affectation, he is in the domestic relations of life most exemplary … a *puritan* in morals … I do not however think that a man's pure conduct at home entitles him to spread poison abroad: and I have no doubt that the poem must be regarded as reprehensible—Vice is much more readily insinuated by such books as the new Eloise & Rimini than by coarser works that call such things more plainly by their names: & it is no justification that Dante first told the story.
>
> (quoted in Roe 1997: 271)[47]

Richardson wrote again to Blackwood two days later:

> There is no doubt, I believe, that Mr L. Hunt can prove himself individually to be almost if not altogether as pure & correct a man as walks the streets of London—& supposing this to be the case—one question which arises is—is the poem [*The Story of Rimini*] of a pure or impure tendency—if a jury will not say that it is impure then you have no case—for if both man & poem be blameless your article is certainly as atrocious a libel as could be penned.
>
> (quoted in Roe 1997: 271)[48]

Kim Wheatley notes that Lockhart attempted to discredit Hunt by 'blurring the identities of the poet and his text' in the first essay on the Cockney School of Poetry (Wheatley 1992: 12). Yet, the equating of poet and poem was common in the period, and the anonymous reviewer of the American edition of *The Story of Rimini* reaches a diametrically opposite conclusion by means of a similar kind of equation:

> Many persons have judged that Lord Byron must possess a bad heart, because he delights in painting the bad and violent passions almost exclusively. By the same rule, Mr. Hunt should be presumed to have a most amiable character, since he so frequently describes frankness, openness, cheerfulness, &c.
>
> ([Tudor] 1816: 281)

Whereas for Lockhart, Hunt's personal style, finery, language, and his affected descriptions of Italy reflect his lack of an upper-class education,[49] and his overtly familiar dedication to Byron represents an attempt to transcend his social background, the American reviewer defends Hunt's character on the basis of his chosen topic and his style of composition. In the fourth essay on the Cockney School published ten months later, Lockhart attacked Keats in ways that make clear his assumption that a similarity with Hunt's *The Story of Rimini* in poetic language indicates a similarity in political views: 'Mr. Keats has adopted the loose, nerveless versification, and Cockney rhymes of the poet of Rimini' ([Lockhart] 1818b: 522). As Roe notes, '[i]n Lockhart's view of Keats, there was no discrimination of the aesthetic and the political; quite the contrary. For him Keats's poetic language was itself reprobate, an insolent challenge to the establishment' (Roe 1995a: 3). The remark is equally descriptive of Lockhart's opinion of Hunt as found in his first review of *The Story of Rimini* and in the other articles devoted to Hunt.

Lockhart's coarse attack in the first article on the Cockney School of Poetry led to the publication of another defense of Hunt's *The Story of Rimini* in a fifty-six-page pamphlet entitled *A Review of Blackwood's Edinburgh Magazine for October 1817*. The bulk of the pamphlet deals with Lockhart's review of *The Story of Rimini*, though the anonymous author also comments negatively on other sections of the October issue of *Blackwood's*, including the 'Chaldee Manuscript' and the review of Coleridge's *Biographia Literaria*. The tone of the pamphlet is as vindictive as that of Lockhart's piece. The author cunningly writes of Lockhart's description of Hunt: 'A mass of rubbish of more gross arrogance, of ridiculous presumption, of weak and silly affectation, we have seldom, nay, we have never seen heaped together' ([Anon.] 1817c: 14). Again following Lockhart's example, he proceeds to an *ad hominem* attack: 'These absurdities could only have emanated from one either totally ignorant of Leigh Hunt's literary character, or, what rather appears the case, from one determined, at every risk, to vilify and misrepresent him' ([Anon.] 1817c: 14–15). The author comments in detail on Lockhart's article, answering Lockhart's allegations point by point, in a systematic defense of Hunt. The author concludes by making strong claims for the poem's moral and aesthetic excellence:

> Rimini, Mr Reviewer and Messrs Conductor and Publisher, has been read, and read attentively; there is not one line, one sentiment introduced in that poem, to warrant such assertions. No, the most delicate and sensible mind, after perusing it, longs again to examine all its beauties, to indulge in its fine descriptions.
>
> ([Anon.] 1817c: 22)

He also declares that Byron and Hunt were friends while Hunt was in prison and thus 'by common courtesy, as well as habits of intimacy, Mr. Hunt was empowered to call him "My dear Byron"' ([Anon.] 1817c: 33).

The series of articles on the Cockney School of Poetry is perhaps, in the words of Patrick Story, 'the most notorious controversy in British literary history' (Story 1980: 191). This series comprised, in any case, the first major negative event of Leigh Hunt's literary career. Hunt had been imprisoned in 1813 for his political beliefs and thus became a political martyr. Because of his views, he experienced calumny and repeated anonymous attacks against him between 1816 and 1825.[50] As Anthony Holden comments, the attacks were 'motivated by political more than literary animus' (Holden 2005: 126). Following the publication of Croker and Gifford's article in the *Quarterly Review*, Hunt had written to Moore on 21 May 1816:

> I was prepared, of course, for a reasonable carbanado from the Government quarters, and even for a good deal of stout objection perhaps from more friendly ones, as far as difference of theory was concerned; but this assault is mere foaming at the mouth.
>
> (quoted in Moore 1853–6: VIII, 215)

Hunt also notes in the preface to his 1832 *Poetical Works*: 'Probably these criticisms [against *Rimini*] were not altogether a matter of climate; for I was a writer of politics as well as verses, and the former (two years ago!) was as illegal as the sallies of phraseology' (Hunt 2003: VI, 80). A few pages later, Hunt also acknowledges the reviewers as being 'not altogether impartial, however, on the political score' (Hunt 2003: VI, 85).

Perhaps more important than the actual reception of the poem, the *Blackwood's* reviews, together with numerous references in articles and reviews published in that journal between 1821 and 1829,[51] linked Hunt definitively with the Cockney School and all the negative connotations implied by this school for the following decade. This association denied him the chance of popular success for several years. Although it can be argued that negative attention was, as in the case of the *Lyrical Ballads*, better than no attention at all, it did not prepare readers for Hunt's success either then or today. Interestingly, as Kim Wheatley remarks, 'Z never addresses the possibility of his reviews functioning as advertisements for Hunt's poetry, nor does he ask himself why, if Hunt is so worthless, he is wasting his time on him' (Wheatley 1992: 8). The answer most likely lies in Lockhart's awareness of the political implications of *The Story of Rimini*, and consequently the need to limit the potential audience by attacking Hunt through calumny of his character and ridicule of the language used in the poem.

Legacy of the Cockney School of Poetry articles

In 1818 Hunt published *Foliage*, a volume of poetry consisting principally of translations and short poems, but also containing two of Hunt's greatest poems: 'To T. L. H.' and 'The Nymphs'.[52] Hunt exposes himself to criticism of the religious opinions he expresses in the preface and in several poems, as well as in his defense of *The Story of Rimini*:

> the moral of [*Rimini*] is not as some would wish it to be,—unjust, and bigoted, and unhappy, sacrificing virtue under pretence of supporting it;—but tolerant and reconciling, recommending men's minds to the consideration of *first* causes in misfortune, and to see the danger of confounding forms

> with justice, of setting authorized selfishness above the natural impulses, and making guilt by mistaking innocence.
>
> (Hunt 1818a: 17)

His controversial political opinions are still apparent throughout *Foliage*, whether in his discussion of the need for a new poetical sensitivity in the preface (Hunt 1818a: 20), or in his repeated use of green imagery in various poems as 'a lyrical expression of the *Examiner*'s oppositional politics' (Roe 1997: 122). Published in the midst of the first wave of attacks on the Cockney School (which went on until October 1819), *Foliage* received some critical attention, but it was primarily hostile and clearly influenced by the reviews in *Blackwood's* and the *Quarterly Review* already discussed.[53] Although the review published in the *British Critic* characterizes some parts of *Foliage* as pleasing, it also refers to 'Mr. Hunt's poetical school' and Hunt's political opinion, and commends him with faint praise for avoiding some of the past offences: 'In these poems ... we have met with no blasphemy or jacobinism, and an unusually small proportion of ribaldry. We cannot part with Mr. Hunt without expressing our high approbation of this part of his labours. As a poet he is at least harmless' ([Anon.] 1818e: 95, 96).[54] the *Eclectic Review* also comments, in more negative terms, on Hunt's political and religious opinions:

> Nothing ... can, for the most part, be more impolitic in the writer of poetry, than for him to obtrude upon his readers those points in his individual character, which relate to differences of religious creed or political opinion, thereby tending to awaken a class of associations opposite to those which it is the business of the poet to excite.
>
> ([Anon.] 1818h: 484)

The *Eclectic* reviewer nevertheless praises 'To T. L. H.' and 'The Nymphs', especially the descriptions of landscape that evoke such painters as Poussin, but he dismisses other poems, in particular the sonnets to Hampstead, for the 'most distressing *cockneyism* [that] pervades Hunt's ideas of the beautiful in scenery' ([Anon.] 1818h: 492–3). The anonymous reviewer for the *Literary Gazette, and Journal of Belles Lettres, Arts, Politics, etc* is more critical of the poems as a whole:

> [W]e candidly own that we think them monstrously insipid. Their model seems to be the meanest of the Italian sonneteers; whose everlasting [effort] at some prettiness or other was sometimes rewarded with a hit, but like Gratiano's reasons, when the object is attained, it is not worth the fatigue of arriving at it.
>
> ([Anon.] 1818c: 210)

Similarly, the *Monthly Magazine* publishes a short notice of the volume which concludes sharply by recommending that Hunt keep his opinions to himself: '[W]e cannot avoid wishing, for his own fame, that Mr. Leigh Hunt had reserved the principal part of this volume as *memoranda* for his port-folio, their appropriate place' ([Anon.] 1818d: 346). The *New Monthly* review reprints several extracts from *Foliage* amidst a series of ruthless comments, including a reference to 'a babbling preface to the mass of crudities' and a mention of the reviewer's 'utter disgust and loathing at the "hail-fellow-well-met" style in which Mr. Hunt addresses these gentlemen [i.e. Byron and Moore]' ([Anon.] 1818f: 162, 164).

Lockhart's review of the volume in the sixth number of his 'Cockney School of Poetry' series is predictably negative. He criticizes the poor quality of the translations, and emphasizes again Hunt's lack of a proper classical education. He also writes derisively of the various sonnets addressed to members of Hunt's circle, and sarcastically states that the familiarity of Hunt's dedication of *The Story of Rimini* to Byron is curiously absent in the dedication to John Swinburne. Lockhart's tone is mean-spirited, and he reveals his own political and class biases in the language he chooses to diminish Hunt's achievement, describing Hunt as 'the most fierce democrat and demagogue of his day, and whose habits and courses [sic] of life were altogether so very vulgar' ([Lockhart] 1819: 70).

John Taylor Coleridge's article in the *Quarterly Review* contains a similarly sarcastic discussion of what he views as the vagueness of thought in Hunt's preface, a harsh attack on Hunt's remarks on Christianity, and numerous negative comments on Hunt's style. As Kim Wheatley remarks, along with the previous assault on *Rimini*, this was the 'only other full-scale attack during Gifford's lifetime' (Wheatley 2003: 186). Coleridge's review continues the previous onslaught on *The Story of Rimini*, with Hunt's language and education again under attack:

> Mr. Hunt's faults are a total want of taste, and of ear for metrical harmony; an indulgence of cant terms to a ridiculous excess, an ignorance of common language, a barbarous and uncouth combination of epithets, an affectation of language and sentiment, and what is a far more serious charge, though it occurs but seldom, an impurity of both.
>
> ([Coleridge J. T.] 1818: 329)

Since Coleridge's review appeared anonymously in the *Quarterly*, Hunt could only blame the editor Gifford by name, as he did in a short article published in *The Examiner* in June 1818—'he is angry at the faults of a work, more angry at its excellences' (Hunt 1818b: 378)—, and again in October in the reprinting of an anonymous letter first published in the *Alfred Exeter* paper, in response to a review of Keats's *Poems* in the *Quarterly Review*.[55] Thus Hunt is not really telling the truth when, in a letter to the Shelleys dated 12 November 1818, he claims to have made

> no answer to Gifford myself, partly out of contempt, partly (I must really say) out of something bordering on a loathing kind of pity, & partly for

the sake of setting an example always praised but seldom or never practiced.

(Reiman 1973–86: VI, 740)

Hunt's hostility towards the *Quarterly* increased in 1819, beginning in February of that year with a brief literary notice announcing Hazlitt's *A Letter to William Gifford, Esq.* (Hunt 1819a: 90),[56] and then in March with a favorable review of Hazlitt's book: 'Mr. Hazlitt has got him [Gifford] fast by the ribs, forcing him, with various ingenuity of grip, to display unwillingly all the deformities of his moral structure' (Hunt 1819b: 156). With references to the *Quarterly* that the reader could easily apply to Hunt's own works, and in particular to *The Story of Rimini*, Hunt writes:

> The letter which consists of 87 closely printed pages, then proceeds to expose the wretched cavilings, wilful falsehoods and omissions, and servile malignity of the well-known articles in the *Quarterly Review* upon the *Round Table*, the *Characters of Shakespeare's Plays*, and the *Lectures on the English Poets*:—and such an exposure!
>
> (Hunt 1819b: 156)

Also in March, Hunt published the anonymous 'Doggerel Verses. By Persons of Distinction [For the Examiner],' which is a satire on Blackwood, Murray, and Gifford ([Anon.] 1819a). In June an additional article on the depiction of America in the *Quarterly Review* appeared in the *Examiner*, where its anonymous author asserts:

> Perhaps there is no Journal that does not deal partially at times; but it was reserved for the *Quarterly Review* to avow its purpose of misrepresenting and vilifying without disguise, to sport with truth, candour, and honesty, and glory in doing so.
>
> ([Anon.] 1819d: 403)[57]

In September 1819, Hunt expounded his views of the *Quarterly* at still greater length in the first part of his response to John Taylor Coleridge's review of *The Revolt of Islam*, an exchange Shelley characterizes as '[t]he droll remarks of the *Quarterly*, and Hunt's kind defence' (Shelley P. B. 1964: II, 126).[58] As is well known, Coleridge's review of the poem was very harsh and full of personal abuse about Shelley's life, but it also included a direct attack on Hunt:

> [Shelley] has not, indeed, all that is odious and contemptible in the character of that person [Hunt]; so far as we have seen he has never exhibited the bustling vulgarity, the ludicrous affectation, the factious flippancy, or the selfish heartlessness, which it is hard for our feelings to treat with the mere contempt they merit.
>
> ([Coleridge J. T.] 1819: 469)

Although Hunt admits that there were two very good articles in this issue of the *Quarterly*,[59] he severely criticizes the review as '[h]eavy, and swelling, and soft with venom, it creeps through the middle of [the issue] like a sulking toad.' He also acknowledges the personal attacks he suffered, together with Shelley, when he writes: 'The Editor, and the other more malignant writers in this Review … only missed their aim, and pitched themselves headlong, with their blind fury, in such articles as that on the *Story of Rimini*' (Hunt 2003: II, 215).

1819 also saw the publication of the first edition of Hunt's *Poetical Works* in three volumes. That this edition was not reviewed in any of the major periodicals of the time is a sign that Hunt the Poet was beginning to be eclipsed entirely by Hunt the Editor and political figure; the absence of reviews may also be another instance of the unfortunate legacy of the 'Cockney School of Poetry' articles. The publication of Hunt's 1819 *Poetical Works* somehow marked a pause in his career as poet, a career that would begin anew in 1832 with the publication of his second *Poetical Works*, which included the revised versions of *The Feast of the Poets* and of *The Story of Rimini*. Although this second edition was well reviewed, and Hunt's position within the London literary scene changed for the better over the following two decades, the stigma of the attacks against *The Story of Rimini* lasted much longer than anyone might have anticipated at the time, and Hunt was now more famous for heading the Cockney School of Poetry than for being the author of *The Story of Rimini*.

4 1821–1828

> Italy is an exhaustless theme to those who, having been long resident there, are familiar with its novel and beauteous aspect.
>
> Mary Shelley, '[English in Italy]' (Shelley M. 1996: II, 159)

Leigh Hunt's life was to undergo some important changes between the years 1821 and 1825. Although he successfully edited two new publications, the *Indicator* (1819–21) and the *Literary Pocket–Book* (1819–23), his finances were once again causing him some distress, as was his health, which had been in decline since the end of the 1810s. Meanwhile, P. B. Shelley, who had been living in Italy with his wife Mary since 1818, had repeatedly invited Hunt to visit them there. Hunt had protested to Shelley for many months that he could not leave London, his brother John, or his work on the *Examiner*, even though John's son Henry had actually been more or less running the *Examiner* on his own from the end of 1820 due to Leigh's problematic health.[1] Poor finances were really the principal reason Hunt had resisted the Shelleys' friendly invitation to come and stay with them in Italy, as his letter to Mary Shelley, dated 9 March 1819, shows:

> 'But what, Hunt, of Italy?' Ah, you see I delay speaking of Italy.— I cannot come; I wish to God I could, & were Shelley & you to be ill so as to want me to help comfort you, I feel almost certain that I would;—but it is next to impossible. My brother John had for some months had an idea of retiring into the country, in order that his sons might be better furnished with means for entering into life; & just as I wrote my last letter, he had finally determined upon it. He & my other brothers dine with me tomorrow, previously to his departure, which takes place in a couple of weeks; & then it will be more than ever necessary that I should be every Saturday at office, where my nephew Henry takes his place.
>
> (Reiman 1973–86: VI, 791)

On 10 July 1821, Hunt explains once more to P. B. Shelley that the sales of the *Examiner* had been 'lamentably falling off' over the last few months, causing great distress to both brothers (Hunt 1862: I, 163).[2]

Yet, in September 1821, Hunt finally agreed to go to Italy, following Byron's invitation to edit a new journal in Italy with Shelley, who had originally suggested including Hunt in this project. Thus, Hunt writes to the Shelleys on 21 September:

> We are coming. I feel the autumn so differently from the summer, and the accounts of the cheapness of living and education at Pisa are so inviting, that, with your kind persuasions, the proposal of Lord Byron, and last, be sure not least, the hope of seeing [you] again and trying to get my health back in your society, my brother as well as myself think I had better go.
>
> (Shelley P. B. 1964: II, 344)

This letter neatly summarizes the reasons that led Hunt to transplant himself and his family from his beloved Hampstead, where the letter was written, to Italy: his financial struggles, Byron's proposal of a new periodical (eventually called the *Liberal*), the desire to be with Shelley again after years of separation, and his (and in fact also his wife Marianne's) failing health.[3] Thus, after many months of hesitation and delay, Hunt had finally agreed to Shelley's proposal to move to Italy and to work on a new publishing venture, which would provide him with a new source of income to supplement the share of profits he expected from the *Examiner*.

Shortly before leaving for Italy, Hunt wrote to Henry Brougham: 'I am about to enter on a literary speculation which I have reason to think will set me free once for all from the difficulties I have long struggled with' (Hunt 1999: 106). Yet, although the tone is hopeful, Hunt ends the letter on a note that shows he was more cautious about the future success of the *Liberal* than is generally acknowledged: 'I still remain connected with the Examiner,— which I tell you that you may not think I have given up a certainty for an uncertainty' (Hunt 1999: 107). When Hunt left for Italy, he was very much aware of Byron's crucial involvement in the planned publication; Byron's name alone could ensure its success. Byron would also contribute new works, which, in Hunt's view, could guarantee the sales of their new periodical, and consequently improve Hunt's finances as well as the printing business of his brother John, as he indicates in a letter to the Shelleys, dated 21 September 1821:

> With regard to the proposed publication of Lord B., about which you talk so modestly, he has it in his power, I believe, to set up not only myself and family in our finances again, but one of the best-hearted men in the world, my brother and his. … I agree to [Byron's] proposal with the less scruple, because I have had a good deal of experience in periodical writing, and know what the getting up of the *machine* requires, as well as the soul of it.
>
> (Hunt 1862: I, 172)[4]

By that stage of his career, Hunt had certainly demonstrated his talent for journalism, as well as his ability to launch new periodicals (although not often financially viable), as his work on the *Examiner*, the *Reflector*, and the *Indicator* amply attest. However, as it turns out, Hunt's finances did not in fact improve. The new periodical was not a success, and Hunt found himself in a new position of financial dependence on Byron.[5]

A further factor that must have played a role in Hunt's decision to move his family from London to Italy had to do with the allure of the country itself. In the summer of 1818 Hunt writes enthusiastically to the Shelleys: 'I long to hear of Rome, & Naples, & the paintings, &c. &c., particularly of the ladies & the out-of-door amusements' (Reiman 1973–86: VI, 610). As Donald H. Reiman notes, 'Only Hunt, among Shelley's English friends, really envied the Shelleys their sojourn in what seemed to him the paradise of the arts' (Reiman 1973–86: VI, 616). By the time Hunt was ready to leave England, he was also extremely familiar with P. B. Shelley's numerous poems dealing with Italy, including *Julian and Maddalo*, *Lines written among the Euganean Hills*, *Ode to Naples*, and *The Cenci* (which evokes Shelley's earlier Gothic novel *Zastrozzi*, also set in Italy).[6] Hunt was also well versed in Italian literature, as he had been an avid reader of Italian prose and poetry ever since his imprisonment at Surrey Gaol and his purchase of *Parnaso Italiano*.[7] *The Story of Rimini* is, to a certain extent, Hunt's homage to Italian literature and to one of its greatest writers, as are his many translations of Italian poems by various authors. An array of essays, notes, and editions further demonstrate his extensive knowledge of Italian authors. The following extract from a letter sent to the Shelleys on 6 April 1820 is but one example of Hunt's ongoing appreciation of Italian writers:

> By the way, a book has been lent me, the pictures in which make me think you [*sic*] of you. It is a life of Boccaccio by a Count Baldelli, containing four views of scenery near Florence, real places which he has described in the Decameron, & in his young rural novel Ameto, which I have the pleasure to have before me also. There is the Valle di Mugnone, the Valle delle Donne, the Villa of Schifanoia, & his native place Certaldo.
>
> (Reiman 1973–86: VIII, 932)[8]

Hunt would assert again, in a letter to Byron dated 27 January 1822, 'I am extremely fond of Italy & Italian literature' (Hunt 1999: 113).

Ultimately, Hunt's journey to Italy would have consequences for Hunt that neither he nor Shelley could have anticipated. Before he left for Italy, Hunt had been away from England only once,[9] and after his return he would never leave his native shores again. At the time of his departure, Hunt was also a well-known public figure who commanded a certain level of respect (as well as animosity) in London literary circles. By the time he came back to London in 1825, Hunt had suffered the second major blow to his career after the Cockney School attack, and his reputation in England was further damaged. From a professional point of view, Hunt's work on the *Liberal* did not make him a more popular writer or editor. He also lost his income from the *Examiner* following an argument with his brother, and he failed to find a new audience for his work, even in his attempts at writing travel literature when travel accounts were amongst the most popular books read through circulating libraries in London (Altick 1957: 217–18). From a personal point of view, Hunt's health did not improve as much as he had hoped, but rather declined due to his poor living conditions and the strain of the demand of producing numerous articles, first for the *Liberal* and then for the 'Wishing Cap' series in the *Examiner*. Finally, Hunt's finances were considerably worse than when he left London four years earlier, when one of the main reasons for his departure in the first place had been to improve them. As a whole, Hunt's stay in Italy had a significant negative impact on Hunt's life and career, especially due to the debacle of the *Liberal*.

The *Liberal*

When the first issue of the *Liberal* appeared on 15 October 1822, most London periodicals had for some time already featured advertisements for it, references to it, and articles about it. As William H. Marshall demonstrates in great detail in his work *Byron, Shelley, Hunt, and The Liberal*, Hunt's new publication received a high level of attention in the London press, as well as in contemporary literary circles, both before and after the publication of the four issues of this short-lived journal (Marshall 1960: 90–134). This level of public interest was not entirely surprising since the three persons who were to collaborate on the project—Shelley, Byron, and Hunt—were all public figures, known for their controversial politics and their own publications.

The result of the (ultimately unsuccessful) collaboration between Hunt and Byron in the *Liberal* has been extensively covered by most biographers of these two authors,[10] in addition to its treatment as the special focus of Marshall's book, where he carefully analyses each issue of the *Liberal* and provides a detailed reception history of this periodical in reviews, letters, and even publications that appeared in direct response to it.[11] Marshall also surveys the essays, poems, and translations that appeared in the four issues of the journal, with a list of authorial attributions. In light of previous studies devoted to the *Liberal*, the focus of the present section is to offer some further understanding as to why this periodical failed.

Marshall propounds several explanations for the failure of the *Liberal*, as do E. M. Earl and James Hogg, who offer a succinct and compelling reading of the whole project:

> One imagines that one just cast into the *Liberal* what one had on hand, and hoped that Byron's name would carry it. His Lordship's temporary fall from public favour and Leigh Hunt's chronic unpopularity with Tory

> readers, allied to John Hunt's lack of experience as a bookseller, sealed the periodical's fate.
>
> (Earl 1998: xiv)

Hunt's 'chronic unpopularity with Tory readers' obviously played a major part in the negative reception of the periodical even before the first issue was actually published. In 1822 Hunt was still a contentious political and literary figure, repeatedly attacked in *Blackwood's* for the licentiousness of his writings (as exemplified in *The Story of Rimini*) and his denunciation in the *Examiner* of many of the Government's decisions. Thus, politics was once again a prominent factor in the failure of one of Hunt's projects. At the same time, the potential threat that the *Liberal* represented for other similar kinds of publications probably played a part in the negative reception that had anticipated the first issue, as this extract from a letter from Charles Ollier to William Blackwood, dated 3 January 1821, indicates:

> Mr Leigh Hunt, we are told, is gone to Pisa: he and his family are to live with Lord Byron in his lordship's house, and they (Ld Byron & Hunt) are, with the assistance of Mr Shelley to write a journal to be published here as the neutralizer of the Quarterly Review and, I suppose, of *Blackwood*
>
> (quoted in Roe 1997: 274)

Meanwhile, Byron at this point was known less for *Childe Harold's Pilgrimage* than for his sacrilegious play *Cain* and the first two 'scandalous' cantos of *Don Juan*—although his reputation was not as tainted as Hunt's. In his 1830 *Life of Lord Byron*, John Galt declares: '[the *Liberal*] disappointed not merely literary men in general, but even the most special admirers of the talents of the contributors. ... But the main cause of the failure was the antipathy formed and fostered against it before it appeared' (Galt 1830: 270–1). And indeed, most members of London literary and political society had already formed an opinion about the result of the collaboration between Hunt and Byron even before the first issue of the *Liberal* appeared, and that view was unsurprisingly negative. The following extract from a letter Wordsworth sent to Walter Savage Landor on 20 April 1822 is quite typical of the prevailing opinion at the time:

> It is reported here that Byron, Shelley, Moore, Leigh Hunt (I do not know if you have heard of all these names) are to lay their heads together in some Town of Italy, for the purpose of conducting a Journal to be directed against everything in religion, in morals and probably in government and literature, which our Forefathers have been accustomed to reverence,—the notion seems very extravagant but perhaps the more likely to be realised on that account.
>
> (Wordsworth and Wordsworth 1978: 124)

Andrew Rutherford suggests that Wordsworth 'was expressing [in this letter] a widely held view of Byron as not merely a profligate and a blasphemer, but a dangerous force of subversion and corruption, moral, religious and political' (Rutherford 1970: 9). Consequently, the very concept of a new periodical edited by Byron, Shelley, and Hunt seemed a threat to morality and the Government even before its publication.

The first issue, which featured Byron's *The Vision of Judgment* as the opening poem, did not disappoint readers' expectations. Carl Woodring remarks that '[p]eriodicals and pamphleteers supporting the Government attacked the *Liberal*, and particularly Byron's satire, more vociferously than any other publication of the Hunts' (Woodring 1970: 196). Alexandre Kilgour's contemporary account also indicates the political nature of the attacks on the *Liberal*:

> Whilst Byron was the friend of Murray, the evil mouths of the party, who were obliged to hate him for his political principles, were shut; but the publishing of one of Byron's works by the Hunts, was the signal for the blood-hounds to shake themselves clear, and pursue, with the utmost speed, their victim. Leigh and John Hunt are not men apt to conciliate the opposite party[.]
>
> (Kilgour 1825: 47)

In the same account, Kilgour provides an instance of the contemporary misunderstanding regarding the origins of the *Liberal*, as well as the overall tediousness of the works, a common focus for criticism:

> The idea of a periodical was suggested by Mr. Hunt; and Byron, in the hope that it would be of some benefit to his friend, agreed to furnish some articles. It was continued for a few months, but, with the exception of a few articles furnished by Lord Byron, was so insufferably dull, that the public threw it up in utter hopelessness.
>
> (Kilgour 1825: 48)

One should also note that, as Donald Reiman points out, if *The Vision of Judgment* is often the main work criticized in contemporary reviews of the *Liberal*, 'Hunt's editorship was the focal point for critical attitudes toward the new journal' (Reiman 1972: II, 670). In fact, Hunt ended up being blamed for Byron's works, in particular *Don Juan*.[12] Thus, William Maginn and John Gibson Lockhart write in their July 1823 review of Cantos VI–VIII of *Don Juan*:

> I feel a moral conviction that his lordship must have taken the *Examiner*, the *Liberal*, the *Rimini*, the *Round Table*, as his models, and endeavoured to write himself down to the level of the capacities and the swinish tastes of those with whom he has the misfortune, originally, I believe, from

> charitable motives, to associate. … Indeed there are some verses which have all the appearance of having been interpolated by the King of the Cockneys.
>
> ([Maginn and Lockhart] 1823: 90)

A few months earlier, *Blackwood's* had published an article that asserted that 'LORD BYRON being a somewhat whimsical nobleman, has lately hired two or three Cockneys as menial servants' ([Anon.] 1823a: 365).

The level of partisanship against Hunt, the *Liberal*, and the potentially subversive politics that the journal represented readily serve to explain attacks of this kind. Even Byron's friends were hostile to his association with Hunt and the *Liberal*, and did their best to stop his collaboration, either by attacking the periodical in reviews or by writing opinionated letters to him. To mention but one instance of the negative view of Byron's collaboration with Hunt, John Wilson Croker wrote to John Murray in March 1820:

> In politics, [Byron] cannot be what he appears, or rather what Messrs. Hobhouse and Leigh Hunt wish to make him appear. A man of his birth, a man of his taste, a man of his talents, a man of his habits, can have nothing in common with such miserable creatures as we now call Radicals.
>
> (quoted in Rutherford 1970: 193–4)

Thus Byron's apparent dismay at the repeated attacks on the *Liberal*, which he expresses in letters to various friends, is somewhat surprising. On 24 February 1823, Byron writes to Mary Shelley:

> I have no other news—but on business—and continual declamation against the Liberal from all parties—literary—amicable—and political—I never heard so persevering an outcry against any work—nor do I know the reason for not even dullness or demerit could authorize the extraordinary tone of reprobation.
>
> (Byron 1973–94: X, 108)

Byron would reiterate his bewilderment in a letter to Bryan Waller Procter, dated 5 March 1823:

> As to 'The Liberal,' I do not know how it is going on; but all my friends of all parties have made a portentous outcry against the whole publication, and so continue, which is a great encouragement. … What *I* have done to displease my aristocratic connections I can quite understand—in this matter; but what the two H[unt]s are guilty of to sanction their invectives is not quite so clear.
>
> (Byron 1973–94: X, 116–17)

However important a role politics played in the negative reception of the *Liberal*, other factors were equally to blame for the failure of this publication. The uneven quality of the writing published in its four issues certainly aided in the periodical's demise. As Phyllis Grosskurth remarks, 'The *Liberal* was a miscellany of disconnected writings without any coordinating tone to unify them in some way. It is not surprising that, after an initial success, it ceased publication after four issues' (Grosskurth 1997: 417). Although some major poems by Byron and essays by Hazlitt (including his famous 'My First Acquaintance with Poets') and Mary Shelley ('A Tale of the Passions') appeared in the pages of the *Liberal*, the bulk of the material was left to Hunt to produce.[13] Hunt wrote more than half of the contributions, and given the difficult times for him and his family, the quality of the writing was predictably uneven. As he himself admitted several years later, in a *Tatler* essay dated 14 January 1831:

> Mr Leigh Hunt willingly concedes that the articles from his own pen in the 'Liberal' are far inferior to what he could have wished them, and were not worthy of the occasion. Ill health, and the calamitous death of his friend, and the new, unlooked-for, and most unpleasant circumstances under which he found himself situated with Lord Byron, may perhaps excuse his doing no better.
>
> (Hunt 1830–32: II, 454)

What emerges as the defining focus of the *Liberal* is the Italian theme, which is sustained throughout the four issues. In fact, as Kenneth Churchill notes,

> [M]uch of the material [in *The Liberal*] is related to Italy: for example, a translation of Ariosto, an article on Casti, stories of medieval Italy, and Hunt's *Letters from Abroad*, the first of which is perhaps the most eloquent and enthusiastic account of the beauties of Pisa to have appeared in English.
>
> (Churchill 1980: 55)

Particularly interesting for the present study are the four articles Hunt published under the heading 'Letters from Abroad'—one in each issue of the *Liberal*[14]—as they constitute a narrative of his stay in Italy and his first-hand impressions of the places and people he had read about so often in the previous decade. This narrative is continued, although with distinct differences, in his two-part article 'On the suburbs of Genoa and the Country about London', published in the *Literary Examiner* in August 1823 (Hunt 1823a and Hunt 1823b). I would like to suggest that, alongside the section of *Lord Byron and Some of his Contemporaries* entitled 'The Author's Visit to Italy, Residence there, and Return to England',[15] these essays engage with, and contribute to, a great tradition of travel writing associated with Italy which developed throughout England and Europe in the early nineteenth century. Herbert Barrows argues that 'the individual tour or sojourn [in Italy] has to be seen against the background of the experience of Italy that was generally available at the time [and] in the context of the individual life, with its specific motivations and needs' (Barrows 1963: 360). For Hunt, part of the context for his work was his love for Italian literature and his interest in the contemporary travel literature available in the first two decades of the nineteenth century.

As mentioned previously, Hunt was already predisposed to take a special interest in Italy, not only via the literature he translated and adapted, including of course *The Story of Rimini*, but also through the travel works he read in connection with the writing of *The Story of Rimini*, many of them provided by Byron, who had himself of course a great interest in Italy, its classical literature, and history, which culminated in the famous and famously influential fourth canto of *Childe Harold's Pilgrimage*. On examining Hunt's writing on Italy, it emerges that, in this genre as in so many others, Hunt's work was likely to offend some of his contemporaries precisely for the quality that should most interest his later readers. In making his contributions to the genre of travel writing about Italy, Hunt was not content to follow conventions of style and context; rather, he had his own independent response to make, both to travel writing and to the English view of Italy itself.

Travel literature and Italy

On 9 February 1820, when Hunt was still considering a journey to Italy but was not yet prepared to leave London, Maria Gisborne writes to Mary Shelley:

> Hunt is prepared to like Italy; he is well acquainted with the style of the country in theory; but yet it will be a new world to him. … Hunt will certainly admire the beautiful little city of Pisa, and its hilly background. (Gisborne 1951: 76)

Gisborne's comment indicates both how different Italy would appear to Hunt when he saw it for himself as well as his extended knowledge of Italy from his reading of primary and secondary works.[16] Indeed, Hunt fits Maura O'Connor's description of the younger generation of English men and women who, in the early part of the nineteenth century, 'learned about Italy secondhand; that is, by reading travel literature and histories and by following accounts of Napoleon's military adventures on the Italian peninsula' (O'Connor 1998: 19). Hunt was obviously very much aware of Napoleon's expeditions, since he had written about them at great length in the *Examiner* over the years. He also was quite familiar with travel literature and historical studies of Italy. Yet, until he actually visited Italy, the country was for him an imaginary one, since his impressions and views of the place had not yet been experienced firsthand.[17]

When the Treaty of Paris was signed at the end of May 1814, English travelers in large numbers began returning to the Continent, and to Italy in particular. In fact, as Brian Barefoot remarks, the urge to travel abroad

> was far greater than it had been in 1763. The frontiers had been closed for longer, and much more effectively closed as well. Since the population was larger, and since wealth was beginning to be distributed more evenly within the population, there were more potential travellers.
>
> (Barefoot 1993: 138)[18]

J. R. Hale also notes that there was a change in the social background of the majority of travelers, and that middle-class visitors were increasingly common (Rogers 1956: 69–70).[19] The rise in English travel to Italy led to larger communities of English abroad, especially in major cities such as Florence and Rome. Byron comments on this growing presence of his fellow countrymen when he writes to Thomas Moore on 25 March 1817 of his plans for travel in Italy:

> I have not the least idea where I am going, nor what I am to do. I wished to have gone to Rome; but at present it is pestilent with English,—a parcel of staring boobies, who go about gaping and wishing to be at once cheap and magnificent.
>
> (Byron 1973–94: V, 187)

In response to this surge in interest, the number of travel books on Italy rose steadily after the Napoleonic Wars, and numerous extracts appeared in newspapers and magazines (Brand 1957: 16).[20] In fact, Italy remained a popular topic for books published between 1810 and 1830; the idea of Italy was still very evocative of culture, history, and a warmer climate in 1828, when Hunt published *Lord Byron and Some of his Contemporaries*. Thus, the anonymous reviewer of Henry Beste's *Italy as it is* asserts in the June 1828 issue of the *Monthly Review*: 'We opened [*Italy as it is*] under the impression of those beguiling fancies, which are always awakened in the mind by the very sound of "Italy"' ([Anon. 1828k: 258).[21] At the same time, any new author was very much aware of the numerous literary precedents, and often tended to justify the publication of a new volume about Italy in his or her preface. For instance, Louis Simond, author of *A Tour of Italy and Sicily* (1828)—a work highly praised by Mary Shelley in her 1829 review[22]—admits that

> an apology may be due, for presuming to publish an account of what I saw in Italy years ago [in 1819], anticipated as I have been, by so many and more recent travellers: but I really thought it might not be quite uninteresting to see what Italy was just on the eve of its revolutions. Contrary to the custom of travellers in Italy, I have said little about the fine arts, and yet I have perhaps said too much; as there is nothing to be gained by any attempt to stem the current of received opinion.
>
> (Simond 1828: x–xi)[23]

Two years earlier, Hazlitt had written in the 'Advertisement' to his *Notes of a Journey through France and Italy*: 'There is little history or antiquities or statistics [in this volume]; nor do I regret the want of them, as it may be abundantly supplied from other sources' (Hazlitt 1930–34: X, 85). The 'received opinion' that Simond evokes in his own account originated in a large number of similar works on Italy published during the eighteenth century and in the even greater number published during the first three decades of the nineteenth century. In fact, as C. P. Brand notes,

> As far as one can judge from the travel-books and articles published, the years 1819–28 formed a peak period. Travel-books on Italy appeared at the rate of about nine each year at this time as compared with an average of four a year between 1829 and 1839, and just over four during the 1840's. Similarly periodical literature during the 1820's is full of references to Italian travel, whereas these occur more rarely in the 1830's and 1840's.
>
> (Brand 1957: 23)

Consequently, it is not surprising that it was determined that travel narratives were to be included in the *Liberal* even before Hunt had arrived in Italy. He writes to Byron on 27 January 1822: '[the journal] might begin, if you pleased, with your account of a land journey to Italy, which I might follow in the next number with that of a sea-one' (Hunt 1999: 113). Although the *Liberal* may have ended up lacking overall coherence, its underlying theme was provided by its location in Italy, and Hunt's idea to exploit the current popularity of travel literature led him to include several essays that are part of this trend.

The first 'Letters from Abroad', entitled 'Letter I.—Pisa', is Hunt's longest contribution to the *Liberal* and reflects his extended knowledge of travel literature about Italy. Hunt indicates in the first paragraph the personal nature of his recollection and how, in his view, an author has to express himself directly and informally to the reader or else '[h]e will not be able to move about with so much freedom, or give the results of his impressions and encounters with such vivacity, as if he were unhampered with a body corporate' (Hunt 1822–3: I, 97). Hunt proceeds to implement this view and to write an entertaining piece about Pisa and the impressions the city made on the author, especially in light of the contrast between the author's expectations of Pisa and Italy in general and the reality of the city. Pisa was, at first, everything Hunt had anticipated:

> Let the reader imagine a small white city, with a tower also white, leaning very distinctly in the distance at one end of it, trees on either side, and blue mountains for the back-ground. Such is the first sight of Pisa, as the traveller sees it in coming from Leghorn. Add to this, in summer-time, fields of corn on all sides, bordered with hedge-row trees, and the festoons of vines, *of which he has so often read*, hanging from tree to tree; and he may judge of the impression made upon an *enthusiastic admirer of*

> *Italy*, who is in Tuscany for the first time. It looks like a thing you have dreamt of, and answers most completely to the imagination.
>
> (Hunt 1822–3: I, 99; my emphasis)

Then, as Hunt remarks, 'The first novelty that strikes you, after your dreams and matter-of-fact have recovered from the surprise of their introduction to one another, is the singular fairness and new look of houses that have been standing hundreds of years' (Hunt 1822–3: I, 100).

This apparent sense of conflict between the imagined city and the real one is not at all unusual for English travelers. In fact, extensive reading about Italy and many long hours spent contemplating famous eighteenth-century depictions of Italian cities was also sometimes the cause of disappointment. Hazlitt, for instance, writes to Landor from Rome on 9 April 1825: 'Rome hardly answers my expectations; the ruins do not prevail enough over the modern buildings, which are commonplace things' (Hazlitt 1978: 338). Hazlitt's biographer Stanley Jones discerningly declares that 'Hazlitt found he could not reconcile modern Rome with the luminous city that had grown in his imagination from such eighteenth-century prints as Claude Lorrain's *Arch of Constantine*, which hung in his room at Winterslow' (Jones 1989: 368).[24] Samuel Rogers, author of *Italy* (1822), was another writer who had been disappointed by his first visit to Italy.[25] The problem originated in Rogers's experience of recognition, rather than the pleasure of discovery, of the places he visited. Indeed, as the editor of Rogers's Italian journals, J. R. Hale, comments:

> So much had been written about Italy, its landscape, its towns, its monuments, and so much of it was known from the works of painters like Claude, Apnini and Salvator Rosa, that the country was familiar even to those who had not yet visited it. The actual places sometimes disappointed.
>
> (Rogers 1956: 94)

Hale could not have been more accurate in his last sentence. Hunt's descriptions of Italy often reflect exactly this state of mind, as is evident in the following extract from 'On the suburbs of Genoa and the country around London':

> When you behold Albaro [a neighboring village of Genoa] from the sea, you cry out, 'What a delicious place to live in!' Imagine a green hill, full of olive trees, vineyards, and country seats, beheld from a blue sea, glittering under a blue sky, and with the Appennines [*sic*] at the back of it. Enter it, and the charm is dissolved.
>
> (Hunt 1823a: 97)

The appearance of Albaro in the perfect setting of 'a blue sea, glittering under a blue sky' is certainly promising. In fact, it corresponds to the image of Italy many English, including Hunt, had in mind. Engravings in guide books, as well as descriptions of the beauties of Italy in most fictional and non-fictional works about the country, helped to build high expectations for Hunt which would sometimes be disappointed by the reality of the landscape.[26] Hunt was aware of these expectations, as he indicates in his description of Pisa quoted earlier, and also in his description of Leghorn in *Lord Byron and Some of his Contemporaries*:

> The country around is uninteresting, when you become acquainted with it; but to a stranger, the realization of any thing he has read about is a delight, especially of such things as vines hanging from trees, and the sight of Apennines.
>
> (Hunt 1828a: 14)

Once past the initial excitement of seeing what one had read about, the reality of the landscape takes over. Thus, the actual decrepitude of houses in Genoa banishes preconceived images of once-colorful houses:

> [I]n some instances, the paintings [had been] done upon stucco, the latter has partly crumbled away; and this gives a shabby, dilapidated appearance to houses otherwise excellent. Nobody seems to think of repairing them. It is the same with many of the houses unpainted, and with common garden walls, most of which must have once made a splendid appearance.
>
> (Hunt 1822–3: I, 282)

Hunt mentions again his frustrated expectations with regard to the Italian cities he visited in his recollections in *Lord Byron* when, after describing Bologna, he states:

> Many cities in Italy disappoint the eye of the traveller. The stucco and plaister outside the houses gets worn, and, together with the open windows, gives them a squalid and deserted appearance.
>
> (Hunt 1828a: 505)[27]

It is fair to say that, after P. B. Shelley's death, Hunt could hardly find anything joyful in Italy—'From that time Italy was a black place for me' (Hunt 1828a: 18)[28]—and this particular passage was written as he was making his way back to England.

Hunt's frankness about his feelings throughout his recollections in *Lord Byron*, as indicated here by the reference to P. B. Shelley's death, is a constant feature of Hunt's writing about Italy. This is in fact one of the major differences between Hunt's essays on Italy and most typical travel literature. This emotional directness emerges in numerous mentions of Hunt's friendship with Shelley, their brief time together in Italy, and other indications of the effects of this sad loss on Hunt, which may be inferred from the first 'Letters from Abroad'. As he is about to describe Pisa's famous Leaning Tower, Hunt inserts the following passage:

> On the Sunday following … I went to see it, and the majestic spot in which it stands, with Mr. Shelley. Good God! what a day that was, compared with all that have followed it! I had my friend with me, arm-in-arm, after a separation of years: he was looking better than I had ever seen him—we talked of a thousand things—we anticipated a thousand pleasures— — —I must plunge again into my writing, that I may try to forget it.
>
> (Hunt 1822–3: I, 103)

Hunt's third 'Letters from Abroad' essay is the text of a letter he addressed to Vincent Novello, and includes many personal references to the love of music and opera Hunt and Novello shared, and things they had discussed together before Hunt's departure for Italy.[29] Similarly, the fourth of these 'Letters from Abroad' is another personal letter, this time addressed to 'C—', in which Hunt again hints at previous discussions that took place between himself and the addressee, as well as other letters they had exchanged since Hunt's move to Italy.[30] The familiar style of the last two essays tends to dominate slightly the information Hunt provides on the popularity in Italy of Rossini versus that of Mozart, and on the dialect spoken by people near Genoa. It is likely, however, that these disconnected outbursts of personal feeling may be the result of the hurried conditions under which Hunt did his work for the *Liberal* rather than a deliberate wish to write in the style of the familiar essays he had published in the *Indicator* a few years earlier, and that he would use again in the *Companion* in 1828.

Another major difference between Hunt's writing on Italy and the other travel literature available at the time has to do with their reflections of their authors' class and educational backgrounds. John Chetwode Eustace's *Tour of Italy, exhibiting a View of its Scenery, Antiquities, and Monuments, particularly as they are objects of Classical Interest* (1813) provides a good example of the standard attitude. Eustace expects his audience to have a background knowledge of Greek and Latin history, and makes passing references to facts and monuments often without providing the reader with any specific information about them. While Eustace's general approach is similar to other travel literature—he describes the best-known landmarks in the major cities, as well as political, literary, and religious aspects of the country—the tone and style clearly indicate the targeted audience. Yet, although Eustace's work would later be attacked for its inaccuracy,[31] it met with great success and became a classic of Italian travel literature during the 1810s.

Another classic work of travel literature that presumes a certain educational background on the part of its audience is Joseph Forsyth's *Remarks on Antiquities, Arts, and Letters, during an Excursion in Italy in the Years 1802 and 1803* (1813). Forsyth was a writer with a strong web of literary connections, having spent most of his eighteen months in Italy among writers in all the major cities he visited. He was knowledgeable in Italian history and poetry, as his work amply demonstrates, and clearly expected his readers to have similar knowledge. Although Hunt mentions having some reservations about Forsyth, he describes him as 'a late traveller of much shrewdness and pith' (Hunt 1822–3: I, 103). He also refers approvingly to *Remarks on Antiquities, Arts, and Letters* several times in the first 'Letters from Abroad', in particular Forsyth's description of specific landmarks of Pisa such as the Leaning Tower and the cathedral, on which subject he quotes at great length from Forsyth's book (Hunt 1822–3: 103, 106–7). However, Forsyth and Hunt differ drastically in their numerous references to Italian authors in the sense that Forsyth expects his readers to know and approve the authors he mentions, whereas Hunt's literary references serve to introduce his audience to works and authors, and to educate his readership in a way similar to his theatrical reviews published in the *News* and the *Examiner*; he clearly does not write with the expectation of an exclusive, highly cultivated audience.

Thus Hunt fills his description of Pisa in the first 'Letters from Abroad' with references to Italian authors that make these authors newly accessible to his readers rather than writing with slight presumptive allusions, as Eustace and Forsyth do. Early in the essay, Hunt comments on his journey to the Leaning Tower, and makes the following passing reference: 'Further up on the same side of the way, is the old ducal palace, said to be the scene of the murder of Don Garcia by his father, which is the subject of one of Alfieri's tragedies' (Hunt 1822–3: I, 100–101).[32] Then, as Hunt describes his visit to the Cathedral of Pisa one evening in August, he writes about Dante (an obvious favorite of his): 'It is impossible to see this profusion of lights [in the cathedral], especially when one knows their symbolical meaning, without being struck with the source from which Dante took his idea of the beatified spirits' (Hunt 1822–3: I, 107–8). Hunt's readers are thus issued an enticing invitation to discover Alfieri, and gently introduced to a Dantesque source. Similarly, Hunt alludes to any literary references called up for him by association with the places he describes in all the essays he penned about Italy. Thus, the first reference to the Italian coasts in his recollection published in *Lord Byron and Some of his Contemporaries* mentions a poet:

> We were now sailing up the angle of the Gulf of Genoa, its shore looking as Italian as possible, with groves and white villages. The names too were alluring,—Oneglia, Albenga, Savona; the last, the birthplace of a sprightly poet, (Frugoni,) whose works I was acquainted with.
>
> (Hunt 1828a: 488)[33]

Hunt had referred to Carlo Frugoni in the second 'Letters from Abroad', where he describes him as 'easy and lively, but [he] wrote a great deal too much [poetry], probably for bread' (Hunt 1822–3: I, 287). Later on in *Lord Byron*, Hunt brings in one of his favorite Italian authors:

> We left Santa Croce to live at Maiano, a village on the slope of one of the Fiesolan hills, about two miles off. I passed there a very disconsolate time; yet the greatest comfort I experienced in Italy was from living in that neighbourhood, and thinking, as I went about, of Boccaccio. Boccaccio's father had a house at Maiano, supposed to have been situate [*sic*] at the Fiesolan extremity of the hamlet. That divine writer ... was so fond of the place, that he has not only laid the two scenes of the Decameron on each side of it, with the valley his company resorted to in the middle, but has made the two little streams that embrace Maiano, the Affrico and the Mensola, the hero and heroine of his Nimphale Fiesolano. A lover and his vestal mistress are changed into them, after the fashion of Ovid.
>
> (Hunt 1828a: 492–3)[34]

While recollecting the time he spent at Maiano, Hunt takes this opportunity to educate his readership about Boccaccio, one of his literary heroes, in an unpretentious fashion, via his own personal experience and identification with the author.

In alluding to literary authors and to various historical details about the locations he describes, Hunt follows the models of travel literature already widely available. Yet, unlike other writers in this genre, he does not use his observations of Italy to reveal his superior taste and education in a self-congratulatory fashion. Instead, he bears witness, with often refreshing honesty, to the particulars of his actual experience as an Englishman, more particularly as a Londoner, in what was, after all, an alien culture. Hunt asserts early on in the recollection of his trip: 'I am thus particular in my daily notices, both to complete the reader's sense of the truth of my narrative, and to give him the benefit of them in case he goes the same road' (Hunt 1828a: 483). Hunt's independent response to the experience of living in Italy is thus remarkable primarily for what is revealed about the author, a self-styled Londoner, in this place and time.

In so doing, Hunt differs markedly from one of the major literary works of the Romantic period dealing with Italy: Lord Byron's fourth canto of *Childe Harold's Pilgrimage*.[35] Although Hunt did not review the poem in the *Examiner* when it was published in April 1818, he singles out the fourth canto in his 'Sketches of the Living Poets. No. 2.—Lord Byron', published in the *Examiner* on 29 July 1821. After drawing a portrait of Byron the man, Hunt proceeds to discuss his poetry, and states that while he finds that Byron's poetic work is 'not of imagination, but of passion and humour', he likes 'nevertheless the last canto of *Childe Harold*' (Hunt 2003: II, 345). As Jerome McGann remarks,

> The poem's historical, artistic, and geographical subjects were almost completely gathered together from B[yron]'s experiences in Italy in 1817—when he was at Venice, on his trip from Venice to Rome, during his stay at Rome, and again when he returned to Venice.
>
> (Byron 1980–92: II, 317)

The last canto opens with Byron's statement: 'I stood in Venice, on the Bridge of Sighs;/A palace and a prison open on each hand' (Canto IV, ll. 1–2; Byron 1980–92: II, 124). Byron goes on to narrate his journey and to portray the places he visited in the 186 stanzas of the canto. In fact, the poem at first appears to be a series of vignettes evoking some guidebooks to Italy.[36] The traditional references to all the major sites are present, along with a discussion of Italy's historical and literary past.[37] Byron's emotional responses are also manifest throughout the poem, where, to quote from Walter Scott's anonymous review, he throws 'before the reader his reflections and opinions, his loves and his hates, his raptures and his sorrows' ([Scott] 1818: 228). Yet, whereas Byron's *Childe Harold* celebrates Italy as a background, fitting in its grandeur as a kind of accompanying illustration for the grand passions of his hero, Hunt usually takes a humorous and down-to-earth view of himself and his own experiences as he describes them in his various essays. Thus, Hunt's view of Italy is correspondingly rendered in life-sized dimensions, as in his descriptions of clothes worn by Italians or of the cost of food: 'In Italy, we also looked for our heaps of fruit; and we had them—in all the luxury of baskets and vine-leaves, and a cheapness that made us laugh' (Hunt 1822–3: I, 273). Hunt also acknowledges his own limitations as guide, and alters statements made in his earlier essays once he has learned more: '[S]ince I have known more of Genoa, I have found out that it possesses multitudes of handsome women; and what surprised me, many of them with beautiful northern complexions' (Hunt 1822–3: II, 52). This is another example of Hunt's frank and independent response to what he sees. These quotations document what might be described as the increasingly articulate cultural self-confidence of someone of Hunt's background.

Standing on a par with Byron's fourth canto of *Childe Harold's Pilgrimage* in terms of its lasting impact on the popular imagination is Madame de Staël's *Corinne ou l'Italie* (1807).[38] De Staël's novel was an immediate and lasting success in France, as well as in Switzerland, Italy, Germany, and England.[39] As late as 1832, Elizabeth Barrett Browning would announce: '*Corinne* is an immortal book, and deserves to be read three score and ten times—that is once every year in the age of man' (Browning 1955: 176). Not only did de Staël's novel entrance contemporary European society with its plot, it also provided a detailed narrative of its hero Oswald's travels from his native Scotland to Italy, as well as descriptions of the major Italian cities and of the character of the Italian people. The anonymous reviewer for the *Edinburgh Review* notes that

> [t]he object of Madame de Staël has been, to intermix, with the incidents of a fictitious narrative, the description of whatever was to be found in Italy most worthy of attention, while that country remained in full enjoyment of the noble patrimony which it inherited from past ages.
>
> ([Anon.] 1807: 183)

The very title of the novel, *Corinne ou l'Italie*, indicates its double intent: it is simultaneously a novel about a woman and an exploration of a country.[40] Madelyn Gutwirth accurately asserts that

> [d]espite the fact that Mme de Staël was by no means the first to interlard her novel with a voyager's observations, her travelogue is at once more extensive and more integrated with her plot than had been the case with similar works.
>
> (Gutwirth 1978: 183)[41]

The book was in fact read by many as a travel guide and studied before a visit to Italy,[42] in particular for its descriptions of Rome, where most of the novel takes place. Throughout *Corinne*, the eponymous heroine lectures Oswald on Italian music, art, and letters in sections of the novel that could almost stand on their own as travelogue (Gutwirth 1978: 161).[43] Hunt refers to one of these sections in his 'Letters from Abroad. Letter II.—Genoa':

> From the Piazza della Fontane Amorose you turn into the Strada Nuova, which leads round through another sumptuous street into the Strada Balbi, fit, says Madame de Staël, for a congress of kings.
>
> (Hunt 1822–3: I, 276)

Hunt follows this reference to de Staël with a rather sarcastic remark on monarchy:

> This has become a poor compliment. It is fit for a congress of men. If intellect, and not childishness, settled the destinies of the world, here might such spirits meet as the Dorias, the Miltons, the Sidneys, the Hôpitals, and the Washingtons, and put an end at once to the tiresome farce of kings being taught to no purpose.
>
> (Hunt 1822–3: I, 276)

Hunt's political commentary here is not atypical of him, but his writing on Italy is actually largely devoid of political references. The allusion to de Staël's *Corinne* might have triggered this observation since her work was quite political in the way it depicted Italy before the Napoleon conquest and in the contrasts she drew between France, Italy, and England through the various conversations conducted among her characters.[44]

Lady Morgan's 1821 *Italy* is another widely read work in which politics permeate the writing.[45] Throughout her two-volume edition, Morgan strongly asserts her own political stance: she repeatedly gives her opinion of the current Italian government,[46] criticizes the papacy, and, in contrast to de Staël, defends Napoleon's legacy in Italy.[47] Morgan's political opinions caused *Italy* to be included in the index of prohibited books in the Vatican,[48] and it was the principal subject of complaint for contemporary reviewers, who generally reviewed the book negatively.[49] One of these reviewers was Albany Fonblanque, who reviewed Morgan's work in the *Examiner* on 1 July 1821. The political dimension of *Italy* not surprisingly constitutes the core of Fonblanque's review, but, after criticizing her political opinions, he nevertheless admits that

> [i]t must not however be imagined, that the interest of Lady Morgan's book is confined to political facts and inferences. On the contrary, it abounds with much pleasant, lively, and vivacious description. Her account of Milan, Florence, Bologna, Rome, and Naples, especially the two latter, are peculiarly pleasant, and interspersed with anecdotes of conspicuous individuals which unequivocally supply the principal charm of this class of tour writing.
>
> ([Fonblanque] 1821b: 413)

Several of these anecdotes were re-published in the *Examiner* on 14 October 1821, and provided Leigh Hunt with another opportunity to enjoy Morgan's work. Hunt had himself read *Italy* and, in his first 'Letters from Abroad', quoted approvingly from Morgan's personal commentaries on the people she met during her travels:

> Lady Morgan has justly remarked the promising countenances of Italian children, compared with what they turn out to be as they grow older; and adds with equal justice, that it is an evident affair of government and education.
>
> (Hunt 1822–3: I, 117–18)

Hunt's style in the recollection included in *Lord Byron and Some of his Contemporaries* also evokes Lady Morgan's attention to physiognomy, as, for instance, in his description of the inhabitants of Bologna and Modena:

> I thought the looks of the Bolognese and Modenese singularly answered to their character in books. What is more, is the extraordinary difference, and nationality of aspect, in the people of two cities at so little distance from one another. The Bolognese have a broad steady look, not without geniality and richness. You can imagine them to give birth to painters. The Modenese are crusty looking and carking, with a dry twinkle at you, and a narrow mouth. They are critics and satirists, on the face of them.
>
> (Hunt 1828a: 506)

However, Hunt's style is more friendly and direct than Lady Morgan's. He jokes with the reader, as he does with the addressee Novello in a letter which he chooses to include unchanged among his recollections. The tone is strikingly self-ironic; Hunt wittily associates the Modenese facial traits ('crusty looking and carking') with those of members of his own profession.

Hunt's very personal style also succeeds in bringing his readers closer to the places depicted, as in his descriptions of Genoa, first in the *Liberal* and then in *Lord Byron and Some of his Contemporaries*:

> GENOA is truly 'Genoa the Superb.' Its finest aspect is from the sea, and from the sea I first beheld it. Imagine a glorious amphitheatre of white houses, with mountains on each side and at the back. The base is composed of the city, with its churches and shipping; the other houses are country seats, looking out, one above the other, up the hill. To the left are the Alps with their snowy tops: to the right, and for the back, are the Appennines [*sic*]. This is Genoa.
>
> (Hunt 1822–3: I, 269)[50]

Hunt's representation of Genoa as seen from a boat is very evocative, and it does justice not only to the geographical aspect of this view but to the colors and shapes Hunt sees. Another aspect of Hunt's familiar style is found in the narration of his first night in Genoa:

> In Genoa you heard nothing in the streets but the talk of money. I hailed it as a good omen in Florence, that the two first words which caught my ears, were Flowers and Women (*Fiori* and *Donne*). The night of our arrival we put up at an hotel in a very public street, and were kept awake (as agreeably as fever would let us be) by songs and guitars. It was one of the pleasantest pieces of the south we had experienced: and, for the moment, we lived in the Italy of books. One performer, to a jovial accompaniment, sang a song about somebody's fair wife (bianca moglie), which set the street in roars of laughter.
>
> (Hunt 1828a: 491)

Hunt's style and personal taste are again evident in this quotation: he asserts that he prefers to hear about 'Flowers and Women' rather than 'talk of money', and he uses a conversational tone to describe his first night in Florence. Addressing the reader as a friend in whom he can confide, Hunt writes a familiar essay that includes both details about the atmosphere of the city and the writer's personal health, underscoring the difficulties of travel, the heat, and the health hazards involved in traveling in summertime. The description of the city filled with laughter is also very vivid, and the whole scene comes to life in the text. This lively prose is reminiscent of Hunt's style in the essays published in the *Indicator* nearly ten years earlier.[51]

If Hunt regularly quotes from Italian writers throughout his essays on Italy, he also refers to English authors, especially Chaucer, Milton and Spenser, both in order to compare the two countries' writers and to use the English descriptions of England to compare with the Italian landscape, as in this reference to Ann Radcliffe in *Lord Byron and Some of his Contemporaries*: 'At Sant-Ambrogio, a little town between Turin and Susa, is a proper castle-topped mountain *à la Radcliffe*, the only one we had met with' (Hunt 1828a: 509). These references to English authors are to be found alongside various mentions of London, at first in order to provide the reader with a point of comparison, and later on as an indication of Hunt's longing to return to his favorite city. In his first 'Letters from Abroad', Hunt refers to London to give a sense of the geographical arrangement around the Leaning Tower: 'With regard to the company in which it stands, let the reader suppose the new square at Westminster Abbey, converted into a broad grass walk, and standing in a much more solitary part of the town' (Hunt 1822–3: I, 105). Then Hunt describes the Campo Santo, '[t]he crowning glory of Pisa' (Hunt 1822–3: I, 109), thus: 'It is an oblong inclosure, about the size of Stratford Place, and surrounded with cloisters wider and lighter than those of Westminster' (Hunt 1822–3: I, 109).[52] Again, in his second 'Letters from Abroad', Hunt compares the streets of Genoa with those of London: 'What surprises you is the narrowness of the streets. As soon as you have passed the gate, you think you have entered upon a lane, remarkably good indeed for a lane—a sort of Bond-street of an alley,—but you have no conception that it is a street, and of the ordinary dimensions' (Hunt 1822–3: I, 274).

Henry Beste declares in his introduction to *Italy as it is* that 'A NARRATIVE of a residence in a foreign country will differ from a tour: the tourist may see and observe; the resident will reflect and compare' (Beste 1828: I). Indeed, Hunt's three-and-a-half-year stay in Italy gave him more opportunities to 'reflect and compare' than a brief tour of the country would have. As time went by, Hunt compared Italy with England, and specifically with London, increasingly often, and it becomes clear that he was increasingly missing England. For instance, he writes in an article from the 'Wishing Cap' series that

> an Englishman in Italy, who loves Italian poetry, and is obliged to be grateful to Italian skies, assures his beloved countrymen (who are not always sensible of the good things they have about them) that there is nothing upon earth so fine as a good, rich English meadow in summer time.
>
> (Hunt 1888: 80)

Earlier in the article, Hunt declares:

> I am in a world of poetry and romance, of vines and olives, and myrtles (which grow wild), of blue mountains and never-ending orchards, with a beautiful city in the middle of it. What signifies? I think of an English field in a sylvan country, a cottage and oaks in the corner, a path and a stile, and a turf full of daisies; and a child's book with a picture in it becomes more precious to me than all the landscapes of Claude. I intended to sprinkle this article with some flowers out of the Italian poets; but positively I will not do it. They are not good. They are not true. The grapes are sour. Commend me to the cockney satisfactions of

> Chaucer, Spenser, and Milton, who talk of 'merry London', of lying whole hours looking at the daisies, and of walking out on Sunday mornings to enjoy the daisies and green fields.
>
> (Hunt 1888: 79)

Though Hunt admits that Italy is a welcoming country and that he is enamored of Italian literature—as he had been for more than twenty years—he expresses his love for English landscape in terms that make clear his longing for England. His recollection of his stay in Maiano, where he wrote the 'Wishing Cap' articles, conveys the same longing for England and London:

> I not only missed 'the town' in Italy; I missed my old trees,—oaks and elms. Tuscany, in point of wood, is nothing but an olive-ground and vineyard. … A tree of reasonable height is a Godsend. The olives are low and hazy-looking, like dry sallows. You have plenty of those; but to an Englishman, looking from a height, they appear little better than brushwood. Then there are no meadows, no proper green lanes (at least, I saw none), no paths leading over field and style, no hay-fields in June, nothing of that luxurious combination of green and russet, of grass, wild flowers, and woods, over which a lover of Nature can stroll for hours with a foot as fresh as the stag's. … In short, (saving a little more settled weather,) we have the best part of Italy in books, be it what it may; and this we can enjoy in England.
>
> (Hunt 1828a: 499–500)[53]

This extract provides another instance of Hunt's recollection of Italy, with numerous details about the places and the surrounding vegetation, but it also shows how London features prominently in his mind and work. Thus, it is not surprising to find Hunt declaring: 'I took leave of Maiano with a dry eye, Boccaccio and the Valley of Ladies notwithstanding' (Hunt 1828a: 502).

Toward the end of his stay in Italy, Hunt wrote a series of essays called 'Wishing Cap' which appeared between 28 March 1824 and 16 October 1825 in the *Examiner*.[54] He was particularly pleased with these pieces, as he writes to Elizabeth Kent in March 1824: 'You must know, modestly speaking, that I think all these articles good, and that I never wrote better prose in my life—I mean good in point of style' (Hunt 1862: I, 214). The 'Wishing Cap' articles do not deal with Italy but rather with London, and clearly indicate Hunt's state of mind in the latter part of his stay in Italy. These articles are, for instance, about Covent Garden, St James's Park, and Piccadilly and the West End. As Hunt remarks in his *Autobiography*, these pieces later became the basis for his book on London, *The Town* (first published in 1848), as well as for a series of articles he published during the 1830s in *Leigh Hunt's London Journal* under the title 'The Streets of London' (Hunt 1850: III, 119).

In his book *English Literary Periodicals* Walter Graham asserts that the *Liberal* was 'an extraordinary literary periodical, and, within a limited circle of readers, the sensation of its day' (Graham 1930: 287). Twentieth-century critics have questioned both its literary quality and the overall lack of a sense of editorial direction. Despite the huge popularity of the *Liberal* in its time, Hunt did not benefit from this publicity, from either a financial or a literary perspective. The reception of the *Liberal* in England was primarily in response to Byron's contributions and the religious and political charges laid against the periodical even before the appearance of its first issue. Consequently, critics neglected Hunt's interesting, unusual and noteworthy contributions to the travel-writing genre. Yet, with the emergence of an increasing number of publications devoted to travel writing in Italy, and the growing popularity of the genre, Hunt's 'Letters from Abroad' and the section of *Lord Byron and Some of his Contemporaries* dealing with the author's stay in Italy had the potential to give Hunt access to a new audience.

Hunt's foray into the travel-writing genre illustrates his awareness of this popular literary trend, and his wish to take advantage of it. His innovations in his writing about Italy are subtler than those introduced through his theatrical criticism or his unconventional ideas about poetic language. For instance, Hunt participates in a genre in which predecessors are acknowledged and often discredited in order to argue for the author's own original contribution to the field. Hunt follows the genre's conventions and refers regularly to previous authors, but he noticeably differs from most writers by remaining positive in these allusions. In fact, although Hunt could be very critical of political, literary and theatrical figures, as reflected in his 'Political Examiner' articles and in his reviews, he opts for constructive descriptions of Italy and the places he visits in order to enlighten the reader, rather than indulge in criticism of previous contributors to the genre. Hunt further differs from other writers of travel literature in the dialogic style he uses throughout his essays. His contribution is intriguing for its informality, particularly his unique way of writing as if to engage the reader in direct conversation.

John Nichol's rather harsh account of the *Liberal* in his 1880 book, *Byron*, takes issue with Hunt's 'gossiping account of Pisa' (Nichol 1880: 162). Yet, Hunt's gossipy style is an aspect of one of his main contributions to the contemporary corpus of writing about Italy, which tended to be rather formulaic in content and stilted in style. In the first two 'Letters from Abroad' essays, Hunt constantly engages the reader in a conversation, and includes anecdotes and personal information. Hunt's essays are a personal guided tour of the places he visits, and they read as if they were addressed to a friend rather than an impersonal reader. In the third and fourth essays, Hunt chooses to reproduce letters he actually addressed to friends, and therefore treats the reader as another friend, welcome to eavesdrop on Hunt's conversations.

Hunt's longing for London and the English landscape became stronger and stronger over time, as the essays he wrote during the second half of his stay in Italy make clear. Hunt's nostalgia, however, does not interfere with his chatty style, and his later travelogue essays offer numerous examples of this characteristic familiar style. For instance, in his essay 'On the suburbs of Genoa and the Country about London', he follows a negative depiction of Genoa and its inhabitants with the amusing interjection:

> Now tell it not in Scotland, lest the Cocknies [*sic*] of the Canongate rejoice; but give, dear N., before all the barren suburbs in the world (bits of mountain included) the green pastures and gentle eminences round about glorious London. *There* we have fields:—there one can walk on real positive turf: there one can get trees that are of no use, and get under trees, and get among trees; and have hedges, stiles, field-paths, sheep and oxen, and other pastoral amenities.
>
> (Hunt 1823a: 98)

Hunt first wrote this self-mocking passage in a letter to his friend Vincent Novello, and chose to publish it in the *Literary Examiner*. Awareness of his reputation in England and of his enemies at *Blackwood's Edinburgh Magazine* are here combined with a good-humored, engaging style which evokes many of the pieces in the 'Wishing Cap' series. Throughout his life, even in times of greatest financial difficulty, Hunt maintained his cheerful tone and his mode of friendly dialogue with the reader, as if writing the kind of conversation in which he might engage as a guest in someone's home. In his essays (published under the penname of Elia), Charles Lamb is arguably more effective in striking a witty, chatty tone than Hunt, but the pieces that Hunt wrote under the heading of the 'Wishing Cap' illustrate his ongoing efforts to bring a more familiar, conversational tone into his writing.

Like many other Romantic writers, Hunt was somewhat disappointed by the reality of Italy when compared with the mental images he had of the country before he arrived. Like many other travel literature writers, he included numerous descriptions of classical sites and evocations of contemporary Italy in his travelogue essays. These essays reveal his awareness of, and his endorsement of, the conventionality of the travel literature genre. Yet, Hunt's familiar style and its engagingly personal, conversational tone constitute his contribution to the genre, and is another example of his literary independence.

Ultimately Hunt's stay in Italy was nothing like what he had hoped for and anticipated: Shelley's death and Hunt's quarrel with Byron were tragic events for him personally, and the Italian people and the country itself generally disappointed him. Hunt remained interested in Italian literature and politics all his life, as his works on Italian authors and his involvement in the Society of the Friends of Italy in 1851 indicate.[55] Nevertheless, in 1825 London was, and would remain, the best place in the world for Hunt. The English capital prevailed as the place he felt most at ease, even in the midst of the difficult times he later went through after his return to England, when the publication of *Lord Byron and Some of his Contemporaries* met with a negative reception and provided Hunt with the third major and final blow to his reputation within London literary circles of the Romantic period.

Lord Byron and Some of his Contemporaries

This section surveys the critical reception of Leigh Hunt's *Lord Byron and Some of his Contemporaries* (1828), the publication of which eventually dealt the final blow to Hunt's public career during the Romantic period. In his introduction, Hunt reports that Byron had asked him to 'look upon him as standing in Mr. Shelley's place, and said that I should find him the same friend that the other had been' (Hunt 1828a: 18). Although Byron had helped Hunt financially during Hunt's stay in Italy, if at times rather grudgingly, they never approached the degree of intimacy of companionship that Shelley and Hunt had known. Hunt's dedication of *The Story of Rimini* to 'My Dear Byron' may have appeared to cross class and social boundaries for reviewers of the poem in 1816, but his relationship with Byron in fact remained very much within these boundaries. The publication of *Lord Byron and Some of his Contemporaries* in late January 1828[56] reveals, among other things, that Hunt did not consider Byron as a friend. Byron's assertion in *Don Juan* that '[d]ead scandals form good subjects for dissection' (Canto I, Stanza 31; Byron 1980–92: V, 57) was to be proven truer than he had probably anticipated.

Lord Byron and Some of his Contemporaries illustrates Hunt's new position within the London literary scene as the third decade of his life as an author ends. It also reveals the consensus of the reading public that Hunt had clearly overstepped the bounds of respectability in writing about the dead, and that he had broken the rules of hospitality. As Chris Hart remarks, '[*Lord Byron*] was to hurl Hunt into the arms of notoriety, earning him an instant reputation as the least savoury literary character in the Romantic period, and excluding him from polite society for several years' (Hart 1996: 164).[57] Most of the critics who discuss *Lord Byron* at length either attack Hunt and his views of Byron or analyze in detail the motivations and consequences of Hunt's decision to publish such a negative account of the major literary figure of the day.[58] My focus here is again on the contemporary reception of Hunt's work, the impact of that reception on Hunt's literary career and its influence on modern interpretations of Hunt's work.

On 14 October 1825, Leigh Hunt, his wife and eight children arrived in London after three-and-a-half years in Italy. Henry Colburn had advanced Hunt the money he needed in exchange for his agreement to write a volume of recollections.[59] Originally, as Hunt writes in the preface to *Lord Byron and Some of his Contemporaries*, the book was 'intended to be nothing but a selection from the Author's writings, preceded by a biographical sketch' (Hunt 1828a: iii). However, Colburn very quickly became more interested in a biographical essay on Byron, or 'the Byron Book' as he would call it, since he judged that this would be more popular with the reading public than Hunt's own personal recollections or his selected writings.[60] Hunt eventually yielded to Colburn's request for a work on Byron and, in 1827, he set down to write the work that would effectively derail his literary career during the Romantic period.

Colburn's insistence on a work about Byron certainly makes sense in the late 1820s when Byron was one of the most popular biographical subjects in England and throughout Europe. Several books on Byron had already appeared in London, including Sir Egerton Brydges' *Letters on the Character and Poetical Genius of Lord Byron* (1824), R. C. Dallas's *Recollections of Lord Byron, from the year 1808 to the end of 1814* (1824), and Thomas Medwin's *Conversations of Lord Byron, noted during a residence with his Lordship at Pisa, in the years 1821 and 1822* (1824), publications that Hunt would refer to and refute in his own recollections of Byron. 'The account of Lord Byron was not intended to stand first in the book', Hunt writes,

> I should have kept it for a climax. My own reminiscences, I fear, coming after it, will be like bringing back the Moselle, after devils and Burgundy. Time also, as well as place, is violated; and the omission of a good part of the auto-biography, and substitution of detached portraits for inserted ones, having given altogether a different look to the publication from what was contemplated at first. But my publisher thought it best; perhaps it is so; and I have only to hope, that in adding to the attractions of the title-page, it will not make the greater part of the work seem unworthy of it.
>
> (Hunt 1828a: vii–viii)

Colburn had clearly great hope for the publishing success of Hunt's book, and he accordingly placed the volume at the top, and in larger print, in advertisements for new books published by his house, as he did, for instance, in the series of advertisements he ran in the *Athenaeum* between 16 January and 29 January 1828, as well as in the *Morning Chronicle* on 9 January. Several extracts from the book were also made available to periodicals in Colburn's journal, the *New Monthly Magazine & Literary Journal*, in the review published on 1 January 1828, as well as in other sources, including the *Morning Chronicle* which offered extracts on 1 and 3 January 1828. Thus, on 5 January 1828, the following comment appeared in the *London Literary Gazette*: 'Extracts from this book, which (however it may be considered when completely before the world) possesses unquestionable interest, having found their way to publicity, we should be sorry not to yield our quota to the contingent of novelty and curiosity' ([Anon.] 1828c: 6).

Colburn's advertising trick of promoting the Byron angle worked all too well: the main interest of the book was Hunt's recollections of Byron, and this section attracted the most severe criticism from reviewers. Yet the Byron section constitutes only forty percent of the whole book, that is to say, as much as the autobiographical section, which received considerably less attention from the public, even though it contains an enlightening portrait of Hunt's early years and the recollections of his trip to Italy. The other sections of *Lord Byron and Some of his Contemporaries* can best be described as Hunt's gallery of portraits in the manner of Hazlitt's *A Spirit of the Age*. Hunt provides a series of individual chapters, varying in length and in familiarity of style, each devoted to one of his contemporaries, including Coleridge, Lamb, Moore, Keats, and P. B. Shelley.

As in the case of the *Liberal*, Hunt's new work was widely advertised before its official publication. So as to puff the book and thereby boost its sales, Colburn published several long extracts from *Lord Byron* in the *New Monthly Magazine*, a periodical owned by Colburn and edited by Thomas Campbell, a friend with whom Hunt had visited weekly since his return to London. These extracts were very quickly republished in other periodicals, as was the current practice at the time, as a form of advance notice which engaged the attention of the literary community, as well as that of members of the general public interested in another book on Byron. As Andrew Elfenbein remarks, '[s]ince reviewers had emphasized that the interest in Byron's poetry depended upon his personality, Byron biographies eventually competed for attention with Byron's poetry' (Elfenbein 1995: 75). That the book was written by Hunt, whose public image was still tarnished by his involvement with the *Examiner* as well as by his role as editor of the *Liberal*, no doubt fuelled the audience's interest in the work and its ultimately negative reception.

Hunt did not approve of the advance publication of these numerous extracts, for he rightly feared that people would get an unfairly biased sense of the book as a whole, and consequently would not purchase it. He wrote to the editor of the *Morning Chronicle* a letter which appeared on 21 January 1828, in which he states his objections to this practice:

> I have been represented as a man capable of violating the confidence of friendship, and giving an unfavourable portrait of a host who had treated me with nothing but kindness. … One does not like to be thought ill of by anybody, much less to be subjected to the hazard of it in the whole heart of a community. I thought of leaving my book to answer for me, and not taking any notice of the misrepresentations, unless repeated after a sight of it; but thousands will have read the extracts who will not see the book; and it is on their account that I shall trouble you with some further remarks.
>
> (Hunt 1828c: 3)

He goes on to add: 'nobody has a right to judge of the spirit of my intercourse with Lord Byron from partial extracts out of the work in question; and that I protest against any opinion of it whatsoever, unproduced by an acquaintance with the work itself' (Hunt 1828c: 3). Hunt also knew that the expensive price of the original quarto edition worked against him as far as getting his work read as a whole was concerned. He thus welcomed a cheaper, two-volume edition published on 8 April of the same year: 'The appearance of this cheaper edition will put an end, I hope, to the misconceptions occasioned by partial extracts: at least with all honest readers who shall see it' (Hunt 1828b: I, xiii). This second edition also allowed him to add another preface to the work in which he was able to explain the composition of the work further, although once again Hunt provided an unsuccessful apology for the existence of the book. In a sense, the publication of this second edition, only a few months after the first, reflects the success of the book, a success no doubt based on the scandalous reputation attached to it, and on the public's eager appetite for works devoted to Byron. Louis Landré remarks that the firm Carey, Lea and Carey published an American edition of *Lord Byron and Some of his Contemporaries* in 1828, and that a three-volume edition also appeared the same year in Paris from the press Galignani, the first work by Hunt to be published in France (Landré 1936: I, 180).[61] This publishing success indicates that Colburn's business instincts, in pushing for the Byron focus, were strong, even if this emphasis had quite negative consequences for Hunt's career in the end.

Among the numerous reviews of *Lord Byron*—this work had the same impressive media coverage as *The Story of Rimini* twelve years earlier—a few are worth noting for their insights into Byron's public stature and their reaction to Hunt's work. The *London Magazine* offers one of the most striking concluding sentences:

> We have no room for further extracts, and can only add, that as a manual of biographical anecdote, relative to the *literati* of an era unparalleled, perhaps, in the annals of time, the present work will be found, at present, and will probably continue to be, unrivalled.
>
> ([Anon.] 1828g: 233)

No other periodicals issued such a positive verdict on Hunt's work; they rather tended to praise Hunt's apparent honesty in writing, but criticized his misapplied judgment. Thus, the anonymous reviewer for the *London Literary Gazette* writes:

> In this quarto the author exhibits himself as a person of considerable talent, and of much literary conceit and affectation. But his deeper offence lies in the essence of the design itself, which appears to us to be one at which an honourable mind would have revolted.
>
> ([Anon.] 1828d: 54)

The vehement defense of Hunt's work in the *New Monthly Magazine* can easily be explained by the fact that Colburn owned this periodical. Therefore, a sentence such as 'for that every word of book is true, no reader can doubt' is very likely excessive in its affirmation ([Anon.] 1828a: 85). Periodicals did tend to be biased one way or another due to their own political agendas, but this specific review is really only a puffing piece designed to promote sales of Hunt's work, with numerous long extracts from the book included before the book's publication in order to increase its market value. John Wilson eventually denounced the publication of the *New Monthly* article in his review of *Lord Byron* for *Blackwood's Edinburgh Magazine*, drawing public attention to the fact that the *New Monthly Magazine* was published by Colburn and edited by Campbell. Wilson also attacked Hunt for his letter in the *Morning Chronicle*, and asserted that the whole thing was nothing but puffery ([Wilson] 1828: 367).

It is interesting to compare the political biases of certain journals that reviewed *Lord Byron*, since they do not fit the same pattern followed by the reviews of *The Story of Rimini*; there is less correlation between support for Hunt's politics and a positive reception of this particular work. Thus, the *Literary Magnet; or Monthly Journal of the Belles Lettres* writes that '[o]f the correctness of Mr. Hunt's principles, with his valuable services in the cause of freedom, we have, ourselves, never had the slightest doubt' ([Anon.] 1828j: 41). The journal nevertheless reproaches Hunt for attacking 'a *friend* and *patron*' ([Anon.] 1828j: 19). The *Literary Chronicle* regrets the absence of qualities typical of Hunt's other works, what the anonymous reviewer describes as the 'vein of genuine and warm-hearted philanthropy by which the writings of Leigh Hunt have been distinguished even more than by their fancy and originality' ([Anon.] 1828e: 50). The review concludes with an assertion that the volume 'has disappointed us in no small degree' and that 'the author sees, or will see, abundant reason to regret having given [it] to the world' ([Anon.] 1828e: 73). In a similar fashion, the *Monthly Review* opens its notice by stating that 'Mr. Hunt has suffered, and severely too, in the cause of liberty', adding a few pages later,

> If we were asked what we think of Mr. Hunt's politics, we should answer, that, generally speaking, we approve of them; liberal measures have always found in him a steady and energetic, and sometimes, even an eloquent defender.
>
> ([Anon.] 1828i: 300, 311)

Despite this frank praise of Hunt's political views, the reviewer severely criticizes Hunt's *Lord Byron* since 'to publish [Byron's] foibles for the sake of gain, and to publish nothing but those, for the sake of spleen, indicate a dereliction of principle, and a destitution of honourable feeling, which we shall not venture to characterise' ([Anon.] 1828i: 304). As this review in the *Monthly Review* makes clear, admiration for Hunt as a political writer and as a man did not prejudice reviewers in favor of *Lord Byron and Some of his Contemporaries*. It is perhaps more than a little ironic that reviewers like these were exemplifying a kind of literary independence that resembled Hunt's own. Another example of this kind of independence appeared in W. E. O. Peabody's review of *Lord Byron* in the *North American Review*, a journal which had favorably reviewed *The Story of Rimini* ten years earlier. Peabody shared the general feeling of distaste for Hunt's apparent motive: '[*Lord Byron*] is addressed, not to that desire which all feel to know something of the familiar life of an eminent man, but to the malicious scrutiny which so often assumes the censorship of virtue' ([Peabody] 1829: 17). Similarly, the anonymous reviewer for the *London Literary Gazette* declares:

> To have gone to enjoy the hospitality of a friend and taste the bounty of a patron, after his death to have made that visit (for avowedly mercenary ends) the source of a long libel upon his memory,—does seem to be very base and unworthy. No resentment of real or fancied ill usage can excuse, far less justify, such a proceeding ...
>
> ([Anon.] 1828d: 54)

The first attack on Hunt's *Lord Byron*, however, was not a review but a small poem entitled 'The "Living Dog" and the "Dead Lion"', which appeared in *The Times* on 22 January 1828. The author was Thomas Moore, Byron's friend (and future 'official' biographer),[62] and the poem is characteristic of Moore's satirical poetry, a genre in which he evidently excels. It narrates how 'the late noble Lion of Exeter Change' [i.e. Byron] once shared his cage with 'a small puppy-dog' [i.e Hunt]. Treated as a friend by the Lion, the dog has the opportunity to observe 'How that animal eats, how he snores, how he drinks' and decides that the Lion is not such a great animal after all. Moore thus concludes:

> 'Tis, indeed, as good fun as a *Cynic* could ask,
> To see how this cockney-bred setter of rabbits
> Takes gravely the Lord of the Forest to task,
> And judge of lions by puppy-dog habits.
> ...
> However, the book's a good book, being rich in
> Examples and warnings to lions high-bred,
> How they suffer small mongrelly curs in their kitchen
> Who'll feed on them living, and foul them when dead.
>
> (Moore 1910: 600)

In this last stanza, Moore portrays Hunt's position as one of dependence on Byron, and strikes at the heart of Hunt's supposed independence in presuming to publish criticisms of a peer of the realm who had been his benefactor. This extract also reflects a class bias, with its references to the 'Lord of the Forest' and the 'cockney-bred setter of rabbits', which is reminiscent of the attacks on *The Story of Rimini*. Moore construes lords like Byron and Cockney commoners like Hunt as members of different species and asserts that the great distance between them renders any true 'friendship' impossible.

The most virulent attack on Hunt's work before the publication of the second edition of *Lord Byron* was written by John Gibson Lockhart, and appeared in the March 1828 issue of the *Quarterly Review*, less than three years after Lockhart had taken over the editorship of that journal. In a letter dated 5

February 1828, Walter Scott encourages Lockhart to write a very harsh review since, in his opinion, 'Hunt has behaved like a hyena to Byron whom he has dug up to girn and howl over him in the same breath' (Scott 1932–6: X, 373–4).[63] Hunt himself singles Lockhart's piece out in his preface, associating it with *Blackwood's* 'for the Review, it seems, is now connected with the unprincipled calumniators, and convicted cowards of that gang, and the article in question has all the marks of being written by one of them' (Hunt 1828b: I: xviii–xix). It is understandable for Hunt to connect the *Quarterly* with *Blackwood's*, as the two journals often echoed one another's opinions, especially regarding criticism of Hunt's works. Lockhart virulently proclaims:

> [*Lord Byron and Some of his Contemporaries*] is the miserable book of a miserable man: the little airy fopperies of its manners are like the fantastic trip and convulsive simpers of some poor worn out wanton, struggling between famine and remorse, leering through her tears. … The coxcombries of Mr. Hunt's style both of thought and language, were these things news, and were they all, might … furnish inextinguishable laughter to the most saturnine of readers. But we had supped full with these absurdities long ago, and have hardly been able to smile for more than a moment at the most egregious specimens of cockneyism which the quarto presents.
> ([Lockhart] 1828: 403)[64]

As in the case of *The Story of Rimini*, Hunt's politics (here dismissed as 'cockneyism') were the true basis for the acrimonious criticism published in the *Quarterly* and *Blackwood's* against that poem. Ten years had passed since the publication of the first article on the 'Cockney School of Poetry', but the strong political antipathy still existed. It had in fact never disappeared: the negatively charged word 'cockney' was used with reference to Hunt throughout the 1820s in these publications. With his attack on Byron, Hunt was once again the enemy of a specific class of British society.

However unjust the treatment of *The Story of Rimini* by the *Quarterly* and *Blackwood's* may have been, in the case of Hunt's *Lord Byron*, they may well have had some basis for their accusations of 'cockneyism'. There is a sense in which Hunt was actually attacking the privileged upper class in *Lord Byron*. Chris Hart suggests that

> Byron was lambasted because Hunt, consciously or not, was in the business of class formation – a process which defined itself by reaction against the aristocracy rather than against the working classes. Although much of his animosity against Byron did undoubtedly result from personal incompatibility, the predisposition to this reaction was probably in place long before the two men met in Italy. *Lord Byron and Some of his Contemporaries* may seem a distasteful libel of a great man: but it was also part of a wider assault on a class.
> (Hart 1996: 165)

If, as I believe, Hunt was unaware that this book constituted an attack against the aristocracy, John Wilson was fully conscious of it. Wilson thus reminds the readers of *Blackwood's* that Hunt had dared to dedicate *The Story of Rimini* to 'My dear Byron', a dedication Wilson considers 'pert, prating, vulgar, and vapid' ([Wilson] 1828: 371). Wilson also describes Hunt's moral values in terms commonly associated with the 'vulgar' lower classes when he recalls that Hunt

> was convicted of a base and brutal libel on his Sovereign…[and that] he is to this day as proud of his crime, and his punishment, as any other patriotic jail-bird; and gives us, in this quarto, all the odious and contemptible details, with the exultation of a martyr.
>
> ([Wilson] 1828: 369)

Wilson recognizes a class difference between people such as Byron and Shelley on one side, and Hunt and Hazlitt on the other. He is explicit in his articulation of *Blackwood's* defense of the former against the latter:

> It was Hazlitt, we believe, who accused us of praising Shelley, because he was a gentleman; and we must confess, that the accusation, however shocking, is far from being untrue, and affords an easy and satisfactory explanation to Hazlitt of much of our censure of himself.
>
> ([Wilson] 1828: 402)

Read 'Byron' for 'Shelley', 'Hunt' for 'Hazlitt', and the socio-political bias of *Blackwood's* against Hunt is confirmed. Wilson repeatedly uses the adjective 'cockney' with its full array of pejorative connotations to make the same point regarding the class discrepancy between Hunt and the subject of his book.[65] A strong desire to defend Byron, and the values associated with his class, coupled with a parallel urge to attack Hunt, explains the extraordinary length of Wilson's review: it consists of forty-six pages—the longest review published that year in *Blackwood's*—when none of the others exceeds seventeen pages. Only the review of Thomas Moore's biography of Byron in 1830—a work directly related to Hunt's volume—would exceed that length among reviews published during the following two years.

The class bias at work in Wilson's and Lockhart's reviews is quite explicit throughout their articles, and even Robert Southey would write reproachfully about it in a letter to Septimus Hodson: 'The article in the *Q.R.* is not more severe on Hunt than he deserves, but there is in it a tone of aristocratic insolence which to me is particularly disgusting' (Southey 1965: II, 326). Lockhart's review ends, however, with a thought-provoking comment:

> The last wriggle of expiring imbecility appears in these days to be a volume of personal Reminiscences; and we have now heard the feeble death-rattle of the once loud-tongued as well as brazen-faced Examiner.
>
> ([Lockhart] 1828: 425)

Lockhart's description of Hunt's position in the London political scene at the end of 1828 was unfortunately accurate: Hunt was no longer the editor of a prominent newspaper, the *Examiner*, and his audience had dwindled greatly in number. The publication of *Lord Byron and Some of his Contemporaries* did not contribute to improving Hunt's literary stature, but on the contrary made him vulnerable to further attacks in Moore's 1830 *Letters and Journals of Lord Byron: with Notices of his Life*, as well as in John Galt's *The Life of Lord Byron*, published the same year, to which Hunt offered in response a series of five articles in the pages of the *Tatler*.[66] By 1830, Hunt had clearly lost the majority of his audience and his finances were at their worst. However, Hunt eventually survived the setbacks of the *Liberal* and *Lord Byron and Some of his Contemporaries*, and he remained more or less true to his principle of independence during the second half of his life which proved to be very fulfilling, both personally and professionally.

Epilogue

> Men die and disappear; the most skilful productions of their ingenuity or labour perish, and are forgotten; and even the most colossal monuments which their admiring contemporaries or successors erect to carry down their names and deeds to posterity, crumble into dust. But books—and books only—can be made to endure for ever.
>
> [Anon.], 'Characteristics of the Present State of English Literature' ([Anon.] 1828b: 1)

After reading Leigh Hunt's *The Town* for the first time, Charlotte Brontë wrote to W. S. Williams on 16 April 1849:

> I was surprised, ere I had read many pages, to find myself enchained by his pleasant, graceful, easy style, varied knowledge, just views and kindly spirit. There is something peculiarly anti-melancholic in Hunt's writings – and yet they are never boisterous – they resemble sunshine – being at once bright and tranquil.
>
> (Brontë 1995–2000: II, 202)

This view of Hunt as the philosopher of cheer and the author of many familiar essays is not atypical of many writers' conceptions of Hunt around 1850, when his *Autobiography* appeared under the imprint of Smith, Elder, and Co. Although based in large part on works previously published, Hunt's *Autobiography* is probably the most important work of his later life, and rightly deserves Thomas Carlyle's praise as being 'by far the best of the autobiographic kind I remember to have read in the English language' (Carlyle and Carlyle 1970–: XXV, 97–8). While a large section of the material included in Hunt's *Autobiography* comes from *Lord Byron and Some of his Contemporaries*, the tone is greatly altered. Whereas *Lord Byron* was very much a statement of personal justification in face of the various attacks Hunt had suffered in publications on Byron, and a reaction against the fulsome praises that the dead poet now garnered from around the country, the *Autobiography* offers a calmer depiction of Hunt's life, imbued with an obvious sense of pleasure in the recollection of past events and friendships. Thus, as Ken A. Bugajski remarks, the textual revisions involved in the writing of the *Autobiography* 'represent or reflect Hunt's changing relationships to the social and literary worlds in which he lived and published' (Bugajski 2002: 133).

Interestingly, just as Hunt's work after 1828 tends not to be considered by modern critics, Hunt himself is curiously silent about the later part of his life. To some extent the rather abrupt truncations of the account of his literary career may be due to the practical necessities of producing copy under pressure of time. The process of revision was certainly cut short by Smith, Hunt's publisher, who insisted, in a new contract dated 7 February 1850, that Hunt should produce the manuscript within three months.[1] The pressure to meet his contractual obligation with the firm in time may also have been a motivation for Hunt to borrow heavily from his previous publications, principally *Lord Byron and Some of his Contemporaries*, the essays on Italy he published in the *Liberal*, and some articles from the *Examiner*.[2]

However, Hunt may also have been attempting to recuperate his stance of independence by revisiting and revising this earlier controversial material into more temperate terms. Since he was most fiercely independent in the early period of his life, it is this period that he spends most time revisiting. Hunt's choice of material for discussion in his *Autobiography* may also suggest that he never considered himself to be part of what is now called the Victorian period. In any case, one can legitimately question whether Hunt should be considered as a Victorian autobiographer as well as a key Romantic figure whom modern periodizations tend to overlook. His life and success under the reign of Queen Victoria complement his pivotal role during the Romantic period, and his *Autobiography* contains much undiscussed material that is relevant to both literary periods. Nevertheless, Hunt's *Autobiography* does not give, to adopt Anthony Trollope's words, 'a record of [Hunt's] inner life' (Trollope 1996: 232), and one needs to turn to his 1853 book *The Religion of the Heart* to find a detailed expression of Hunt's personal beliefs.[3]

Many changes in Hunt's life had an impact on his position within literary circles between 1830 and 1859. He made new friends and lost most of his enemies; his advancing age also had an impact on the stamina he could invest in new literary projects such as running a periodical or going to the theater every night. His reputation as a well-known and respected personality grew during these years, and brought him many visitors from around the country as well as from America, where his works had been regularly published and reviewed since *Juvenilia*,[4] in the same way that those of Coleridge and Wordsworth had been between 1830 and 1850. Yet, all throughout the second half of his life, Hunt retained a keen political sense and a sharp critical judgment, which motivated him to promote both new poetical voices such as Tennyson and D. G. Rossetti, as well as past authors, in his critical anthologies and editions *Imagination and Fancy* (1844), *Wit and Humour* (1846), *Stories from the Italian Poets* (1846), and *Beaumont and Fletcher* (1855).

Notes

Introduction

1 As for the impact of reviews on sales, it is worth bearing in mind William St Clair's remark that

> the influence of the reviews appears to have been greatly exaggerated both at the time and by subsequent writers. Given the time difference between the publication, selling, and reading of a book and the appearance and circulation of the review notices in the literary reviews, it would be misleading to regard them as normally intermediating in the market like the book pages of modern newspapers.
>
> (St Clair 2004: 189)

2 William Mudford actually defends anonymous reviews in his biography of the playwright Richard Cumberland:

> In reading an anonymous criticism we read it without any undue bias or partiality; if it have merit, that merit is allowed to have its fair influence upon our minds. We judge of it by itself without any reference to the presumed qualifications of the author; we are not subdued by the authority of a *name*.
>
> (Mudford 1812: 570)

Interestingly, Cumberland would himself attempt to put an end to the practice of anonymous criticism in his unsuccessful *London Review*, published in 1809.

3 For a longer discussion of the reception of Shelley's poems, see Behrendt 1989 and Wheatley 1999. For Shelley's reactions to contemporary reviews as found in his prefaces, see my article '"I *will* live beyond this life": Shelley, Prefaces and Reviewers' (Laplace-Sinatra 1999).

4 For more information on Hunt's involvement with the *Monthly Repository*, see Mineka 1972.

5 As Roe remarks, 'Hunt, once the most articulate radical journalist in England, was doomed by Dickens to eternal childishness' (Roe 1997: 228). Many critics have discussed Hunt's relationship with Dickens and the Skimpole caricature, but I would recommend consulting the following two: Luther A. Brewer's *Leigh Hunt and Charles Dickens: The Skimpole Caricature* (Brewer 1930), and Richard D. Altick's 'Harold Skimpole Revisited' (Altick 1984).

6 Mizukoshi offers a detailed reading of *The Literary Pocket-Book* and Hunt's intention to 'cultivate the middle-class taste for literature in an accessible and democratic form' (Mizukoshi 2001: 34; see also 33–38). Keach and Roe also discuss *The Literary Pocket-Book*, but more specifically for Keats's involvement; see Keach 1986, and Roe 1995b: 201–5.

Chapter 1

1 In his 1774 *Essay upon the Harmony of Language, intended to illustrate that of the English Language*, William Mitford states: 'Hundreds of such lines might be found in Shakespear, calculated not be red [sic], but to be acted; and few, perhaps none, will even conceive their full force and beauty who have not seen Mr Garrick in Shakespear's principal characters' (Mitford 1774: 118). Hunt's marginalia found in his copy in the Brewer–Leigh Hunt collection reads: 'Oh incapable critic! When will this subject be handled by any body who really understand it?'. Hunt eventually took on this task himself.

2 While Hunt wrote theatrical criticism earlier than Coleridge, Lamb, and Hazlitt did, I do not claim that he was more experienced with the theatrical world than they were when they started publishing reviews. Lamb and Coleridge had both written plays, and, as P. P. Howe points out, '[u]nlike the generality of dramatic critics; Hazlitt attended the theatre for twenty years before he began to write about it' (Hazlitt 1930–4: V, 399). Similarly, Lamb went to his first play in 1781 and started going to the theater regularly in 1789, although his first extensive discussion of drama, 'Theatralia. No. I.—On Garrick, and Acting; and the Plays of Shakespeare, considered with references to their fitness for Stage Representation', appeared in Hunt's *Reflector* in 1811. (Lamb's review of George Crooke's performance as Richard III in the *Morning Post* for 8 January 1802 cannot be considered as a theoretically informed, critical review.) Although Coleridge started lecturing on Shakespeare in 1811, he never published his lectures. He would discuss Shakespeare at greater length in *Biographia Literaria* (1817) and, as an exemplar of what he called 'method', in the 1818 edition of the *Friend*. I am grateful to Nicholas Halmi for drawing my attention to this reference in the *Friend*.

3 The first issue of Dutton's *Dramatic Censor; or, Weekly Theatrical Report* was published 4 January 1800. The journal changed its format after six months, and, from July 1800 until September 1801, it became *The Dramatic Censor; or, Monthly Epitome of Taste, Fashion, and Manners*. It finally reverted to a weekly publication as *The Dramatic and Literary Censor*, from 9 October to 18 December 1801. Throughout its two years of existence, Dutton's *Dramatic Censor* contained the germs of independent journalism that the Hunts put into practice in the *News*. Although it offered occasionally lengthy reviews of performances, short notices remained its principal form. For more information on Dutton's journal and other periodicals devoted to theater criticism in the 1810s and 1820s, see Chapter 2 of Jonathan Mulrooney's unpublished thesis (Mulrooney 2001).

4 Thomas Holcroft's the *Theatrical Recorder* ran from December 1804 to May 1806. It contained mainly short notices of performances, typically reproduced from other newspapers. Holcroft also included new dramas and biographies in his monthly publication, as well as essays on the art of acting, which often dealt with the character of Hamlet and the intrinsic difficulty of performing it properly. It is worth pointing out that Holcroft was also a playwright, who was personally acquainted with actors, as his memoirs amply demonstrate (Holcroft 1816).

5 Two rare instances of Hunt's liking a contemporary play are to be found in his review of Tobin's *The Curfew*, published in the *News* on 22 February and 1 March 1807 (Hunt 1807c), and of Colman's *The Africans; or, War, Love, and Duty*, published in the *Examiner* on 31 July 1808 (Hunt 2003: I, 64–8). Hunt obviously respected the latter play's denunciation of slavery.

6 Two years later, Cumberland would positively review Hunt's *Critical Essays* in a lengthy piece published in the *London Review*, a quarterly in which Cumberland identified the author of each review against contemporary practices (Cumberland 1809).

7 In his *Autobiography*, Hunt humorously recalls that the playwright Thomas Dibdin sent him a hostile letter, that Charles Incledon, a leading tenor of the time, called him the 'd—d boy', and that George Colman the Younger attacked him indirectly in the prologue to one of his plays (Hunt 1850: I, 290). Colman's lines are: 'If we give trash, as some few pertlings say, / Why flocks an audience nightly to our play?' (quoted in Stout 1928: 26). For

more information on Colman, see Thomson, P. 1971: 67–82. Hunt published Dibdin's letter in the *News* on 26 April 1807 in which the latter asserts that he is not the author of *Ogre and Little Thumb*, a play negatively reviewed by Hunt the previous week. Dibdin declares: 'You have been pleased to drag my name forward for the purpose of loading it with unmerited censure, on the subject of a piece, the composition or production of which I never directly or indirectly had the least concern in'. Hunt's response is particularly sharp: 'But if a bad writer persist in the exercise of his pen, is it not natural that bad productions should be attributed to him even when they are not of his composition?' (Hunt 1807d: 135).

8 Although the date 1807 appears on the title page of *Critical Essays*, the volume was published in January 1808, as shown by the advertisement in the *Times* (19 January 1808) and the prospectus for the *Examiner* included in *Critical Essays*, which indicates that '[t]he first number of this Paper appeared on the 3rd January, 1808'.

9 As late as 1860, Hunt's theatrical criticism would still be praised by the *Saturday Review* as 'the best guide to the merits of playwrights and performers, and playgoers had certainly reason to be thankful for a writer who had ... courage and sense' ([Anon.] 1860: 115).

10 Lorne Kruger's *The National Stage: Theatre and Cultural Legitimation in England, France, and America* presents an illuminating overview of national politics and theater in England (Kruger 1992). Hunt writes in his copy of Ninian Pinkney's 1814 *Travels through the South of France* next to a section praising the English versus the French: 'doubtless the English have solid virtues, but the French have them too' (Pinkney 1814: 21). Hunt repeatedly defends the French in his annotations to this volume. Hunt himself is quite fond of French writers, in particular Voltaire and Molière. His copy of the two-volume edition of *The Works of Moliere, French and English* is heavily annotated throughout in the original French, with most of his comments and approving lines in the margins to be found in *Les précieuses ridicules* in volume 2 (Molière 1739). In his 1844 *Imagination and Fancy*, Hunt publicly praises Molière as 'the greatest writer of comedy that the world has seen' (Hunt 2003: IV, 242).

11 Hunt referred to the intricate relationship between playwrights and journalists as early as January 1805 in a letter to Hunter about the recent attack on a play by Thomas Holt: 'The party against him [Holt] was very strong; all the modern play manufacturers, and their friends the editors of newspapers, whom the severity of his criticism in Bell's paper [i.e. *Bell's Weekly Messenger*] had made his personal enemies, came with a determination, as I very well know, to damn the piece' (Hunt 1862: I, 16).

12 Kemble's *Macbeth Reconsidered* was reissued in 1817 in an extended version to include a study of the character of Richard III.

13 See Linda Kelly's *The Kemble Era* for a detailed overview of Kemble's life and career (Kelly 1980).

14 For one of the best overviews of theater during Garrick's time, see Auburn 1995.

15 Hunt asserts that it was 'a critical religion in those times to admire Mr. Kemble' (Hunt 1850: I, 282). Similarly, Hazlitt writes in the *Examiner* for 8 December 1816: 'We wish we had never seen Mr. KEAN. He has destroyed the KEMBLE religion; and it is the religion in which we were brought up' (Hazlitt 1930–4: V, 345). This comment should not hide the fact that Hazlitt was a great admirer of Kean, as his numerous theatrical reviews printed in *The Examiner* and other newspapers show. For an illuminating discussion of Coleridge's famous comment on Kean, see Davis 1995; see also Jonathan Mulrooney's 'Keats in the Company of Kean' (Mulrooney 2003).

16 John Ambrose Williams remarks in his *Memoirs of John Philip Kemble* that 'Mr. Kemble's pronunciation has been the subject of much controversy and ridicule. His orthöepy has frequently been different from the established rule; as in the well-known instance of the word *aches*, which he pronounces as two syllables' (Williams 1817: 75).

17 Hunt's view of Kemble's pronunciation had already been challenged in the *News* on 4 January 1807 by an anonymous correspondent (writing under the name of 'Philo-Dramaticus') who argues that Kemble is right in pronouncing the *I* in *Coriolanus* long. Hunt responds that he sticks to his opinion and ends his response: 'when we meet with

scarcely a single person who pronounces it like the actor, and scarcely a single line that warrants such a pronunciation, we had rather hold sacred both the custom and the poet' (Hunt 1807b: 7).

18 Six months earlier, Hunt had written in the *News*:

> It has often surprised us, that this character is so perpetually chosen for a first appearance in London, for not only is the metropolis prepared to make comparisons with the most admired performers, but the character in itself is the most difficult one on the Stage. … The representation of *Hamlet* demands three great requisites, which are most rarely united on the stage: the actor must be the tragedian, the humourist and the gentleman.
>
> (Hunt 1807e: 208)

19 Twenty years after the publication of his *Critical Essays* piece, Hunt still ranked *Hamlet* as the most difficult of Shakespeare's plays to perform. In 22 October 1830 *Tatler* column 'The Play-Goer', he would comment that he had never seen a representation of *Hamlet* that did justice to the play, nor was he expecting to see one. He felt that '[Hamlet] is a character, though quite in nature, made up of too many qualities than are likely to be represented by any but a *Hamlet* himself' (Hunt 1830–2: I, 167).

20 Terence Allan Hoagwood suggests that the contemporary censorship of passages in certain Shakespeare plays (such as *King Lear*) under political pressure might be another reason for Lamb's preference for reading the plays as opposed to seeing them performed (Hoagwood 1998: 27; 52 n20).

21 For a list of Kemble's adaptations, see Ellis 1985: 145. For a detailed analysis of Kemble's adaptations of Shakespeare's plays, see Child 1935.

22 I agree with George Taylor that Coleridge may have adopted 'a position of patronising superiority with regard to popular theatrical success' (Taylor 2000: 178), but I would not assert, as Taylor does, that Hunt shared a similar sense of superiority.

23 For a detailed discussion of the various techniques of stage illusion at the turn of the nineteenth century, see Burwick 1990.

24 Hunt had published this essay in three parts in the *News* on 23 August 1807, 30 August 1807, and 6 September 1807. The final section appeared with an extra penultimate paragraph missing from the *Critical Essays* version, most likely because Hunt had already made this point clear earlier in *Critical Essays*:

> Let Englishmen never forget, that all history has united the depravation of public taste with that of public virtue, and that the most flourishing times of independence have been the most glorious times of literature. Weak instruments very often preserve powerful means; what is gained by the sword is preserved and glorified by the pen: when the pen has lost its powers, it is because there is nothing in its country to excite them. But are we come to this? No, no: the Muse's features are only distorted; and it is a convulsion that must be remedied by treatment apparently harsh.
>
> (Hunt 1807f: 289)

25 Commenting upon the biographical notices included in editions of Sheridan's plays during the nineteenth century, E. H. Mikhail observes that '[t]he most noted of these is perhaps the "Biographical and Critical Sketch" of Leigh Hunt, which does not, however, pretend to any new light, and is entirely unsympathetic. Hunt undertakes to explain the waste of Sheridan's gifts, remarking his early habits of delay, his high animated spirits, and his love for luxury' (Mikhail 1989: xiii). Hunt had already criticized Sheridan in a note to *The Feast of the Poets*: 'Mr. Sheridan, upon the whole, appears to me to have been overrated as an observer' (Hunt 2003: V, 50).

26 Hunt wrote again about the absence of independence in contemporary newspapers in his March 1808 'Political Examiner N°10. Rules for the Conduct of Newspaper Editors with respect to Politics and News' (Hunt 1808).

27 See also Cox and Kucich's detailed headnote to the prospectus of the *Examiner* (Hunt 2003: I, 25–31).

28 Charles Cowden Clarke fondly recalls his reading of the *Examiner* in his *Recollections of Writers*: 'My father had taken in the *Examiner* newspaper from its commencement, he and I week after week revelling in the liberty-loving, liberty-advocating, liberty-eloquent articles of the young editor' (Clarke and Clarke 1878: 16).

29 Roe repeatedly refers to the *Examiner* in his study of Keats's poetry (Roe 1997), and Kenneth Neill Cameron states that 'for the modern reader [the *Examiner*] is also the most valuable background source, because it not only related the events as they actually happened but held views similar to Shelley's' (Cameron 1974: 363).

30 As Kenneth Kendall notes in his detailed study of this journal, 'Two-third of [Hunt's] material [in the first issue] is politically oriented, and to emphasise the importance of politics, the opening article takes a long-range view of politics in England in the preceding decade or so' (Kendall 1971: 24). Though short-lived, the *Reflector* contains several articles that demonstrate the extent of Hunt's committed engagement in political matters, both national and international. Published on 1 January 1811, the essay which opens the first issue, 'Art. I.—The English considered as a thinking People, in reference to late Years', illustrates Hunt's progress as political journalist since the beginning of the *Examiner*. He considers in detail the various political events of 1810 and is critical of Pitt's fiscal and political policies, a topic he had discussed several times in the 'Political Examiner' that year. However, the format and length (16 pages) of the *Reflector* essay gives Hunt the opportunity to reflect on the events as a whole and to suggest that the government should reform its attitude in the war with France and towards the repression of expression. Hunt's opinion of the government is unsurprisingly negative, and his tone is as combative as his political articles in the *Examiner*: 'Thirty years of debauched, money-wasting, and most unfortunate policy, have at length brought us to the climax of absurdity and corruption' (Hunt 1812a: I, 3). Throughout his piece, Hunt presents a logical argument, accompanied by references to illustrious authors such as Locke and Hume to contrast the present state of the country. Kendall comments further that '[Hunt's] Retrospect articles are skillfully written narratives interspersed with editorial comment, for reform is never far from the surface of things in Hunt's writings of this period' (Kendall 1971: 36).

31 The events that followed the publication of Hunt's article 'The Prince on St. Patrick's Day' (see Hunt 2003: I, 215–22), and which led to the Hunts' trial on the charge of committing seditious libel against the Prince Regent, in December 1812—a trial which Frederick W. Hackwood describes as one of the 'historic struggles for the freedom of political comment' (Hackwood 1912: 170)—are well known to Romantic scholars, and have been assessed in great detail in Edmund Blunden's Leigh Hunt's 'Examiner' Examined (Blunden 1928) and George Dumas Stout's *The Political History of Leigh Hunt's* Examiner, *together with an Account of 'The Book'* (Stout 1949), as well as by every biographer of Hunt, including most recently Anthony Holden in The Wit in the Dungeon (Holden 2005).

32 Hunt mentions in his 1860 *Autobiography* James Perry's offer to use the threat of *The Book*, a manuscript 'connected with some important state and court secrets, and well known and dreaded by the Regent' (Hunt 1949a: 235), to pressure the Government into dropping its sentence. The Hunts, however, did not accept his offer. Hunt also mentions his being in possession of 'a particular "Book" in [his] library' in the 'Political Examiner' of 8 March 1812 entitled 'Princely Qualities' (Hunt 1812c). For a longer discussion of *The Book*, see Stout 1949:110–35.

33 For an enriching reading of Hunt's 'effeminate' behavior, see Kucich 1999.

34 See, for instance, 'Political Examiner N°259—Sentence against the Examiner (continued from last week),'the *Examiner*, 268 (14 February 1813) 97–99; 'Political Examiner N°265—Mr. Whitbread and Lord Ellenborough,' the *Examiner*, 274 (28 March 1813) 193–7; 'Political Examiner N°275—Visit of the Princess to the Opera,' the *Examiner*, 284 (6 June 1813) 353–4; 'Political Examiner N°279—The British Court,' the *Examiner*, 288 (4 July 1813) 417–18; 'Political Examiner N°299—Courts and Cabinets—A Fatal Error

noticed in the Conduct of some of our Journals,' *The Examiner*, 308 (21 November 1813) 737–8. For a detailed discussion of Hunt's continuing political attacks on the government during his stay in Surrey Gaol, see Kucich 1999.

Chapter 2

1 In his biography of Edward John Trelawny, David Crane comments on Hunt's grave thus: 'A little further to the south can be found another of the Pisan Circle, Leigh Hunt, true to himself even in death beneath a monument "raised by public subscription"' (Crane 1998: 322).

2 As Nicholas Roe and others have amply demonstrated, Keats had a long-time interest in Hunt's politics and shared many of his views. Andrew Motion's biography *Keats*, Roe's *John Keats and the Culture of Dissent*, and Cox's *Poetry and Politics in the Cockney School* are but three among several publications dealing with Keats's politics and the importance of Hunt in his life and political opinions. (Roe is particularly useful in showing Keats's reading of *The Examiner* at Enfield School; see Roe 1997: 27–50.) John Brown also alludes to Hunt's imprisonment in his poem *Psyche: or, The Soul, A Poem. In Seven Cantos* (1818); see Roe 1995c: 185–6.

3 For the dating of the first publication of *The Feast of the Poets*, see Landré 1936: II, 487. For a longer discussion of the *Reflector*, see Kendall 1971: 11–59.

4 Hunt's view of poets '*who have prostituted their genius*' anticipates the language of Shelley's comment on Wordsworth in the preface to *Alastor*. The final section of Hunt's plan for 'Groundwork of the Planet of Poets' also contains a rather eerie reference to a meeting with 'the rising spirit of a young poet, who died prematurely.' Hunt certainly thought that Keats was a young poet with great promise, as can be seen in his well-known 1816 'Young Poets' article (to take one example from many). For a thought-provoking reading of Hunt's article, as well as Keats's poems in the *Examiner*, see Kandl 1995.

5 For a discussion of several other possible poetical sources for Hunt's *Feast of the Poets*, see Edgecombe 1994: 153–64.

6 I thus agree with Clarence DeWitt Thorpe's assertion that *The Feast of the Poets* was 'written no doubt much under the influence of Byron' (Thorpe 1956: 33).

7 Following his quarrel with Byron and the bitterness that led to the publication of *Lord Byron and Some of his Contemporaries*, Hunt removed this passage in the 1832 version and from all following republications of the poem.

8 Although Byron did not comment specifically on Hunt's lines, he wrote Hunt that he had enjoyed the *Reflector* version of *The Feast of the Poets*, and he praised several sections of the 1814 version (Byron 1973–94: IV, 50). Byron gave Hunt an annotated edition of *English Bards and Scotch Reviewers* in October 1815, with a note: 'There are in it *many* opinions I have altered—& some which I retain—upon the whole I wish that it had never been written' (Byron 1973–94: IV, 318). Hunt may have appreciated the relevance of this comment a few years later when he in turn regretted some of his own attacks in *The Feast of the Poets*.

9 That Hunt would rather see 'Kemble in love' clearly indicates his low opinion of contemporary poetry since, as I indicate in my first chapter, he was not one of Kemble's admirers, and particularly not of Kemble acting in the role of a lover.

10 For further information on the *Analectic Magazine*, see Edgar 1975: 103–4, and Mott 1970: 279–83.

11 Although Byron, Hobhouse, and Hunt spell Cawthorn's name 'Cawthorne', I use the spelling found on the title pages of works Cawthorn published, as well as on the London register of printers (see Timperley 1839 and Todd 1972).

12 Byron wrote to Cawthorn on 21 October 1814: 'I should not permit others to publish what I refused you.—Of course my mind remains unaltered on the subject of publication—it must *not* proceed on any account' (Byron 1973–94: IV, 221). Cawthorn did issue 'a series of spurious edition between 1812 and 1819' without Byron's approval (Byron 1980–92: I, 397), even though Murray intervened, and invoked power of attorney, to

prevent any further publication; see Byron's letters to Murray dated 28 August 1816, 30 September 1816, and 23 October 1817 (Byron 1973–94: V, 91, 108–9, 270).

13 Earlier that month, Hunt wrote to Marianne that 'Mr. Cawthorne is a very civil man, & would let me send you as many [books] as you pleased' (4 May 1813, Hunt 1999: 33). Cawthorn also gave him a copy of Hobhouse's travel book *A Journey through Albania, and Other Provinces of Turkey in Europe and Asia, to Constantinople, during the Years 1809 and 1810*, as Hunt reports in another letter to Marianne on 29 May 1813 (Hunt 1999: 44).

14 Moore had already praised the *Reflector* version in a letter to Hunt, to which Hunt had responded on 13 September 1812: 'You gratify me much by liking my verses in the "Reflector," and infinitely more (highly as I value your praise) by ratifying, with your own mouth, the conclusions they had drawn from the character of your later poetry' (quoted in Moore 1853–6: VIII, 120).

15 Van Winkle and Wiley were also the publishers of the *American Medical and Philosophical Register* (from July 1813 to April 1814) and, more relevant to Hunt scholars, the printers of *Cobbett's American Political Register* (from 1816 to 1818).

16 The Brewer–Leigh Hunt Collection has a copy of the 1811 version of *The Feast of the Poets*, printed from the same setting of type as that used in the *Boston Weekly Messenger* (21 May 1813). This copy is stitched, and contains an unsigned one-page note from the *Boston Weekly Messenger*, which states

> We have not so much as heard a conjecture as to the author of this piece, which is certainly above mediocrity. We believe it made its first appearance at Edinburgh. It will be observed, that the critical creed contained in it, is in general that of the Edinburgh Review—the same partiality for Campbell and captious criticism of Scott; and in general, with few exceptions, the same defects and beauties are attributed to each poet. Our readers will probably agree with this nameless bard in his quadruple assignment of the laurel. Gifford and Sheridan, and Rogers and Crabbe, have reason to complain of their treatment—but they may easily console themselves, when Pope is made to have corrupted the public taste with *cuckoo-song verses*. It is to be wished that the silly affectation of questioning Pope's title to the name of a poet, and denying the merit of his poems, may some time or other be abandoned. To banish him from Parnassus, is the very ostracism of poetry.
>
> (Brewer–Leigh Hunt Collection PR4812.F339 1813)

17 On 19 August 1816, Hunt wrote to Archibald Constable to offer him the copyright of *The Story of Rimini* and to explain how he came to owe money to Gale, Curtis, and Fenner. He also records: 'I put them in possess[ion] at once of 250 copies remaining of the first edition of the Feast of the Poets' (Hunt 1999: 78). Gale, Curtis, and Fenner were also the publisher of Hunt's *Descent of Liberty* (1815).

18 The *Reflector* versions has 'Or at least my Lord Colley with all his grand brothers' for line 228 and 'three or four others' for line 229.

19 Muriel J. Mellown also asserts that '[a]t the beginning of the nineteenth century Wordsworth and Coleridge were deemed less important than Southey, who, having published far more than they, was considered the leader of the new school' (Mellown 1981: 85).

20 Hunt had already referred publicly to Southey as 'that true poet' in a review published in the *News* on 1 November 1807 (Hunt 1807g: 349), his earliest printed commentary on that poet.

21 Hunt would eventually change his mind regarding the Laureateship, and actually attempt to be named Poet Laureate after Southey's death in 1844.

22 Thomas Love Peacock also complained of Southey's appointment in his poem *Sir Proteus: A Satirical Ballad*, published under the pseudonym of P. M. O'Donovan in March 1814. Carl Dawson rightly points out that Southey is Peacock's main target in the poem, but that he also attacks Scott, Coleridge, Wordsworth, and Byron (Dawson 1970: 42). An illustration of Peacock's verse on Southey and his laureateship shows similarities with Hunt's views:

"Here shall CORRUPTION's *laureate wreath*,
By ancient DULLNESS twined
With flowers that courtly influence breathe,
Thy votive temples bind.
Amid the thick LETHEAN fen
The dull DWARF-LAUREL springs,
To bind the brows of venal men,
The tuneful slaves of kings.["]

(Peacock 1814: 70–1)

23 See, for instance, Hunt 2003: V, 17–9, 22–4; Hunt 1814c; Hunt 1817a; Hunt 1817b, and Hunt 1820a. Hunt also referred sarcastically to Wordsworth's dedication of *Peter Bell* to Southey in his review of the poem: 'The poem is dedicated in an odd shy way, that has any thing but the look of sincerity, to "Robert Southey, Esq. P. L.", that is to say, (for Mr. Wordsworth has left it unexplained) not *Precious Looby*, but *Poet Laureat*' (Hunt 2003: II, 189). Southey is again attacked for his *Vision of Judgment* in Albany Fonblanque's review, under the pseudonym 'Q', of Byron's *The Two Foscari*, where Byron's own long note against the Laureate is reprinted. Fonblanque also writes:

> The monstrous absurdity of that *Vision of Judgment*—to be equalled only by the grossness of its irreligion, the arrogance of its assumption, and the excess of its rancour, will secure it a bad immortality, by rendering it the laughing stock of ages. The author of such a *thing* to be one of those who aspire to guide the taste of the world of letters—Excellent!

([Fonblanque] 1821c: 810)

24 See Hazlitt's reviews of *Christabel* ('Literary Notices N°1. *Christabel;—Kubla Khan, a Vision; The Pains of Sleep. By S. T. Coleridge, Esq.'*, the *Examiner*, 440 [2 June 1816] 348–90); of *A Lay Sermon* ('Literary Notices N°11. *A Lay-Sermon on the Distresses of the Country addressed to the Middle and Higher Orders. By S. T. Coleridge'*, the *Examiner*, 454 [8 September 1816] 571–3); and of *The Statesman's Manual* ('Literary Notices N°21. *The Statesman's Manual; or the Bible the best Guide to Political Skill and Foresight. A Lay Sermon, addressed to the Higher Classes of Society. By S. T. Coleridge, Esq.'*, the *Examiner*, 470 [29 December 1816] 824–7).

25 In a diary entry dated 17 January 1812, Henry Crabb Robinson writes: 'I found [Lamb and Hunt] had had a discussion about Coleridge, whom Hunt had spoken of as a bad writer, while Lamb thought him the first man he ever knew' (Robinson 1869: I, 370).

26 I am grateful to Chris Koenig-Woodyard for directing me to this reference.

27 Hunt refers several times to Coleridge's poetry in his introductory essay, 'An Answer to the Question What is Poetry?', always in very laudatory terms. He also praises *Christabel* in the preface to his 1855 *Stories in Verse* as 'the best of all modes and measures for reducing a narrative to its most poetic element, and so producing the quintessence of a story' (Hunt 2003: IV, 266).

28 Hunt again criticized *The Friend* in his 'Sketches of the Living Poets. N°4.—Mr. COLERIDGE': 'In many passages … it is impossible not to recognize that weakness of the will, or liability to the same amount of impression from all views of a question, which has been observed by a critic [i.e. Hazlitt] better able to speak of him' (Hunt 2003: II, 352).

29 Hunt himself would ultimately praise *Biographia Literaria* as 'the most masterly criticism on poetry in this language' (Hunt 1860: 441).

30 In his heavily annotated copy of Ugo Foscolo's 1825 *La Commedia di Dante Alighieri*, Hunt writes 'Coleridge' next to the following sentence which he underlines: 'Se non che la metafisica sarà sempre mirabilmente arrendevole a tutto ed a tutti' (Foscolo 1825: 376). This seems quite relevant to Hunt's opinion of Coleridge and the latter's metaphysical mind: 'Except that metaphysics are always admiringly conciliating with everything and everyone'. I am grateful to Elena Benelli for her help with the translation.

31 In June and December 1835, Hunt reviewed Coleridge's *Table Talk and Letters, Conversations, and Recollections of S. T. Coleridge* in his periodical *Leigh Hunt's London Journal and the Printing Machine* (see Hunt 2003: III, 305–10, and Hunt 1835). On both occasions, Hunt is very critical of these works that, in his view, are not worthy of Coleridge's true poetic genius. See also Hunt 1999: 381; Hunt's 'Preface' to the 1844 edition of his *Poetical Works* (Hunt 1844: vii–viii); and 'An Essay on the Cultivation, History, and Varieties of the Species of Poem called the Sonnet' (Hunt 1867: I, 83). William Bell Scott also reports in his *Autobiography* following his meetings with Hunt in 1837: 'As a perfectionist in poetry, whose thought and rhythm were one, [Hunt] seemed to hold Coleridge above all others. Nor did he limit his high praise to the four or five exceptional poems we all hold so high, a small modicum out of the mass, but included others as equally admirable, though much less interesting' (Scott W. B. 1892: 128–9).

32 Gill indicates that Wordsworth was parodied in, among others, James and Horace Smith's *Rejected Addresses* (1812), John Hamilton Reynolds's *Leaves of Laurel: or, New Probationary Odes, for the Vacant Laureatship* (1813), John Agg's *Rejected Odes: or, Poetical Hops, Steps, and Jumps of a Dozen Popular Bards* (1813) (Gill 1989: 289–90). See also Nicola Trott's insightful article 'Wordsworth and the Parodic School of Criticism' (Trott 2003).

33 Wordsworth was obviously fond of calling great critics 'Coxcomb' since he also qualifies Hunt thus in a letter to Edward Moxon dated 13 June 1831: 'Mr. Leigh Hunt is a Coxcomb, was a Coxcomb, and ever will be a Coxcomb' (Wordsworth and Wordsworth 1979: 401).

34 See the autograph letter from J. H. Reynolds to Wordsworth, dated August 1816, in which he mentions being lent a copy of *A Letter to a Friend of Robert Burns* by Hunt in the summer of 1816 (Reynolds 1816: n. pag.)

35 See 'The Political Examiner' N°s114, 115, and 116, published in the *Examiner*, 116 (18 March 1810): 161–3 (rpt. in Hunt 2003: I, 128–33); 117 (25 March 1810): 177–81; and 118 (1 April 1810): 193–5.

36 In the first three versions of *The Feast of the Poets*, Hunt humorously makes Gifford exclaim: 'So stupid, in gen'ral, the natives are grown,/They really prefer Scotch reviews to their own' (ll. 140–1; Hunt 2003: V, 36). Gifford thus seemed to agree with Byron, who had attacked Jeffrey quite violently in *English Bards and Scotch Reviewers* as the 'Self-constituted Judge of Poesy' (l. 62; Byron 1980–92: I, 231).

37 Hunt had accepted the idea of a Lake school between the *Reflector* version and the 1814 one, as these lines were 'But another bright promise must fairly be lost,/And the gifts of a God by this madman be crost' in the *Reflector* poem (ll. 195–6; Hunt 1812a: II, 319). Yet, by 1815 Hunt rejected this critical grouping and dropped the lines altogether, probably as he had come to have a better appreciation of the differences between Southey, Coleridge, and Wordsworth. The former he now derides because of his laureateship. Hunt still gently disregards Coleridge as conscious of his own mistakes, and he finally acclaims Wordsworth.

38 Hazlitt reports Wordsworth's alleged comment on this review in *A Reply to Z*: 'What did they know about his poetry? What could they know about it? It was presumption in the highest degree for these cockney writers to pretend to criticise a Lake poet' (Hazlitt 1930–4: IX, 6).

39 Mary Moorman notes that '[i]f Wordsworth's presentation copy had been given with a hope of a favourable review in the *Examiner*, he was disappointed, for the poems were not noticed at all except for a scathing reference by Hazlitt, in a review of a performance of *Comus* in the issue of June 11th' (Moorman 1965: 279). Duncan Wu argues that Wordsworth sent the copy following 'a visit to Lowther in September 1814 [where] he met Hunt's defence counsel, Henry Brougham', who reported that Hunt valued Wordsworth's writings (Wu 1996: 80). For information on Wordsworth's own knowledge of Hunt's *Feast of the Poets*, see Wu 1995: 114–15.

40 For the dating of Wordsworth's gift to Hunt, and Hunt's response, see Roe 1981.

41 Only two months before he died, Hunt expressed his pride at Wordsworth's positive appreciation of his poetry in a letter to George James de Wilde dated 6 June 1859:

> What made me so desirous of recovering these verses ['On the Summer of 1818' that de Wilde sent to Hunt in a previous letter], is that Wordsworth expressed a regard for them;—*no habit*, you know, of his, towards any verses; which gives one a kind of sneaking satisfaction, when approbation comes. I felt once the same shabby pleasure, when told of his taking down my Poems from a shelf at a bookseller; to show some persons present how swimming ought to be described;—to wit, after the manner of the passage in "Hero & Leander".
>
> (Hunt 1859: n. pag.)

42 Robert J. Griffin argues for an 'ironic presence of Pope' (Griffin 1995: 93) in the 'Essay, Supplementary to the Preface', which I do not find fully convincing. I would in fact agree with Seamus Perry who, in his review of Griffin's book, expresses some reservations about Griffin's assertion of 'Pope's repressed but central imaginative presence for Wordsworth's poetry' (Perry 1996: n. pag.).

43 As it happens, Jeffrey's piece precedes his review of Hunt's *Rimini* in this issue of the *Edinburgh Review*.

44 For more information on the number of copies sold of Wordsworth's *The Excursion* and 1815 *Poems*, see Owen 1957.

45 Hazlitt's reviews appeared in the *Examiner*, 347 (21 August 1814), 541–2; 348 (28 August 1814), 555–8, and 353 (2 October 1814), 36–8.

46 Hunt reprints, under different titles, 'November 1, 1815' in the *Examiner*, 422 (28 January 1816), 57; 'September 1815' in the *Examiner*, 424 (11 February 1816), 92; 'To R.B. Haydon, Esq.' and 'Anacreon's Sprightly Old Age' in the *Examiner*, 413 (31 March 1816), 203. Wordsworth had enclosed these sonnets in a letter to Haydon, dated 21 December 1815. Haydon in turn gave them to Hunt, to whom he had introduced Wordsworth in the first half of 1815 (Finney 1963: I, 146). Following the publication of his sonnets in the *Examiner*, Wordsworth wrote to Gillies: 'I have great respect for the *Talents* of its Editor' (Wordsworth and Wordsworth 1969–70: II, 299).

47 See Hunt 2003: II, 56–61.

48 Hunt describes the *Selections from the Poem of Mr. Wordsworth* that Moxon published as 'containing some of the best things of the best poet of his time' (Hunt 2003: III, 181). The fact that Hunt was friend with Moxon, who would publish a new edition of his *Poetical Works* in 1832, may have of course influenced his positive review.

49 Hunt eventually complimented Wordsworth without a negative political reference in his 1835 article 'Chat with the Magazines. Wordsworth's Sonnets': 'With the exception of Shakespeare (who included everybody), Wordsworth has proved himself the greatest contemplative poet this country has produced. His facility is wonderful. He never wants the fittest words for the finest thoughts' (Hunt 2003: III, 302).

Chapter 3

1 In a letter dated 30 October 1815, Byron had strongly discouraged Hunt from publishing *Rimini* in a quarto format: '[D]on't let your bookseller publish in *Quarto* it is the worst size possible for circulation—I say this on Bibliopolical authority—' (Byron 1973–94: IV, 326).

2 Hunt seems to imply in his *Autobiography* that he first conceived the idea for *Rimini* in prison, but he actually began *Rimini* some time in late 1811, as Clarice Short notes (Short 1972–3: 207). It is nevertheless true that he did not start working seriously on the poem before his imprisonment in Surrey Gaol. The entry for 17 March 1813 in his journal states: 'I had left it standing at the conclusion of the preceding paragraph [Canto I, ll. 241–65] for six months, without being able to touch it' (Hunt 1862: I, 81). During his time in prison, Hunt did most of his reading for the poem, as well as the writing of the first two cantos.

3 As Michael O'Neill remarks, 'Hunt "unfortunately chose" a subject in a way that wryly mirrors the tragically unfortunate choice of reading matter made by Paolo and Francesca' (O'Neill 2003: 141).

4 For a discussion of the importance of Henry Francis Cary's *The Vision*, the acclaimed translation of the *Divine Comedy* first published in 1814, for Romantic writers, see Pite 1994 and Braida 2005. It is also worth noting that, while discussing the value of Dante's poetry in an article published in the *Monthly Magazine* in February 1818, the anonymous author praised Hunt's *Rimini*: 'To those who wish to know more of this affecting story [the tale of Francesca da Rimini], we recommend the perusal of Mr. Leigh Hunt's 'Tale of Rimini,' of which it is the subject' ([Anon.] 1818b: 20). The fame of Hunt's *Rimini* is also partly responsible for Coleridge's lectures on European literature at the Philosophical Society in January to March 1818. As Richard Holmes observes, 'Coleridge was responding to the interests of the younger generation of writers who, with the publication of Leigh Hunt's *The Story of Rimini* ... were turning back to Italian models' (Holmes 1998: 467).

5 Hunt would later provide a prose translation of the entire *Divine Comedy*, and a translation of the Paolo and Francesca episode in the terza rima of the original, in his *Stories from the Italian Poets*; see Hunt 1846: I, 81–279, 393–5. Hunt also provides accounts by different writers of the circumstances relating to the Paolo and Francesca story; see Hunt 1846: I, 395–401.

6 For an analysis of the language used by Francesca and the light it sheds on her and on Dante, see Kirkpatrick 1987: 82–94.

7 For an illuminating discussion of the theme of Robin Hood during the Romantic period, see Roe 1997: 140–55. As Roe remarks, 'The Sherwood pastoral represented the values of a "happy age" which Hunt sought to revive in *The Story of Rimini, Foliage*, and in his four "Songs of Robin Hood" published in the *Indicator*, Nov. 1820' (Roe 1997: 141). See also Thomas R. Mitchell, 'Keats's "outlawry" in "Robin Hood"' (Mitchell 1994). I am grateful to Jeffrey N. Cox for recommending I consult Mitchell's essay.

8 I would like to thank David H. Stam for suggesting this to me.

9 In a note to Canto III, l. 7, Hunt wrote in the 1855 edition that 'the state of my health was such as to render confinement more than ordinarily injurious' (Hunt 1923: 670).

10 Similarly, Robert Gittings writes: 'Poor Hunt succeeded in producing some ludicrous effects in this poem [*Rimini*], by a mixture of naïvety and over-confidence; but he was certainly read and quoted, sometimes even with approval, by his young disciple [i.e. Keats]' (Gittings 1956: 128). For the perceived influence of Hunt in contemporary reviews of *Endymion*, see Bennett 1994: 145–6. For a discussion of the influence of *Rimini* and *The Descent of Liberty* on Keats's *Endymion* and *Hyperion*, see Newey 1995. For a discussion of Hunt's influence on Keats's writings, and in particular 'On First Looking into Chapman's Homer', see Turley 1998: 115–18. Of course, Keats himself worried in October 1817 about having the reputation of being Hunt's *élève* (Keats 1958: I, 170). One may also note that Keats slightly misquoted two lines from *Rimini* in a letter to George and Georgiana Keats, dated 14 October 1818: 'And had been kept from men of pleasure's cares/By dint of feeling still more warm than theirs' (Canto III, ll. 121–2; Hunt 2003: V, 184). It is indicative of Keats's ambivalent feelings about the influence of Hunt that he misattributes these lines to Byron, and commends them as 'one of the finest things [Byron] has said' (Keats 1958: I, 396). For an alternative reading of Keats's reactions to reviews of his poems and of his relationship with Hunt, see Franta 1999.

11 Claude Lee Finney shrewdly remarks that in his notes to *The Feast of the Poets*, Hunt had censured

> the smooth closed heroic couplets of the school of Pope upon the principle that harmony in verse depends upon a proper mixture of uniformity and variety, a principle that had been defined by the poets and rhetoricians of the school of taste.
>
> (Finney 1963: I, 85)

Walter Jackson Bate argues further that 'Despite a slightly looser treatment of [closed-couplet] by some writers during the latter half of the eighteenth century, it remained largely for Hunt to break the couplet entirely and at the same time add extreme variety of caesural placing' (Bate W. J. 1962: 20).

12 Hunt also includes several triplets in *Rimini* that emphasize the sound quality of his poem; see for instance I, 216–18; I, 279–81; I, 306–8; II, 14–16; II, 224–6; II, 241–3; III, 11–13. Hunt was quite fond of triplets in general, and he defends this particular propensity in the preface to the 1832 edition of his *Poetical Works*: 'it expresses continuity of some sort, whether for the purpose of extension, or inclusion' (Hunt 2003: VI, 80–2). In the same preface, Hunt refers to Milton's and Spenser's use of the double rhyme and states: 'the use of which I have made of double rhymes [in *The Story of Rimini*] is a revival, not an innovation' (Hunt 2003: VI, 81).

13 See, for instance, Hunt's use of words such as 'bright-eyed face' (I, 14), 'a grassy plot' (I, 78), and 'feeling turf again' (II, 177).

14 Drawing on Solzhenitzyn's novel, *The First Circle*, Seamus Heaney writes that 'a voice is like a fingerprint, possessing a constant and unique signature that can, like fingerprint, be recorded and employed for identification' (Heaney 1980: 43). Heaney develops this idea of 'verbal fingerprint' further in the rest of his essay.

15 It is worth noting that, as late as 1857, S. Adams Lee felt the need to justify the subject of *The Story of Rimini* to his American readers, asserting that '[I]t may be a question whether such a story is to be told at all, but if told, it certainly ought to embody the emotions which naturally belong to it' (Hunt 1857: I, xix).

16 Hazlitt particularly liked the third canto, as his quotations in this letter and his inclusion of the whole canto in his 1824 *Select British Poets* illustrate. Mary Shelley reported to Hunt that Charles Lamb was pleased by Hazlitt's decision to include 'the Canto of the Fatal Passion from Rimini' in his selection (Shelley M. 1980–8: I, 379). Hazlitt also declares in *The Spirit of the Age*: 'We will venture to oppose his Third Canto of the *Story of Rimini* for classic elegance and natural feeling to any equal number of lines from Mr. Southey's Epics or from Mr. Moore's *Lallah Rook*' (Hazlitt 1930–4: XI, 177). Mary Shelley herself much enjoyed *Rimini*, as her repeated use of epigraphs from the poem in her novel *Lodore* demonstrates. I am grateful to Fiona Stafford for bringing this to my attention.

17 Hunt declares Byron 'a young man it is true,—but of acknowledged genius, and with a keen sight in particular for human nature' (Hunt 1816a: 49). Hunt also reprints anonymously Byron's 'Ode on the Star of the "Legion of Honour"' in the *Examiner* on 7 April 1816 , a poem that Stephen Cheeke describes as 'an exercise in dramatic monologue rather than an actual translation' (Cheeke 2003: 74). As John Clubbe notes, '[d]espite Hunt's coy disclaimer, many immediately recognized Byron as the author' (Clubbe 1997: n. pag.). Hunt had already published Byron's 'Napoleon's Farewell' the previous year on 30 July, as well as his 'Ode to Napoleon' on 25 April 1814 in his 'Political Examiner: The Joy of the Public – Bonaparte' (Hunt 2003: I, 323–8).

18 Another instance showing that Byron did not find Hunt's dedication offensive comes in a letter that Byron sent to Hunt on 14 March 1816 which included six orchestra tickets for Drury Lane, 'the best place in the house' (Byron 1973–94: V, 50).

19 An unwarranted effect of Hunt's dedication to Byron was to diminish the value of Coleridge's reference to Byron in the preface to his 1816 volume *Christabel, Kubla Khan, a Vision; The Pains of Sleep*. The anonymous reviewer for the *Scourge and Satirist* declares that Byron has brought himself to

> miserable degradation; to be a pandar to the false pretensions of scribblers of nauseous doggerel, of an individual who possesses the same feeling of poetic beauty that a blind man enjoys of colours, and mistakes the prattle of a pert and conceited boy for the language of simplicity inspired by genius. We verily believe that human talent, employed in framing a burlesque of all that is delicate in thought, beautiful in diction, and harmonious in versification, could not, by any efforts, have produced a more ludicrous example of the bathos than Hunt's Rimini.
>
> ([Anon.] 1816f: 60–1)

The reviewer goes on to assert: 'Mr. Coleridge can feel, in the privacy of his closet, but little gratification from the eulogies of a nobleman who approves the verses of Leigh Hunt, and permits that unfortunate poetaster to select him as the patron of his effusions' ([Anon.] 1816f: 62).

20 Hunt's comment in the *Examiner* appears in a small piece published after Albany Fonblanque's review of Byron's *Letter to* **** ***** *on the Rev. W. L. Bowles' Strictures on the Life and Writings of Pope* ([Fonblanque] 1821a: 269). As late as 1822, Hunt would still address Byron as 'My dear Byron' in a letter sent from Plymouth on 27 January 1822, which begins: 'For I will not abate a jot of my democracy, at least on occasions of letter-writing' (Hunt 1999: 111).

21 Byron's marginalia are reproduced in Nicholson's edition of his miscellaneous prose (Byron 1991: 541–2).

22 Byron again writes to Hunt on 30 October 1815: 'Pray let me have the rest of 'Rimini[']' you have 2 excellent points in that poem—originality—& Italianism' (Byron 1973–94: IV, 326). In addition, on 4 November 1815, Byron tells Moore: 'Leigh Hunt has written a *real good* and *very original Poem*, which I think will be a great hit. You can have no notion how very well it is written, nor should I, had I not redde it' (Byron 1973–94: IV, 330).

23 Thomas Medwin reports that Byron once told him: 'A friend of mine [Moore] calls "Rimini," *Nimini Pimini*; and "Foliage," Follyage. Perhaps he had a tumble in "climbing the trees in the Hesperides!" But "Rimini" has a great deal of merit. There were never so many fine things spoiled as in "Rimini"' (Medwin 1966: 254).

24 Byron evokes this dispute in a letter to Murray dated 9 April 1817: 'You & L[eig]h Hunt have quarrelled then it seems; I introduce him & his poem to you—in the hope that (malgré politics) the union would be beneficial to both—and the end is eternal enmity' (Byron 1973–94: V, 208). Five years later, Byron acknowledges that the relationship between Murray and Hunt has not improved: 'I do not propose to you to be the publisher—because I know you are unfriends' (Byron 1973–94: IX, 182).

25 The second edition of *Rimini* appeared with the imprint of Taylor and Hessey, R. Triphook, and C. and J. Ollier. The third one was published by C. and J. Ollier in duodecimo format. It includes an advertisement for *Hero and Leander*, and *Bacchus and Ariadne*, and *Foliage*, also published by the Olliers. For Hunt's financial difficulty with Taylor and Hessey, see Shelley P. B. 1964: II, 1n. 2, Stout 1925, and Reiman 1973–86: VII, 530–9 (Reiman reproduces the draft of John Taylor's angry letter to Hunt).

26 Tom Shuffleton is a character from the play by George Colman the Younger, *John Bull* (1803). Shuffleton borrows money from everybody, and thus the association of Hunt and a money-borrowing character was made long before Harold Skimpole in *Bleak House*. The reference here, however, has more to do with the language used by Shuffleton than his actual financial habits.

27 Conder would refer again positively to *The Story of Rimini* and Hunt's 'poetical genius' in his review of Keats's 1817 *Poems*, although not to Keats's benefit ([Conder] 1817: 270).

28 John Donovan attests the extent to which incest was a fashionable theme between 1815 and 1818 (Donovan 1987), and Richard Cronin's essay 'Shelleyan Incest and the Romantic Legacy' considers incest in several of P. B. Shelley's poems, and provides a good context for reading Hunt's *Rimini* (Cronin 1996b).

29 I base my attribution of this review to Roberts on John O. Hayden's assertion that, based on the account of Roberts's son in *The Life, Letters, and Opinions of William Roberts*, 'all of the reviews of Byron's works [in the *British Critic*] were attributed to Roberts' (Hayden 1969: 52).

30 Hunt himself claims this debt in his *Autobiography*: 'I had the pleasure of supplying my friendly critic, Lord Byron, with a point for his *Parisina* (the incident of the heroine talking in her sleep)' (Hunt 1850: II, 171). Andrew Nicholson however disagrees with that claim in his edition of Byron's miscellaneous prose, asserting instead 'there is no evidence to suggest that B ever saw canto iv of *The Story of Rimini* before its publication, by which time *Parisina* had already been published' (Byron 1991: 540).

31 Roberts declares: 'We solemnly proscribe [*Parisina*] from the English fire-side, and summon all that religion, morality, and policy enjoin, to give authority to the interdict. We are

happy to say that in this instance, that the subject is no more objectionable than the poetry is contemptible' ([Roberts] 1816: 463).

32 On 4–6 November 1815, Byron wrote Hunt: 'I have not time nor paper to *attack* your *system*—which ought to be done—were it only because it is a *system*' (Byron 1973–94: IV, 332). And on 1 June 1818, he wrote to Thomas Moore: 'When I saw "Rimini" in MSS., I told [Hunt] that I deemed it good poetry at bottom, disfigured only by a strange style. His answer was, that his style was a system, or *upon system*, or some such cant; and, when a man talks of system, his case is hopeless: so I said no more to him, and very little to any one else' (Byron 1973–94: VI, 46).

33 Many of Hunt's contemporaries believed Hazlitt to be the author of the *Edinburgh Review* article on *Rimini*. For instance, discussing the independence of his new periodical, the anonymous editor of the *Stage* declared on 16 November 1816:

> [A]s an instance [of biased criticism] we may quote the favourable mention which was made (in the Edinburgh) of Mr. Hunt's 'Rimini,' a work without exception the most ridiculous that ever issued from the press. It was reviewed by Mr. Hazlitt a writer for Mr. Hunt's political catch-penny 'The Examiner,' of course it was eulogized—so much for the impartiality of 'The Edinburgh Review'.
>
> ([Anon.] 1816h: 749)

Hunt himself thought that Hazlitt was the author of the review, as he wrote to Jeffrey: '[N]othing can be falser than what is said [in *Blackwood's*] respecting my having asked and pestered Mr. Hazlitt to write an article upon my poem in the *Edinburgh Review*' (Hunt 1862: I, 103). Hazlitt himself did write to Hunt in April 1821, 'I praised you in the Edinburgh Review' (Hazlitt 1978: 204) but, as Stanley Jones remarks, '[the] article [was] so drastically revised by Jeffrey that it is usually excluded from the Hazlitt canon' (Jones 1989: 212).

34 For a political reading of Moore's *Lalla Rookh*, see Jeffery Vail's article 'The Standard of Revolt: Revolution and National Independence in Moore's *Lalla Rookh*' (Vail 2005).

35 One may note that, two years later, Jeffrey would still refer positively to *Rimini* in his review of Barry Cornwall's *A Sicilian Story*. At one point, Jeffrey expressed doubt whether Cornwall 'could have written any thing so good, on the whole, as the beautiful story of *Rimini*' ([Jeffrey] 1818: 146). Although Hunt announces to John Booth on 17 September 1816 that he is 'about to commence Edinburgh Reviewer' (Reiman 1973–86: VII, 70), his only publication appeared in the *Edinburgh Review* for December 1816. Francis Jeffrey writes Hunt on 20 October 1816 regarding this publication, and invites him to contribute another essay: 'It will give me great pleasure to have an article from you of more original speculation, and it will be obliging in you when you have fixed upon a subject to let me know what it is as soon as possible' (Jeffrey 1816b: n. pag.). However, as Donald H. Reiman notes, Hunt never contributed another article to that journal (Reiman 1973–86: VII, 71–4).

36 Although Hunt had the opportunity to make some revisions to the poem before the second edition was published in June 1817, he only changed the lines 'She had stout notions on the marrying score,/And where the match unequal prospect bore' to 'She had a sense of marriage, just and free;/And where the match looked ill for harmony'. As he did with *The Feast of the Poets*, Hunt made many more extensive changes in the version he included in his 1832 *Poetical Works*, again in his 1844 edition, and finally in his 1860 edition, as well as in his 1855 *Stories in Verse*. These changes, as I argued in my previous chapter, were made principally in order to accommodate his audience, as Hunt himself acknowledges in his preface to *Stories in Verse*: 'I have done this [change] in compliance not only with my own judgment, but with that (as far as I could ascertain it) of the majority of my readers' (Hunt 2003: IV, 264).

37 It should be noted that being on the verge of poetical success did not equate with financial success. In fact, Hunt spent the advance money he got from Murray to pay off previous

debts. Hunt writes about his financial difficulties in a letter to Charles Ollier dated 26 November 1816:

> I console myself as well as I can, and find my poetry a solid good in the way of comfort if not of acquirement; but I would rather not see so many overbearing mansions of booksellers about me if I could help it, when I think that there are Wordsworth, Tom Moore, and I all living in cottages and as poor as the rats that infest them.
>
> (quoted in Brewer 1922: 19)

In 1817, Hunt's finances were again in a rather critical condition. This would of course happen repeatedly throughout Hunt's life. Holden's recent biography offers an accurate and sympathetic account of Hunt's recurring monetary problems (Holden 2005).

38 In this article, Lockhart particularly attacked the sexual politics present in 'the obscene and traitorous pages' of *Rimini* ([Lockhart] 1818a: 201). He also declares: 'No woman who has not either lost her chastity, or is not desirous of losing it, ever read "The Story of Rimini" without the flushing of shame and self-reproach' ([Lockhart] 1818a: 200).

39 Kim Wheatley also suggests that, although the negative remarks on Hunt's language in *The Story of Rimini* published in the *Quarterly Review* 'may be seen as politically motivated, the reviewers seem to have been content to exploit *Rimini* primarily for entertainment' (Wheatley 2003: 185).

40 In her detailed study of William Blackwood, Margaret Oliphant remarks that, with the publication of their first issue, John Gibson Lockhart and John Wilson Croker wanted 'something to sting and to startle, and make every reader hold his breath' (Oliphant 1897: I, 114). For a discussion of the relationship between Blackwood and P. B. Shelley, see Robinson 1983. For a more neutral description of Blackwood than Oliphant's study, see de Montluzin 1987.

41 To quote from but one of these critics, de Montluzin writes:

> The resultant literary war launched by *Blackwood's Magazine* against the Cockney poets is justly notorious for its ferocity, its venom, and its journalistic overkill. It was a rhetorical assault clearly out of proportion to the aesthetic needs of legitimate literary criticism, an assault characterized by cruelty, pettiness, mean-spirited conceit, manipulation of the truth, and inexcusable attacks upon personalities.
>
> (de Montluzin 1998: 107)

As can be expected, every biography of Leigh Hunt and John Keats contains a discussion of the Cockney School of Poetry, from Walter Jackson Bate's classic *John Keats* to Andrew Motion's *Keats* and Anthony Holden's *The Wit in the Dungeon* (Bate W. J. 1963; Motion 1997; Holden 2005). The Cockney School debate was of course still very much alive in 1821 when *Adonais* was published, as Susan Wolfson demonstrates (Wolfson 1995).

42 John Hunt had also written to Robert Baldwin, the London publisher and agent for Blackwood on 3 November 1817:

> Mr John Hunt calls upon Mr Baldwin to procure for him the Name and Residence of the Writer of an article in Blackwood's Magazine for October 1817—signed Z containing the most false, malignant, and altogether infamous assertions on the Character of Mr Leigh Hunt, the Editor of the Examiner.
>
> (quoted in Roe 1997: 270)

Following John Hunt's visit to their shop, Baldwin and Cradock wrote to William Blackwood on 3 November 1817:

> We were much surprised and hurt this morning at receiving a visit from Mr John Hunt, complaining on behalf of his brother of an article in your new Magazine signed

Z. Not having had time since the arrival of the copies to read the number, we were entirely ignorant of the nature of the article of which he complained; but, on examining it, we certainly think that it contains expressions which ought not to have been used.

(quoted in Oliphant 1897: I, 134–5)

43 Byron would also single out the *Quarterly* piece in a letter to Moore dated 11 April 1817:

There was a devil of a review of [Hunt] in the Quarterly, a year ago, which he answered. All answers are imprudent: but to be sure, poetical flesh and blood must have the last word—that's certain. I thought, and think, very highly of his Poem; but I warned him of the row his favourite antique phraseology would bring him into.

(Byron 1973–94: V, 211)

44 One may note that, though he was certainly no friend of Hunt, Southey objected to Murray about the severe personal attacks printed in the reviews of the *Quarterly*, in a letter dated 8 April 1818:

The cursed system of acrimonious criticism has prevailed too generally and too long: keep it for the culprits of literature, for pretenders in philosophy, incendiaries in politics, scoffers in religion. ... But any undue severity, any gratuitous attack, any wound wantonly inflicted makes a man your enemy, when he might as well have been your friend. Above all let us do ample justice to those who are most obnoxious: *more* than justice has been done to Bp Watson ... this is erring on the right side: less than justice was done to Leigh Hunt, a conceited writer, and a man of the most villainous principles, but of no inconsiderable powers. Let us differ from the *Edinburgh* as much in our principles of criticism as in every thing else.

(Southey 1965: II, 184)

See also his letter to Murray dated 24 August 1816, where he approves of a review 'which may redeem the *Quarterly* from the stigma brought upon it by such articles as those upon Galts Tragedies, and Leigh Hunts *Rimini*' (Southey 1965: II, 141).

45 Hunt removed these two lines referring specifically to his imprisonment in the 1832 version of the poem, another instance of Hunt's attempt to present a public face removed from political connotations to his contemporaries.

46 Charles Cowden Clarke sees the review as '[a] perverse misrepresentation,—[a] real, or affected want of comprehension,—[a] flimsily disguised envy and malignity' ([Clarke] 1816: 18). Ironically, forty years later, Croker wrote to Lord Russell about the publication of Thomas Moore's *Diary*:

The discretion allowed to an editor is never better employed than in keeping domestic life separate from what you yourself describe as the 'idle gossip and calumnies of the day,'—the squabbles of authorship, and the hot conflict of political parties.

(Croker 1854: 10)

47 Several years later, Charles Lamb again defended Hunt's reputation in his 'Letter of Elia to Robert Southey, Oct. 1823':

I was admitted to his [Hunt's] household for some years, and do most solemnly aver that I believe him to be in his domestic relations as correct as any man. He chose an ill-judged subject for a poem [*Rimini*]; the peccant humours of which have been visited on him tenfold by the artful use, which his adversaries have made, of an *equivocal term*. Dante started the subject itself, but better because brieflier treated of. But the crime of the Lovers, in the Italian and the English poet, with its aggravated enormity

> of circumstance, is not of a kind (as the critic of the latter well knew) with those conjunctions, for which Nature herself has provided no excuse, because no temptation.
>
> (Lamb and Lamb 1903–5: V, 210)

48 Since she was a friend of the Blackwood family, it does not come as a surprise that Mrs Oliphant admitted that the attack on Hunt was unjustifiable but that, in any case, Hunt was 'as evil-tongued a critic as could be found, so that there is little cause for pity'. She even states that the real cause for pity was that 'such a man as Lockhart should ever have been tempted to indulge in abuse so unworthy of himself' (Oliphant 1897: I, 133).

49 Byron also noted Hunt's 'poor' education as a probable reason for his lack of poetical achievement:

> Hunt would have made a fine writer, for he has a great deal of fancy and feeling, if he had not been spoiled by circumstances. He was brought up at the Blue-coat foundation, and had never till lately been ten miles from St. Paul's. What poetry is to be expected from such a course of education? He has his school, however, and a host of disciples.
>
> (quoted in Medwin 1966: 254)

50 The first piece in the series of articles 'On the Cockney School of Poetry' appeared in *Blackwood's Edinburgh Magazine*, II, VII (October 1817): 38–41. Another seven articles appeared between 1817 and 1825; see *Blackwood's Edinburgh Magazine*, II, VIII (November 1817): 194–201; III, XVI (July 1818): 453–6; III, XVIII (August 1818): 519–24; V, XXV (April 1819): 97–100; VI, XXXI (October 1819): 70–6; and XVIII, CIII (August 1825): 155–60.

51 See, for instance, the approving mention of Hunt being 'the laughing-stock of all gentlemen and ladies' following Z's attacks ([Anon.] 1820a: 690), the negative description of the *Examiner*'s success because 'it was the only cleverish paper printed on a Sunday about town' ([Anon.] 1820b: 318), the criticisms against the *Indicator* ([Anon.] 1820c), the reference to *Rimini* and Hunt's principles 'with his coming-up mouth, and his "showery smile," and his "clipsome waist"' ([Anon.] 1821: 674); the assertion that 'LORD BYRON being a somewhat whimsical nobleman, has lately hired two or three Cockneys as menial servants' ([Anon.] 1823a: 365); the review of Hunt's *Bacchus in Tuscany* explicitly titled 'The Cockney School of Poetry. N°VIII' ([Lockhart] 1825); the review of *Lord Byron and Some of his Contemporaries* ([Wilson] 1828); and the assertion 'After killing a Cockney, why run away, and more especially in a mask? Let the fair deed be perpetrated at noon-day, and on a crowded street, not a human creature will seek to detain you' ([Anon.] 1829: 524).

52 On 22 March 1818, P. B. Shelley writes to Hunt: 'What a delightful poem the "Nymphs" is! especially the second part. It is truly *poetical*, in the intense and emphatic sense of the word' (Shelley P. B. 1964: II, 2–3). Shelley would again praise the poem in a letter dated 14–18 November 1819 (Shelley P. B. 1964: II, 152). For one of the rare detailed readings of this poem, see Thorpe 1959.

53 Hunt had sent Byron a copy of *Foliage* through P. B. Shelley (Shelley P. B. 1964: II, 13), and the latter would write to Mary on 23 August 1818 that Byron 'quizzes [*Foliage*] immoderately' (Shelley P. B. 1964: II, 37). For Byron's possible attack on 'The Nymphs' and *Endymion* in the first canto of *Don Juan*, see Barnard 1988.

54 *The British Critic* had published a very negative review of *The Round Table* a year earlier, stating on the first page that '[a] production less improving, or less gratifying, we have seldom perused: whether the taste, the tone of mind, or the morality which they display, be upon the most disgusting and contemptible, we should find it not easy to determine' ([Anon.] 1817b: 554).

55 The anonymous author criticizes the tone and content of the review, and declares:

> Reviewers are creatures that 'stab men in the dark:'—young and enthusiastic spirits are their dearest prey. Our readers will not easily forget the brutality with which the Quarterly Reviewers, in a late number of their ministerial book, commented on the work of an intelligent and patriotic woman [i.e. Lady Morgan], whose ardour and independence happened to be high enough to make them her enemies.
>
> ([Anon.] 1818g: 648)

Hunt had already published a letter from an unknown correspondent in the 2 November 1817 *Examiner* attacking the *Quarterly Review*, and specifically Gifford, in response to the review of Lady Morgan's *France*; see [Anon.] 1817a.

56 In the other column on that page, nearly at the same level, appears another short notice, signed 'Scotsman', which reads: 'Mr. HAZLITT's action against the Publishers of *Blackwood's Magazine* has been withdrawn, they having agreed to pay him a certain sum as damages, and all expenses.—'.

57 This article is signed 'Scotsman', the same name that appeared four months earlier in the notice regarding Hazlitt and *Blackwood's Magazine*; see note 56 above.

58 See Hunt 2003: II, 214–21 for a reprint of Hunt's articles in 'The Quarterly Review, and Revolt of Islam' and 'The Quarterly Review, and Revolt of Islam (Concluded from last week)'.

59 Hunt is referring to 'Art. I—Lectures on the History of Literature, Ancient and Modern, from the German of Frederick Schlegel' ([Anon.] 1819b), and 'Art. IX—1. Prospectus and Specimens of an intended National Work by William and Robert Whistlecraft 2. The Court of Beasts, freely translated from the Animali Parlanti of Giambattista Casti, a Poem, in seven Cantos' ([Anon.] 1819c). The sub-heading of the latter article probably appealed to Hunt in particular: 'Narrative and Romantic Poems of the Italians'.

Chapter 4

1 Hunt's famous 'hand' signature became rarer in the pages of the *Examiner* from the end of 1820 onward, and the *Indicator* was cancelled on 21 March 1821 because of Hunt's health; see Hunt 1862: I, 163. Henry Hunt took an active role in the running of the *Examiner* from 1819 onward, when he took over his father's duty and began assisting Leigh in his editorial task when the latter was unwell. Henry eventually took over his father's firm in 1825 when John retired, and added a partner to it a year later when the firm was renamed Hunt & Clark. For details of the history of John Hunt's various business ventures, see Brown, P. A. H. 1982: 95.

2 Hunt would advance the necessity of his staying in London and working on the *Examiner* again in another letter to P. B. Shelley dated 28 August 1821:

> But you talk of the *Examiner*. Alas! my dear friend, the whole difficulty lies there. It had got to so low a pitch, and my absence reduced it to me so much lower that we [i.e. John and Leigh] feared for its very existence, and upon this depends not only my family, but my brother's.
>
> (Hunt 1862: I, 167)

3 Marianne's health was so bad when they arrived in Italy that Andre Vaccà Berlinghiera, a celebrated surgeon, announced that she had only a few months to live. Yet, as Hunt recalls with some humor in his 1860 *Autobiography*, 'She lived till the year 1857, and Vaccà had been dead many years before' (Hunt 1949a: 325). Hunt had referred to Vaccà in his first 'Letters from Abroad' as 'a man in the prime of life, with an intelligent and pleasing countenance [who] is known all over Europe' (Hunt 1822–3: I, 98).

4 Byron would also indicate in a letter to Douglas Kinnaird, dated 10 March 1823, that 'L[eigh] H[unt] says that it will do him great harm if that Journal stops' (Byron 1973–94: X, 121).

5 Most biographies of Byron usually include a section on the relationship between Hunt and Byron, and what a recent biographer describes as 'Hunt's complete dependence on Byron's largesse' (Eisler 1999: 706). Byron's biographers obviously tend to side with their subject. Similarly, Hunt's biographers put the situation in perspective from Hunt's side and deplore his subordination to Byron during the first part of his stay in Italy; see, for instance, Blainey 1985: 129–36, and Chapter 8 of Holden's biography (Holden 2005). Of course, as Steven Zani remarks, '[a]ny close reading of Byron biography reveals examples of exaggerated contradiction' (Zani 2004: 35).

6 For a discussion of the poems P. B. Shelley wrote during his four-year stay that had a clear Italian influence, be it literary, geographical, or political, see Weinberg 1991.

7 *Parnaso Italiano* was a collection of poetry in fifty-six volumes adorned with vignettes, which Hunt bought while in prison. The *Parnasso Italiano* volumes were still prominent in Hunt's library as late as 1837, when William Bell Scott started visiting him at his Chelsea address, as Scott notes in his *Autobiography*:

> I found Leigh Hunt living at Chelsea in a quiet street, near Carlyle,—a small house with two windows to the drawing-room, in which he appeared to live, and which consequently contained his books—a small collection, mostly Italian, in which the fifty-six volumes of the Parnasso Italiano was most important—and his piano, a venerable instrument.
>
> (Scott W. B. 1892: 125)

8 Reiman identifies the work Hunt mentions as Giovanbattista Baldelli Boni's *La Vita di Giovanni Boccaccio* (1806). Other instances of Hunt's knowledge of Italian authors include a letter to Mary Shelley dated 4 August 1818 (Hunt 1862: I, 121–3), where he mentions Ariosto, Petrarch, and Pulci.

9 Hunt states in *Lord Byron and Some of his Contemporaries*: 'I had never been out of England before; except, when a child, to the coast of France' (Hunt 1828a: 98).

10 For more information on the collaboration between Hunt and Byron on *The Liberal*, see also Miller 1910: 88–120, Gross 2001: 153–70, and Chapter 8 of Holden's biography (Holden 2005).

11 See, for instance, Marshall's discussion and reprint of the sixteen-page pamphlet *The Illiberal* (Marshall 1960: 120–1, 217–27). See also the anonymous publication, *The Press, or Literary Chit–Chat. A Satire* for its discussion of the *Liberal* and the relationship between 'Harold and Rimini, a noble pair' (l. 276; [Anon.] 1822: 19–22). The anonymous author of *A Critique of 'The Liberal'* also announces that the blasphemic tone of Byron's 'Vision of Judgment' compelled him to publish his pamphlet as public condemnation of both the poem and *The Liberal* ([Anon.] 1823b: 3).

12 It is therefore somewhat ironic that Hunt would assert in his 1830 review of Byron's *Werner* that 'Lord Byron's real genius is to be found in *Don Juan*' (Hunt 2003: III, 144).

13 Marshall indicates the authorship of the various articles throughout his study, and he includes two tables listing the number of articles and the number of pages per author (Marshall 1960: 239).

14 The articles published in the *Liberal* under the heading 'Letters from Abroad' are 'Letter I.—Pisa' (Hunt 1822–3: I, 97–120), 'Letter II.—Genoa' (Hunt 1822–3: I, 269–88), 'Letter III.—Italy' (Hunt 1822–3: II, 47–65), and 'Letter IV' (Hunt 1822–3: II, 251–64).

15 Since this section of *Lord Byron and Some of his Contemporaries* is obviously based on the journal Hunt kept during his time in Italy, I choose to consider it alongside Hunt's 'Letters from Abroad' and his *Literary Examiner* article. Furthermore, while every reviewer of Hunt's *Lord Byron and Some of his Contemporaries* discusses his account of Byron, only two reviewers mention the autobiographical section of Hunt's work. The anonymous reviewer for the *Athenaeum* briefly discusses the 200 pages devoted to Hunt's memoirs, including his recollections of Italy ([Anon.] 1828f: 70). The anonymous reviewer for the *London Magazine* is the only one to refer specifically to Hunt's voyage to Italy and to praise his narration as 'one

of the most amusing, as well as natural descriptions of a sea voyage, by a landsman' ([Anon.] 1828g: 224).

16 Hunt's life in Italy led him to revise *The Story of Rimini* in his 1844 *Poetical Works* because, as he explains in the preface to that volume, 'he wrote it before he had visited Italy, and made it in some respects too English. … The landscapes are now freed from northern inconsistencies' (Hunt 1844: iv).

17 Alison Chapman and Jane Stabler rightly observe that 'Italy had been portrayed as a dream-like haven for male northern travellers since Milton's *Paradise Lost* presented Eden as an Italianate garden of unfallen sexuality' (Chapman and Stabler 2003: 4).

18 Barefoot's chapter 'To Rome for the Winter: From the Napoleonic Wars to 1870' provides a good survey of the major works on Italy written during this period, as well as a discussion of the major authors who sojourned in Italy; see Barefoot 1993: 135–95.

19 Hale offers a detailed account of the English travelers in Italy in that period, including the various means available to get to the country, board and lodging facilities, and the itineraries; see Rogers 1956: 56–99.

20 Brand discusses the English interest in Italy, as well as publications on Italy in prose and poetry, and the major literary figures associated with this country (Brand 1957: 7–25; see also Avitabile 1959).

21 The anonymous author of the combined review of Samuel Rogers's *Italy. Poem. Part the Second* and William Sotheby's *Italy, and other Poems* (Sotheby 1828) also describes the topic of these volumes as 'the fair and ever fascinating land of Italy' ([Anon.] 1828l: 397). For a more cynical view on books about Italy, see the anonymous review of Louis Simond's *Voyage en Italie et en Sicile* in the *Monthly Review* ([Anon.] 1828h).

22 Mary Shelley asserts: 'If all travellers wrote and described as [Simond] does, their productions would attain the highest places in the literary scale' (Shelley M. 1996: II, 187).

23 Simond's account presents the reader with an intimate view of the country, an informative presentation of Italian politics, and some personal reminiscences, which evoke Hunt's style and opinion.

24 Note also that Hazlitt famously begins his *New Monthly Magazine* essay of June 1828 by stating: 'I am one of those who do not think that much is to be gained in point either of temper or understanding by travelling abroad' (Hazlitt 1930–4: XVII, 332).

25 Despite the fact that the first part of Rogers' *Italy* appeared in 1822, during the great vogue that Italian travel literature then still enjoyed, the poem proved unsuccessful, as did successive editions. The second part of *Italy*, published in 1828, was also unsuccessful, even though both parts possess all the attributes common to other, more successful recollections of Italy previously published. In his poem, Rogers tells of his journeys to Italy and describes the impressions that Italian art and history have made upon his mind. He also acquaints his readers, as P. W. Clayden notes, with 'the scenes which had stimulated his poetical fancy and gratified his artistic taste' (Clayden 1889: II, 2). Avery F. Gaskins accurately summarizes the poem when he states that '[t]he book intersperses prose and poetry in a series of impressions of places, people, and regional character. Rogers is less interested in the Italy of ancient Rome than he is in medieval Italy, especially the gothic aspects of life' (Gaskins 1985: 148; see also Holcomb 1988).

Drawing on his personal wealth, Rogers was able to buy and destroy all the unsold copies of the poem before proceeding to revise it carefully for a new edition, published in 1830. On 4 June 1831, Hunt declares in his *Tatler* essay 'Mr. Moxon's Publications' that Edward Moxon 'had astonished us with Mr. Rogers's poems on *Italy*, full of beautiful plates after Turner and Stothard—a golden volume' (Hunt 1830–32: II, 937). Thanks largely to the quantity and quality of the illustrations by J. M. W. Turner and Thomas Stothard that Hunt mentions, this new edition of *Italy* was a great success, and would remain so for many years. Indeed, as J. R. Hale asserts, '[f]or two generations [*Italy*] remained the ideal present for those about to leave for Italy or who had just come back. It appeared in edition after edition, simple and elaborate' (Rogers 1956: 111). Kenneth Churchill writes further that '[i]t is these vignettes which have made the volume famous, not only as a stage in the development in Turner's career but, especially, for the impression they made on the young Ruskin' (Churchill 1980: 50). For a longer discussion of Rogers' poem, see Giddey 1959.

26 I say *sometimes* because Hunt would also find places that matched or exceeded the beauty of their representations in the *Parnaso Italiano*, as he told Elizabeth Kent in a letter:

> You remember how we used to look at the poor little vignettes in the *Parnaso Italiano*, and fancy Italy. You cannot conceive—yes, yes, you can,—how delightful it was to find a number of features exactly the same, though greatly heightened in beauty.
> (Hunt 1862: I, 187)

27 Italian cities, unsurprisingly, did not correspond to the English picturesque tradition, but this tradition probably affected Hunt's appreciation of Italian urban landscape. Wordsworth describes the necessity of houses (and their colors) blending in with the landscape in his *Guide through the District of the Lakes in the North of England* (Wordsworth 1968: 96), and the harmony of houses and their natural surroundings was a necessary aspect and convention of English landscaping, as Humphrey Repton discusses at length in *Observations on the Theory and Practice of Landscape Gardening, including some Remarks on Grecian and Gothic Architecture* (Repton 1803). I am grateful to Joel Pace for suggesting I consult Repton's work.

28 As early as 9 April 1823, Hunt wrote to Horace Smith: 'This country has been such a melancholy one to me, since [Shelley] has gone, that I have nothing pleasant to tell you of it' (Hunt 1862: I, 195). Hunt still felt similarly eighteen months later when he wrote to T. J. Hogg of 'this dreary country, where I have suffered nothing but torture' in a letter dated 17 December 1824 (quoted in Scott W. S. 1943: 72).

29 Richard D. Altick concisely describes Hunt's relationship with Novello in his book on the Cowden Clarkes:

> half-English, half-Italian, educated in France, married to a lady of German and Irish extraction, he was, as Hunt himself was in taste if not in lineage, a cosmopolitan. Novello had pronouncedly Italianate tastes, and Hunt's heart had Italy engraved inside it. At the Novellos' there was constant music; Hunt here could drink his fill of his own adored Haydn, Mozart, and Purcell. No wonder, then, that later, during his Italian exile, his dreams were constantly returning to the snug musicales.
> (Altick 1948: 32)

30 An anonymous review of the fourth issue of the *Liberal* in the *Literary Examiner*, most likely written by Albany Fonblanque, describes the fourth 'Letters from Abroad' as conveying 'a variety of information that can be acquired by organs of a refined and peculiar construction alone'. The reviewer adds: 'Descriptive epistles of this class, close up the rear matter-of-fact travellers with the happiest effect—a liqueur after dinner' ([Fonblanque] 1823: 52). Although the reviewer is obviously biased in favor of this essay and the whole issue, which is quoted from at great length, he does draw a good analogy between Hunt's essay and 'a liqueur after dinner': in the same way that a liqueur is a complement to a meal and is pleasing to the palate without being a main course, Hunt's essay gives the feeling of providing some information but not as much as an entire work on the subject would.

31 In one of the notes to the fourth canto of *Childe Harold's Pilgrimage*, John Cam Hobhouse warns the reader that 'however [the *Classical Tour*] may adorn his library, it will be of little or no service to him in his carriage' (Byron 1980–92: II, 263). P. B. Shelley certainly agreed with Hobhouse, as his letter to Thomas Peacock dated 9 November 1818 shows: 'Consult Eustace if you want to know nothing about Italy' (Shelley P. B. 1964: II, 54). Similarly, Charlotte Ann Waldie (afterwards Mrs Eaton) asserts in the preface to her *Rome in the Nineteenth Century*: 'Of the two most popular writers [of travel literature], Eustace is inaccurate, and Forsyth inadequate' (Waldie 1820: I, vi–viii). Eaton's work, first published anonymously in 1820, met with some success and was reprinted in 1822, and again in

1823. Eaton offers a detailed account of Rome, with numerous commentaries on archaeology and religion, but also on Italian politics. Mary Shelley praised Eaton's *Rome in the Nineteenth Century* as 'an inestimable guide to all who visit the Eternal City' in her article for the October 1826 issue of the *Westminster Review* (Shelley M. 1996: II, 159).

32 The work referred to here is Alfieri's *Don Garzia* (1789), a play in which Alfieri criticizes parental tyranny. The plot runs thus:

> Cosimo, the father-tyrant, orders his son, Don Garzia, to kill Salviati, his enemy, or sacrifice his love for Salviati's daughter, Giulia. Don Garzia sets out to carry out the order but by mistake kills his own brother, Diego. Cosimo, in fury on learning that Salviati's life was not taken, murders Don Garzia.
>
> (Mezaro 1975: 44)

Hunt was well versed on Alfieri and he included 'Epigram of Alfieri', 'Alfieri's Benediction', and 'Portrait of Alfieri' in the second number of the *Liberal* (Hunt 1822–3: I, 163, 395, and 399). He inserted the original text and his own translation of two more of Alfieri's poems in his third 'Letters from Abroad'; see Hunt 1822–3: II, 59–62 and 65. He also wrote Byron in October 1822 that he was 'translating a *trampling* satire of Alfieri's upon trade and money-getting' (MS, John Murray Archive, quoted in Stabler 2002: 179).

33 Incidentally, that Hunt records that the shore looked 'as Italian as possible, with groves and white villages' indicates once again the preconceived idea he holds of the country and its landscape.

34 Hunt also mentions Boccaccio's house in a letter to Kent; see Hunt 1862: I, 220. Hunt was evidently an admirer of Boccaccio, as his praise of this author a few years earlier in the preface to his 1825 *Bacchus in Tuscany* shows.

35 There are obviously many other fictional works published during the Romantic period in which Italy figures as an important element, especially in the very popular Gothic novels of Ann Radcliffe (*The Mysteries of Udolpho*, *A Sicilian Romance*, and *The Italian*). Jane Waldie declares in her travel account about Italy that '[t]hese fictitious narratives gave a better idea of the peculiar characteristics of Italian scenery and Italian habits, than many more detailed and regular accounts' (Waldie 1820: I, 157).

36 Jeanne Moskal points out the importance of Mariana Starke in the creation of the modern guidebooks with her 1820 *Information and Directions for Travellers on the Continent* (Moskall 2000).

37 Carolyn Springer considers in detail the section of Canto IV devoted to Rome, especially Byron's representation of Roman ruins, in her book *The Marble Wilderness: Ruins and Representation in Italian Romanticism, 1775–1850* (Springer 1987: 4–8). Italy is also an important country for Byron because of its politics, particularly in contrast to the British politics that Byron evokes in his dedication to Hobhouse. Hobhouse's notes to the poem reinforce its political dimension. Although these notes were already quite numerous in the published version of *Childe Harold's Pilgrimage*, Hobhouse felt he had to write another work to explore more fully the issues he wished to confront, hence the publication of *Historical Illustrations of the Fourth Canto of Childe Harold: containing Dissertations on the Ruins of Rome; and an Essay on Italian Literature* (1818). As David Blayney Brown notes in his catalogue to the exhibition 'Turner and Byron', Hobhouse's *Historical Illustrations* 'were a substantial amplification of the text [of the poem], providing a wealth of antiquarian and literary information' (Brown D. B. 1992: 26). For more information on Hobhouse's notes, see Rutherford 1961. For Foscolo's part in the *Historical Illustrations*, see Vincent 1949.

38 De Staël's *Corinne* had an extended influence on many other fictional and non-fictional works published in the early part of the nineteenth century. The importance of de Staël for the second generation of Romantic writers is undeniable, although not yet fully explored by Romantic scholars. For the present study, I will mention Byron's note to *Childe Harold, Canto IV* where he discusses de Staël/Corinne (Byron 1980–92: II, 235–6) and Ernest

Giddey's essay 'Byron and Madame de Staël' (Giddey 1982). The Shelleys read de Staël's works, both fictional and non-fictional, during the 1810s, and Mary Shelley uses epigrams from de Staël's novels in several of her works. Shelley also corresponded with John Murray about writing a biography of de Staël in 1829, and again in 1830; see Shelley 1980–8: II, 89, 105, 110, and 113. She eventually published a biographical essay on de Staël in the second volume of Lardner's *Lives of the Most Eminent Literary and Scientific Men of France* (1839).

39 For a discussion of the reception of *Corinne*, as well as a synopsis of the novel, see Besser 1994: 77–92. Maura O'Connor points out that *Corinne* was published at a time when travel between England and Italy was greatly restricted, and that de Staël's story 'spoke directly to the English traveller and reader' (O'Connor 1998: 29).

40 Charlotte Hogsett observes that

> [t]he novel is at once a story of lovers and a guide to Italy—its monuments, its characters, its literature, its artistic achievements. Staël takes care to unite these two parts of her book into a whole by having the events of her story happen in places that reflect or symbolize the particular nature of the event.
>
> (Hogsett 1987: 109)

41 Simone Balayé discusses Staël's own travel in Italy in 1805 in her book *Les Carnets de voyage de Madame de Staël*; see Balayé 1971: 93–259.

42 In his preface to his *Tour of Italy*, Eustace strongly encourages future travelers to Italy to treat de Staël's novel as a companion to their journeys (Eustace 1821: I, xxxvi).

43 *Corinne* was actually listed as a travel guide in the Bibliothèque Nationale de Paris until the end of the nineteenth century (Vallois 1985: 76).

44 Napoleon himself did not approve of de Staël's decision to set the story in 1795, since it reflected negatively on his territorial subjugation and the removal of many works of art from Italian museums and churches under his direction. For de Staël's discussion of politics in *Corinne*, see Gennari 1947: 123–242. Napoleon had already prevented the publication of de Staël's *De l'Allemagne* in 1810. The book was eventually published in French by John Murray in 1813.

45 As Mary Cambell remarks, when Henry Colburn published *Italy* after heavily publicizing it, Morgan was at the height of her literary fame, with her previous controversial work, *France*, having gone through several editions in England, France, and America (Cambell 1988: 177).

46 Although Mary Shelley asserts in her preface to *Rambles in Germany and Italy* (1844) that Morgan's book *Italy* 'is dear to the Italians' (Shelley M. 1996: VIII, 66), the same could not be said for Morgan's contemporaries. Shelley's own book is a rather political work and, as Jeanne Moskal notes, it exposes 'the cause of Italian nationalism, excusing the excesses of its advocates, the Carbonari, and promoting recent Italian literature with a nationalist agenda' (Moskal 1999: 188). Shelley's work was of course primarily a travel narrative focused on Italy, and was praised extensively by reviewers. This, in itself, was no small achievement at a time when, as Moskal points out, 'travel memoirists needed to differentiate their works from a new genre of travel handbooks or guides' (Shelley M. 1996: VIII, 51). For more information on *Rambles in Germany and Italy*, see also Orr 1998 and Kautz 2000.

47 As the editor of Morgan's *Autobiography* remarks, 'Lady Morgan's work is full of eloquent lamentation and description of the change for the worse that had come over everything [after Napoleon's departure]' (Owenson 1862: II, 144).

48 For a detailed discussion of Morgan's politics and advocacy of Napoleon in *Italy*, see Moskal 1995: 191–3.

49 A second edition of *Italy* appeared in January 1822, with a long preface by Morgan defending her work against the severe criticisms that had appeared in the press. One of the most severe attacks came from Croker in the July 1821 *Quarterly Review* ([Croker] 1821). (Hill Shine and Helen Chadwick Shine attributes this review to Croker; see Shine 1949: 75.) Byron was one of the few persons to praise Morgan's work, as this reference in a letter to

Moore, dated 24 August 1821, indicates: 'Her work is fearless and excellent on the subject of Italy—pray tell her so—and I know the country' (Byron 1973–94: VIII, 189).

50 Interestingly, when Hunt integrated the text of *Lord Byron and Some of his Contemporaries* into his *Autobiography*, he changed the sentence: 'Genoa again! With what different feelings we beheld it the first time!' (Hunt 1828a: 61), referring to the description just quoted as well as to the sadness he then associated with Italy following Shelley's death, to 'Genoa again!—With what different feelings we beheld it *from those which enchanted us* the first time!' (Hunt 1850: III, 57, my emphasis). In so doing, Hunt is more truthful to his first impression of the city, as he expressed in a letter to P. B. Shelley, dated 15 June 1822: '[I]f anything could console us for this last tantalising delay, it is the sight of this glorious and at the same time lovely city' (Hunt 1862: I, 181–2).

51 I am thinking particularly of Hunt's essays 'A Tale for Chimney Corner' (Hunt 1819c), 'Deaths of Little Children' (Hunt 1820b), 'Of the Sight of Shops' (Hunt 1820c), and 'Coaches' (Hunt 1820d).

52 In a letter to Hunt dated 3 March 1823, Vincent Novello, the addressee of Hunt's third 'Letters from Abroad', writes: 'Your description of the "Campo Santo" was so very vivid, that I could fancy I had the very spot before me—or that I was reading an account of some place that I had seen before, and with which I was perfectly familiar' (quoted in Marshall 1960: 170).

53 Hunt also manifests this longing for England in a letter to Elizabeth Kent, dated 16 April 1825: '[N]othing can make up to me for the want of proper *treey* trees and grass walks. I am often seized with a desire to walk through particular spots in England, generally a path in a field' (Hunt 1862: I, 237).

54 The 'Wishing Cap' essays are another instance of Hunt's contribution to travel writing, although they are unusual in that while written from Italy, they deal with the subject of London. Hunt's familiar style would again be present in the *Companion*, especially his essays 'A Walk from Dulwich to Brockham' and 'Of the Sight of Shops'.

55 See, for instance, *Stories from the Italian Poets* (Hunt 1846), and *A Jar of Honey from Mount Hybla* (Hunt 1848). Hunt's name appears in the list of original members of the council for this society, established to promote the cause of Italian politics in view of the unification of the country. For more information on the Society of the Friends of Italy, see O'Connor 1988: 77–9. In an undated letter most likely written in the same period, Joseph Mazzini invites Hunt to join the council of this association:

> Your name is known to many of my countrymen; it would, no doubt, impart additional value to the thought embodied in the League. It is the name, not only of a patriot, but of a high literary man and of a poet. It would show at once that *national* questions are questions not merely of *political* tendencies, but of feelings, eternal truth and god-like poetry. It would show that poets understand their active mission down, and that they are the prophets and apostles of 'things to come'.
>
> (Mazzini ?1851: n. pag.)

56 *Lord Byron* was published between 22 and 28 January 1828. The work is announced as 'published today' in the *Morning Chronicle* of 22, 24 and 26 January 1828. On 29 January, Hunt's second letter to the editor of the *Morning Chronicle* appeared, in which he refers to the book then being available.

57 Hunt's 'instant reputation' may have contributed to his being depicted as Mr Eavesdrop in Thomas Love Peacock's 1831 *Crotchet Castle*. As Claude A. Prance indicates, Eavesdrop is '[a] literary character who portrayed his acquaintances in his writings [and who is generally] thought to be based on Leigh Hunt' (Prance 1992: 21). Marilyn Butler notes further that 'Mr Eavesdrop, who publishes gossip about his friends, evokes a common enough type, but would certainly have been identified by Peacock's contemporaries as one or other of the two friends of Byron who had recently published their reminiscences of him: Leigh Hunt and Thomas Moore' (Butler 1979: 184).

58 See, for instance, Jane Blumberg, who announces that 'Hunt revenged himself [upon Byron] in 1828 when he published *Lord Byron and Some of His Contemporaries*, taking advantage of their former intimacy to savage the poet's character' (Blumberg 1992: 61), or Jeffery W. Vail, who describes Hunt's book as 'the most exaggerated hostile portrait of Byron ever produced' (Vail 2000: 230).

59 Hunt had already established a business relationship with Colburn, having published a series of articles, as Harry Honeycomb, under the title 'The Family Journal' in Colburn's *New Monthly Magazine*; see Hunt 1862: I, 236. On 16 June 1825, Hunt wrote to Vincent Novello: 'Colburn has done all, and more than I expected; and I am glad of the polite and cordial manner in which he behaved. … I shall set him down as the most *engaging* of publishers' (Hunt 1862: I, 246).

60 In an undated letter probably written in the Fall of 1827, Colburn wrote to Hunt:

> I am so extremely anxious that you should make all possible *additions* and corrections to the Byron Book that I have determined to send you another 20£ on acct of *that work* and I rely accordingly on your best *exertions* to fulfil my wishes … . I trust in the course of the *next week* I shall receive the 1st Vol. of Byron and the 2nd Vol. the following week.
>
> (quoted in Landré 1936: I, 177)

61 The Brewer–Leigh Hunt Collection has copies of these two foreign editions, along with an Italian edition which reprints the Byron section of Hunt's book: *Lord Byron. Frammenti Critico-Storici Tratti Dall' Opera di M. Leigh Hunt Intitolate Lord Byron and Some of his Contemporaries* (Milano: Co 'Torshi D'Omobono Manini, Ne 'Tre Re, N°4085, 1828).

62 On 28 February 1828, Moore writes in his journal: 'The late infamous book of Leigh Hunt has induced [Murray] to change his mind with respect to the publication of Lord Bs papers' (Moore 1853–6: V, 255). Hunt's work thus ultimately 'acted in Moore's favour' (MacCarthy 2002: 541). Indeed, as Andrew Elfenbein contends, 'Hunt's negative interpretation so outraged Murray that he commissioned Byron's friend Thomas Moore to write a response. Moore's official biography … was published in two volumes by Murray in 1830, and quickly established itself as the standard biography' (Elfenbein 1995: 78). For more on the relationship between Byron and Moore, see Vail 2000.

63 Probably due to Hunt's disparaging comments about him in *Lord Byron and Some of his Contemporaries*, Scott makes his feelings clear to Lockhart: 'I am speaking in the idea that you are taking Leigh Hunt in hand which he richly deserves. Only remember the lash is administered with most cutting severity when the executioner keeps his temper' (Scott 1932–6: X, 373).

64 Elizabeth Jones rightly notes the echo of the earlier articles in the Cockney School essays and their argument that the Cockneys 'were intent upon corrupting domestic life' in Lockhart's review, in particular in the way he 'drew upon the disreputable reputation of London's suburbs' (Jones 2003: 81, 82).

65 The anonymous reviewer for the *London Literary Gazette* also uses 'Cockney' in a pejorative sense when he describes Hunt's behavior as 'the pert vulgarity and miserable low-mindedness of Cockney-land' ([Anon.] 1828d: 54).

66 See Hunt's article 'Lord Byron—Mr Moore—and Mr Leigh Hunt', published in five parts between 11 January and 15 January 1831 in the *Tatler* (Hunt 1830–2: II, 441–3, 445–6, 449–51, 453–5, 457–8).

Epilogue

1 The arrangement between Smith and Hunt is at the Brewer–Leigh Hunt Collection; see also Landré 1936: I, 253.

2 J. E. Morpurgo's edition of Hunt's *Autobiography* contains a very useful appendix which identifies all the passages in the *Autobiography* that are reproduced *verbatim* from earlier

sources; among these, *Lord Byron and Some of his Contemporaries* is the main instance; see Hunt 1949a: 496–8.

3 For a discussion of Hunt's *Religion of the Heart*, see my article '"A natural piety": Leigh Hunt's *The Religion of the Heart*' (Laplace-Sinatra 1998) and Tim Webb's 'Religion of the Heart: Leigh Hunt's Unpublished Tribute to Shelley' (Webb 1992).

4 Nathaniel Hawthorne is a famous example of one of Hunt's American visitors. Hawthorne describes his meeting with Hunt, complete with amusing descriptive details of Hunt's study, in *Our Old Home: A Series of English Sketches* (Hawthorne 1855). B. W. Procter had written the letter of introduction to Hunt on 2 October 1855:

> The bearer of this is Mr. Hawthorne, an American gentleman, for whom & for whose writings I (in common with the rest of the world) have a great respect. His books are excellent[.] He is better than his books. Give him a warm place in the corner of your heart. His defect is that single defect common to poets—his want of assurance. You know how to deal with this, & how to make him welcome.
>
> (Photostat of autograph letter; Brewer–Leigh Hunt Collection Ms. H94ph)

Until his death, Hunt received American visitors, as this letter dated May 1859 from the American poet and artist Thomas Buchanan Read shows:

> Jas: T: Fields, of the firm Ticknor & Fields, publishers, Boston — leaves in a few days, accompanied by Mrs. Field, for a visit to Europe;— wishing to show my friends some mark of kindness before their departure I could think of nothing more acceptable to them than to make them acquainted with you.
>
> That I cannot join them and spend one more pleasant evening with you at your cottage in Hammersmith is [my] only regret[.]
>
> (Read 1859: n. pag.)

Bibliography

Alighieri, D. (1844) *The Vision; or Hell, Purgatory, & Paradise of Dante Alighieri, translated by the Rev. Henry Francis Cary, A. M. – With the Life of Dante, Chronological View of his Age, Additional Notes, Etc. From the Last Corrected London Edition; with the Translator's Latest Corrections and Additions*, trans. Henry Francis Cary, New York: Hurst & Co.

——— (1990) '*De Vulgari Eloquentia*', in *De Vulgari Eloquentia – Dante's Book of Exile*, ed. M. Shapiro, Lincoln and London: U of Nebraska P.

Altick, R. D. (1948) *The Cowden Clarkes*, London, New York, and Toronto: Oxford UP.

——— (1957) *The English Common Reader: A Social History of the Mass Reading Public, 1800–1900*, Chicago: Chicago UP.

——— (1984) 'Harold Skimpole Revisited', in *The Life and Times of Leigh Hunt*, ed. R. A. McCown, Iowa City: Friends of the U of Iowa Libraries.

[Anon.] (1807) 'Art. XII. *Corinne ou L'Italie. Par Madame de Staël Holstein*', *Edinburgh Review*, XI, 21 (October): 183–95.

[Anon.] (1808) 'Article IV—Critical Essays—The Performers of the London Theatres', *The Critical Review*, 14 (August): 374–9.

[Anon.] (1809a) 'Critical Essays on the Performers of the London Theatres', *The Cabinet*, 6 (February): 141–8.

[Anon.] (1809b) 'Review of *Critical Essays*', *Anti-Jacobin Review and Magazine*, 33 (June): 191.

[Anon.] (1812) 'State of Public Affairs', *The Universal Magazine*, XVIII, CIX (December): 501–7.

[Anon.] (1814a) '*The* Sporting Journalist', *The Satirist, or Monthly Meteor*, XIV (1 January): 63–4.

[Anon.] (1814b) 'Review of *The Feast of the Poets, with Notes, and other Pieces in Verse, by the Editor of the Examiner*', *The Champion*, 59 (20 February): 62–3.

[Anon.] (1814c) 'Review of *The Feast of the Poets, with Notes, and other Pieces in Verse, by the Editor of the Examiner*', *The Satirist, or Monthly Meteor*, XIV (1 April): 327–34.

[Anon.] (1814d) 'Review of *The Feast of the Poets, with Notes, and other Pieces in Verse, by the Editor of the Examiner*', *Monthly Review; or Literary Journal*, LXXV (September): 100–3.

[Anon.] (1814e) 'Review of *The Feast of the Poets, with Notes, and other Pieces in Verse. By Leigh Hunt*', *Analectic Magazine*, VI (September): 243–9.

[Anon.] (1815a) 'Review of William Wordsworth, *The Excursion*', *British Critic*, 3 (May): 450–4.

[Anon.] (1815b) 'Review of William Wordsworth, *Poems*', *Monthly Review*, 78 (November): 221–7.

[Anon.] (1816a) 'Review of *The Story of Rimini*', *The New Monthly Magazine*, 26 (1 March): 149.

[Anon.] (1816b) '*The Story of Rimini*', *The British Lady's Magazine*, 16 (April): 239–42.

[Anon.] (1816c) 'Art. II.—*The Story of Rimini*', *Augustan Review* (May): 474–9.

[Anon.] (1816d) 'Art. III. *The Story of Rimini*', *Monthly Review; or Literary Journal* (June): 138–47.

[Anon.] (1816e) '*The Story of Rimini: a Poem*. By Leigh Hunt', *Dublin Examiner*, I (June): 141–7.

[Anon.] (1816f) 'Coleridge's *Christabel, Kubla Khan, a Vision; The Pains of Sleep*', *Scourge and Satirist*, XII (July): 60–2.

[Anon.] (1816g) '*The Story of Rimini*', *Literary Panorama*, 4 (September): 936–44.

[Anon.] (ed.) (1816h) *The Stage – From January to November 1816*, London: T. J. Wooler.

[Anon.] (1817a) 'Letter to the Editor of the Examiner: Lady Morgan and the Quarterly Reviewers', *The Examiner*, 514 (2 November): 698–9.

[Anon.] (1817b) 'Art. III. *The Round Table; a Collection of Essays on Literature, Men, and Manners. By Wm. Hazlitt*', *The British Critic*, VII (June): 552–5.

[Anon.] (1817c) *A Review of Blackwood's Edinburgh Magazine, for October 1817*, Edinburgh: John Moir.

[Anon.] (1818a) 'Review of Biagioli's edition of *The Divina Commedia* and Cary's *Vision of Dante*', *Edinburgh Review*, XXIX (February): 452–9.

[Anon.] (1818b) 'L'Ape Italiana. No. IV.—Dante', *Monthly Magazine*, 45 (February): 13–22.

[Anon.] (1818c) 'FOLIAGE; *or Poems Original and Translated*. By Leigh Hunt', *The Literary Gazette, and Journal of Belles Lettres, Arts, Politics, etc*, 63 (4 April): 210–2.

[Anon.] (1818d) 'New Publications in April; with an Historical and Critical Proëmium', *The Monthly Magazine*, 311, 45 (1 May): 346.

[Anon.] (1818e) 'Art. X. *Foliage; or Poems Original and Translated. By Leigh Hunt*', *The British Critic*, X (July): 90–6.

[Anon.] (1818f) 'III.—*Foliage; or Poems Originals and Translated*, by Leigh Hunt', *New Monthly Magazine*, X (September): 162–5.

[Anon.] (1818g) 'Literary Notices N°44. The Quarterly Review,—Mr. Keats', *The Examiner*, 563 (11 October): 648.

[Anon.] (1818h) 'Art. X. *Foliage*; or Poems, Original and Translated: By Leigh Hunt', *The Eclectic Review* (November): 484–93.

[Anon.] (1819a) 'Doggerel Verses. By Persons of Distinction [For the Examiner]', *The Examiner*, 585 (14 March): 169.

[Anon.] (1819b) 'Art. I—Lectures on the History of Literature, Ancient and Modern, from the German of Frederick Schlegel', *Quarterly Review*, XXI (April): 271–320.

[Anon.] (1819c) 'Art. IX—1. Prospectus and Specimens of an intended National Work by William and Robert Whistlecraft 2. The Court of Beasts, freely translated from the Animali Parlanti of Giambattista Casti, a Poem, in seven Cantos', *Quarterly Review*, XXI (April): 486–556.

[Anon.] (1819d) 'America and the Quarterly Reviewer', *The Examiner*, 600 (27 June): 403.

[Anon.] (1820a) 'Extracts from Mr. Wastle's Diary. N°I', *Blackwood's Edinburgh Magazine*, IV, XXXV (March): 688–91.

[Anon.] (1820b) 'Extracts from Mr. Wastle's Diary. N°II', *Blackwood's Edinburgh Magazine*, VII, XXXIX (June): 317–23.

[Anon.] (1820c) 'Extracts from Mr. Wastle's Diary. N°III', *Blackwood's Edinburgh Magazine*, VII, XLII (September): 663–7.

[Anon.] (1821) 'Letter to Pierce Egan, Esq. Confidential', *Blackwood's Edinburgh Magazine*, VIII, XLVIII (March): 674.

[Anon.] (ed.) (1822) *The Press, or Literary Chit–Chat. A Satire*, London: Lupton Relfe.

[Anon.] (1823a) 'On the Scotch Character—By a Flunky', *Blackwood's Edinburgh Magazine*, XII, LXXIV (March): 365.

[Anon.] (1823b) *A Critique of 'The Liberal'*, London: William Day.

[Anon.] (1824) 'Art. II.—*The Works of Sir John Suckling, containing his Poems, Letters, and Plays*', *The Retrospective Review*, IX: 19–38.

[Anon.] (1828a) 'Lord Byron and Some of his Contemporaries', *The New Monthly Magazine & Literary Journal*, 22 (1 January): 84–96.

[Anon.] (1828b) 'Characteristics of the Present State of English Literature', *The Athenaeum*, 1 (2 January): 1–12.

[Anon.] (1828c) 'Leigh Hunt's Memoirs of Byron, &c, *The London Literary Gazette; and Journal of Belles Lettres, Arts, Sciences, &c.*, 572 (5 January): 6–8.

[Anon.] (1828d) '*Lord Byron and Some of his Contemporaries; with Recollections of the Author's Life, and of his Visit to Italy*', *The London Literary Gazette; and Journal of Belles Lettres, Arts, Sciences, &c.*, 575 (26 January): 54–6.

[Anon.] (1828e) 'Review of New Books: *Lord Byron and some of his Contemporaries*', *The Literary Chronicle and Weekly Review*, 454 (26 January): 46–52.

[Anon.] (1828f) 'Lord Byron and Some of his Contemporaries', *The Athenaeum*, 5 (29 January): 70–71.

[Anon.] (1828g) 'Leigh Hunt's Lord Byron', *London Magazine*, 38 (1 February): 211–33.

[Anon.] (1828h) 'Louis Simond, *Voyage en Italie et en Sicile*', *Monthly Review*, 30 (February): 256–9.

[Anon.] (1828i) 'Art. II.—*Lord Byron and some of his Contemporaries*', *Monthly Review*, 31 (March): 300–12.

[Anon.] (1828j) 'Lord Byron, and Some of his Contemporaries, by Leigh Hunt', *The Literary Magnet; or Monthly Journal of the Belles Lettres*, 5 (April): 18–87.

[Anon.] (1828k) 'Art. XI.—*Italy as it is; or, Narrative of an English Family's Residence for Three Years in that Country*', *Monthly Review*, 34 (June): 249–58.

[Anon.] (1828l) 'Art. XI.—*Italy. A Poem.* By Samuel Rogers. *Part the Second. – Italy, and other Poems.* By William Sotheby', *Monthly Review*, 35 (July): 396–407.

[Anon.] (1829) 'The Loves of the Poets', *Blackwood's Edinburgh Magazine*, XXVI, CLVI (September): 524.

[Anon.] (1832) 'Leigh Hunt's *Poetical Works*', *Literary Gazette and Journals of Belles Lettres*, 832 (29 December): 823.

[Anon.] (1833) 'Review of *Poetical Works*', *National Standard*, 3 (19 January): 38.

[Anon.] (1860) 'Review of *The Autobiography of Leigh Hunt*', *Saturday Review*, 9 (28 January): 115–16.

Auburn, M. (1995) 'Theatre in the Age of Garrick and Sheridan', in *Sheridan Studies*, eds J. Morwood and D. Crane, Cambridge: Cambridge UP.

Avitabile, G. (1959) *The Controversy on Romanticism in Italy: First Phase 1816–1823*, New York: S. F. Vanni.

Balayé, S. (1971) *Les Carnets de voyage de Madame de Staël: Contribution à la genèse de ses oeuvres*, préface de la comtesse Jean de Pange, Genève: Librairie Droz.

Barefoot, B. (1993) *The English Road to Rome*, Upton-upon-Severn: Images.

Barnard, J. (1988) 'Byron's Use of *Endymion* in *Don Juan*, Canto I', *Keats–Shelley Review*, 3: 62–9.

——— (1997) 'Charles Cowden Clarke and the Leigh Hunt Circle 1812–1818', *Romanticism*, 3.1: 66–90.

Barrows, H. (1963) 'Convention and Novelty in the Romantic Generation's Experience of Italy', *Bulletin of the New York Public Library*, 67: 360–75.

Bate, J. (1989) *Shakespearean Constitutions: Politics, Theatre, Criticism 1730–1830*, Oxford: Clarendon P.

Bate, W. J. (1962) *The Stylistic Development of Keats*, New York: Humanities P.

——— (1963) *John Keats*, Cambridge, Mass.: The Belknap Press of Harvard UP.

Beaty, F. L. (1960) 'Byron and the Story of Francesca da Rimini', *PMLA*, LXXV, 4: 395–401.

Behrendt, S. C. (1989) *Shelley and his Audience*, Lincoln and London: U of Nebraska P.

Bennett, A. (1994) *Keats, Narrative and Audience: The Posthumous Life of Writing*, Cambridge: Cambridge UP.

Besser, G. R. (1994) *Germaine de Staël Revisited*, New York: Twayne Publishers.

Beste, H. (1828) *Italy as it is; or Narrative of an English Family's Residence for Three Years in that Country*, London: Henry Colburn.

Blainey, A. (1985) *Immortal Boy: A Portrait of Leigh Hunt*, London and Sydney: Croom Helm.

Blumberg, J. (1992) *Byron and the Shelleys: The Story of a Friendship*, London: Collins & Brown Limited.

Blunden, E. (1922) 'Leigh Hunt', *The Times Literary Supplement* (16 November): 733–4.

——— (1928) *Leigh Hunt's 'Examiner' Examined, comprising Some Account of that Celebrated Newspaper's Contents, &c. 1808–25 and Selections, by or concerning, Leigh Hunt, Lamb, Keats, Shelley and Byron, illustrating the Literary History of that Time, for the most part previously unreprinted*, New York: Archon Books.

——— (1930) *Leigh Hunt: A Biography*, London: Cobden-Sanderson.

Braida, A. (2005) *Dante and the Romantics*, Basingstoke: Palgrave.

Brand, C. P. (1957) *Italy and the English Romantics: The Italian Fashion in Early Nineteenth-Century England*, Cambridge: Cambridge UP.

Brewer, L. A. (1922) *Leaves from a Leigh Hunt Note-Book*, Cedar Rapids, Iowa: Privately printed for the Friends of the Torch Press and of Luther Albertus and Elinore Taylor Brewer.

——— (1930) *Leigh Hunt and Charles Dickens: The Skimpole Caricature*, Cedar Rapids, Iowa: The Torch P.

Brontë, C. (1995–2000) *The Letters of Charlotte Brontë*, ed. M. Smith, 2 vols, Oxford: Clarendon P.

Brown, D. B. (1992) *Turner and Byron*, London: Tate Gallery.

Brown, P. A. H. (1982) *London Publishers and Printers: c.1800–1870*, Dorking: Adlard & Son Ltd.

Browning, E. B. (1955) *Unpublished Letters of Elizabeth Barrett Browning to Hugh Stuart Boyd*, ed. B. P. MacCarthy, London: John Murray.

Bugajski, K. J. (2002) '"The Men and Women merely Players": Performing the Self in Nineteenth-Century Literary Autobiography', unpublished thesis, Texas A&M U.

Burwick, F. (1990) 'Romantic Drama: From Optics to Illusion', in *Literature and Science: Theory & Practice*, ed. Stuart Peterfreund, Boston: Northeastern UP.

——— (1991) *Illusion and the Drama: Critical Theory of the Enlightenment and Romantic Era*, University Park, Pennsylvania: The Pennsylvania State UP.

Butler, M. (1979) *Peacock Displayed: A Satirist in his Context*, London, Boston, and Henley: Routledge & Kegan Paul.

Byron, G. G. N. (1973–94) *Letters and Journal*, ed. L. A. Marchand, 13 vols, London: John Murray.

——— (1980–92) *The Complete Poetical Works*, ed. J. McGann, 7 vols, Oxford: Clarendon P.

——— (1991) *The Complete Miscellaneus Prose*, ed. A. Nicholson, Oxford: Clarendon P.

Cameron, K. N. (ed.) (1961–70) *Shelley and His Circle, 1773–1822*: vols 1–4, Cambridge, Mass.: Harvard UP.

——— (1974) *Shelley: The Golden Years*, Cambridge, Mass.: Harvard UP.

Campbell, M. (1988) *Lady Morgan: The Life and Times of Sydney Owenson*, London, Sydney, and Wellington: Pandora.

Carlyle, T. and J. Welsh Carlyle (1970–) *The Collected Letters of Thomas and Jane Welsh Carlyle*, gen. ed. C. R. Sanders, 30 vols, Durham, NC: Duke UP.

Chandler, J. (1987) '"Wordsworth" after Waterloo', in *The Age of William Wordsworth: Critical Essays on the Romantic Tradition*, eds K. R. Johnston and G. W. Ruoff, New Brunswick and London: Rutgers UP.

Chapman, A. and J. Stabler (2003) 'Introduction', in *Unfolding the South: Nineteenth-Century British Women Writers and Artists in Italy*, eds A. Chapman and J. Stabler, Manchester: Manchester UP.

Cheeke, S. (2003) *Byron and Place: History, Translation, Nostalgia*, New York: Palgrave Macmillan.

Child, H. (1935) *The Shakespearean Productions of John Philip Kemble*, London: Humphrey Milford.

Churchill, K. (1980) *Italy and English Literature, 1764–1930*, London and Basingstoke: Macmillan.

[Clarke, C. C.] (1816) *An Address to that Quarterly Reviewer who Touched upon Mr. Hunt's 'The Story of Rimini'*, London: R. Jennings.

——— and M. Cowden Clarke (1878) *Recollections of Writers, by Charles and Mary Cowden Clarke, with Letters of Charles Lamb, Leigh Hunt, Douglas Jerrold, and Charles Dickens; and a Preface by Mary Cowden Clarke*, second edition, London: Sampson Low, Marston, Searle & Rivington.

Clayden, P. W. (1889) *Rogers and his Contemporaries*, 2 vols, London: Smith, Elder, & Co.

Clubbe, J. (1997) 'Between Emperor and Exile: Byron and Napoleon 1814–1816', *Journal of Napoleonic Scholarship*, 1, 1; reprinted in *NapoleonSeries.org*. Online. Available HTTP: <http://www.napoleonseries.org/articles/misc_art/byron.cfm> (accessed 10/09/04).

[Coleridge, J. T.] (1818) 'Art. III. *Foliage; or, Poems Original and Translated.* By Leigh Hunt', *Quarterly Review*, XVIII (January): 324–35.

[———] (1819) 'Art. VII. 1. *Laon and Cythna, or the Revolution of the Golden City. A Vision of the Nineteenth Century, in the Stanza of Spenser.* 2. *The Revolt of Islam. A Poem in Twelve Cantos*', *Quarterly Review*, XXI (April): 460–71.

Coleridge, S. T. (1956–71) *The Collected Letters of Samuel Taylor Coleridge*, ed. E. L. Griggs, 6 vols, Oxford: Clarendon P.

——— (1983) *Biographia Literaria*, eds J. Engell and W. Jackson Bate, 2 vols, Princeton: Princeton UP.

——— (1987) *Lectures 1808–1819: On Literature*, ed. R. A. Foakes, 2 vols, Princeton: Princeton UP.

——— (1990) *Table-Talk Recorded by Henry Nelson Coleridge (and John Taylor Coleridge)*, ed. C. Woodring, 2 vols, Princeton: Princeton UP.

——— (1995) *Shorter Works and Fragments of Samuel Taylor Coleridge*, eds H. J. Jackson and J. R. de J. Jackson, 2 vols, Princeton: Princeton UP.

[Conder, J.] (1816) 'Art. VIII. *The Story of Rimini*', *The Eclectic Review*, V (April): 380–5.

[———] (1817) 'Art. V. *Poems*. By John Keats', *The Electic Review*, VIII (September): 267–75.

Cox, J. N. (ed.) (1992) *Seven Gothic Dramas, 1789–1825*, Athens: Ohio UP.

——— (1998) *Poetry and Politics in the Cockney School: Keats, Shelley, Hunt and their Circle*, Cambridge: Cambridge UP.

——— (1999) 'Leigh Hunt's Cockney School: The Lakers' 'Other". *Romanticism on the Net*, 14 (May): n. pag. Online. Available HTTP: <http://www.erudit.org/revue/ron/1999/v/n14/005859ar.html> (accessed 12/1/04).

——— (2003) 'Leigh Hunt's *Foliage*: a Cockney Manifesto', in *Leigh Hunt: Life, Poetics, Politics*, ed. N. Roe, London and New York: Routledge.

Crane, D. (1998) *Lord Byron's Jackal: The Life of Edward John Trelawny*, London: HarperCollins P.

[Croker, J. W. and W. Gifford] (1816) 'Art. IX. *The Story of Rimini*', *Quarterly Review*, XV (January): 473–81.

[———] (1821) '*Italy. By Lady Morgan*', *Quarterly Review*, XXV (July): 529–34.

——— (1854) *Correspondence between the Right Hon. J. W. Croker and the Right Hon. Lord John Russell, on Some Passages of 'Moore's Diary'*, London: John Murray.

Cronin, R. (1996a) 'Keats and the Politics of Cockney Style', *Studies in English Language*, 36.4: 785–806.

——— (1996b) 'Shelleyan Incest and the Romantic Legacy', *Keats–Shelley Journal*, XLV: 61–76.

Cumberland, R. (1807) *Supplement to the Memoirs of Richard Cumberland*, London: Lackington, Allen, & Co.

——— (1809) 'Review of *Critical Essays on the Performers of the London Theatres*', *London Review*, 2 (August): 1–21.

David, S. (1998) *Prince of Pleasure: The Prince of Wales and the Making of the Regency*, London: Little, Brown & Company.

Davis, T. C. (1995) '"Reading Shakespeare by flashes of lightning": Challenging the Foundations of Romantic Acting Theory', *English Literary History*, 62.4: 933–54.

Dawson, C. (1970) *His Fine Wit: A Study of Thomas Love Peacock*, London: Routledge & Kegan Paul.

Deguchi, Y. (1996) 'Introduction', in *The Examiner – Volume I: 1808*, London: William Pickering.

Donohue, J. W. (1975) *Theatre in the Age of Kean*, Oxford: Basil Blackwell.

Donovan, J. (1987) 'Incest in *Laon and Cythna*: Nature, Culture, and Desire', *Keats–Shelley Review*, 2: 47–90.

Dyer, G. (1997) *British Satire and the Politics of Style, 1789–1832*, Cambridge: Cambridge UP.

Earl, E. M. and J. Hogg (eds) (1998) *Byron and Southey: Vision of Judgment*, Salzburg, Oxford, and Portland: U of Salzburg.

Edgar, N. L. (1975) *A History and Bibliography of American Magazines 1810–1820*, Metuchen, N. J.: The Scarecrow P, Inc.

Edgecombe, R. S. (1994) *Leigh Hunt and the Poetry of Fancy*, London and Toronto: Associated UP.

Eisler, B. (1999) *Byron: Child of Passion, Fool of Fame*, New York: Alfred A. Knopf.

Elfenbein, A. (1995) *Byron and the Victorians*, Cambridge: Cambridge UP.

Eliot, T. S. (1965) *To Criticize the Critic and Other Writings by T. S. Eliot*, London: Faber and Faber.

Ellis, J. (ed.) (1985) *English Drama of the Nineteenth Century: An Index and Finding Guide*, New Cannan, Connecticut: Readex Books.

Eustace, J. C. (1821) *Tour of Italy, exhibiting a View of its Scenery, Antiquities, and Monuments, particularly as they are objects of Classical Interest*, sixth edition, 4 vols, London: J. Mawman.

Fenner, T. (1972) *Leigh Hunt and Opera Criticism: The 'Examiner' Years, 1808–1821*, Lawrence, Manhattan, and Wichita: The UP of Kansas.

——— (1994) *Opera in London: Views of the Press, 1785–1830*, Carbondale and Edwardsville, Southern Illinois UP.

Finney, C. L. (1963) *The Evolution of Keats's Poetry*, 2 vols, New York: Russell & Russell, Inc.

[Fonblanque, A.] (1821a) '*Letter to **** ***** on the Rev. W. L. Bowles' Strictures on the Life and Writings of Pope*', *The Examiner*, 695 (29 April): 269–70.

[———] (1821b) 'Literary Notices N°56. *Italy. By Lady Morgan*', *The Examiner*, 704 (1 July): 411–2.

[———] (1821c) 'Literary Notices: *Sardanapalus, a Tragedy. The Two Foscari, a Tragedy. Cain, a Mystery*. By Lord Byron', *The Examiner*, 726 (23 December): 808–10.

[———] (1823) 'Review of Books. *The Liberal, No. IV*', *The Literary Examiner*, IV (26 July): 47–53.

Foscolo, Ugo (1825) *La Commedia di Dante Alighieri*, Londra: Guglielmo Pickering. Brewer–Leigh Hunt Collection 858D192Ffo.

Franta, A. (1999) 'Keats and the Review Aesthetic', *Studies in Romanticism*, 38.3: 343–64.

Galt, J. (1830) *The Life of Lord Byron*, London: Colburn and Bentley.

Garnett, M. (1997) '"One that Loved his Fellow-men": The Politics of Leigh Hunt', *The Charles Lamb Bulletin*, 97: 2–8.

Gaskins, A. F. (1985) 'Samuel Rogers: A Revaluation'. *The Wordsworth Circle*, 16.3: 146–9.

Gennari, G. (1947) *Le premier voyage de Madame de Staël en Italie et la genèse de Corinne*, Paris: Boivin & Cie.

Giddey, E. (1959) *Samuel Rogers et son poème 'Italie'*, Genève: Librairie E. Droz.

——— (1982) 'Byron and Madame de Staël', in *Lord Byron and His Contemporaries: Essays from the Sixth International Byron Seminar*, ed. C. E. Robinson, Newark: U of Delaware P; London and Toronto: Associated UP.

Gifford, W. (1795) *The Baviad, and Maeviad*, London: J. Wright.

Gill, S. (1989) *William Wordsworth: A Life*, Oxford and New York: Oxford UP.

Gilmartin, K. (1996) *Print Politics: The Press and Radical Opposition in Early Nineteenth-Century England*, Cambridge: Cambridge UP.

Gisborne, M. (1951) *Maria Gisborne and Edward E. Williams: Shelley's Friends – Their Journals and Letters*, ed. F. L. Jones, Norman: U of Oklahoma P.

Gittings, R. (1956) *The Mask of Keats: A Study of Problems*, Melbourne, London, Toronto: William Heinemann, Ltd.

Graham, W. (1930) *English Literary Periodicals*, New York: Thomas Nelson & Sons.

Grayson, C. (1962) 'Dante and the Renaissance', in *Italian Studies Presented to E. R. Vincent on his Retirement from the Chair of Italian at Cambridge*, eds C. P. Brand, K. Foster, and U. Limentam. Cambridge: Heffer.

Griffin, R. (1995) *Wordsworth's Pope: A Study in Literary Historiography*, Cambridge: Cambridge UP.

Gross, J. D. (2001) *Byron: The Erotic Liberal*, Oxford: Rowman & Littlefield.

Grosskurth, P. (1997) *Byron: The Flawed Angel*, London: Hodder & Stoughton.

Gutwirth, M. (1978) *Madame de Staël, Novelist: The Emergence of the Artist as Woman*, Urbana, Chicago, and London: U of Illinois P.

Hackwood, F. W. (1912) *William Hone: His Life and Times*, London: T. Fisher Unwin.

Hart, Chris (ed.) (1996) *Lives of the Great Romantics by their Contemporaries – Volume 2: Byron*, London: William Pickering.

Hawthorne, N. (1855) *Our Old Home: A Series of English Sketches*, Boston: Ticknor & Fields.

Hayden, J. O. (1969) *The Romantic Reviewers, 1802–1824*, Chicago: The U of Chicago P.

——— (1987) 'Leigh Hunt's *Story of Rimini*: Reloading the Romantic Canon', *Durham University Journal*, 48, 2: 279–87.

Haydon, B. R. (1817) 'Autograph letter to William Wordsworth', 15 April, Dove Cottage Library DC WL MS A – Haydon.

Hazlitt, W. (1930–4) *The Complete Works of William Hazlitt*, ed. P. P. Howe, 21 vols, London and Toronto: J. M. Dent and Sons, Ltd.

——— (1978) *The Letters of William Hazlitt*, ed. H. Moreland Sikes. New York: New York UP.

——— (1998) *The Selected Writings of William Hazlitt*, ed. D. Wu, 9 vols, London: Pickering & Chatto (Publishers) Limited.

Heaney, S. (1980) *Preoccupations: Selected Prose, 1968–1978*, London and Boston: Faber and Faber.

Heller, J. R. (1990) *Coleridge, Lamb, Hazlitt, and the Reader of Drama*, Columbia and London: U of Missouri.

Hoagwood, T. A. (1998) 'Romantic Drama and Historical Hermeneutics', in *British Romantic Drama: Historical and Critical Essays*, eds T. A. Hoagwood and D. P. Watkins, London: Associated UP.

Hobhouse, J. C. (1818) *Historical Illustrations of the Fourth Canto of Childe Harold: Containing Dissertations on the Ruins of Rome; and an Essay on Italian Literature*, second edition, revised and corrected, London: John Murray.

——— (1984) *Byron's Bulldog: The Letters of John Cam Hobhouse to Lord Byron*, ed. P. W. Graham, Columbus: Ohio State UP.

Hogsett, C. (1987) *The Literary Existence of Germaine de Staël*, foreword by Madelyn Gutwirth, Carbondale and Edwardsville: Southern Illinois UP.

Holcomb, A. M. (1988) 'Turner and Rogers' *Italy* Revisited', *Studies in Romanticism*, 27,.1: 63–95.

Holcroft, T. (1816) *Memoirs of the Late Thomas Holcroft, Written by himself, and Continued to the Times of his Death, from his Diary, Notes, and other Papers*, ed. W. Hazlitt, 3 vols, London: Longman, Hurst, Rees, Orme, and Brown.

Holden, A. (2005) *The Wit in the Dungeon: Leigh Hunt and his Circle*, London and New York: Little, Brown, and Company.

Holmes, R. (1998) *Coleridge: Darker Reflections*, London: HarperCollins Publishers.

Horace (1929) *Satires, Epistles, and Ars Poetica*, ed. and trans. H. Rushton Fairclough, second edition, Cambridge, Mass.: Harvard UP.

Horne, R. H. (1907) *A New Spirit of the Age*, with an introduction by W. Jerrold, London, New York and Toronto: Oxford UP.

Howitt, W. (1847) *Home and Haunts of the Most Eminent British Poets*, 2 vols, London: Richard Bentley.

Hunt, L. (1807a) *Critical Essays on the Performers of the London Theatres, including General Observations on the Practice and Genius of the Stage*, London: John Hunt.

——— (1807b) 'Theatricals', *The News*, 86 (4 January): 7.

——— (1807c) 'Theatricals', *The News*, 93 (22 February): 62.

——— (1807d) 'Theatricals', *The News*, 102 (26 April): 135.

——— (1807e) 'Theatricals', *The News*, 111 (28 June): 208.

——— (1807f) 'An Essay on the Appearance, Causes, and Consequences of the Decline of British Comedy', *The News*, 120 [for 121] (6 September): 289.

——— (1807g) 'Theatricals', *The News*, 128 [for 129] (1 November): 349.

——— (1808) 'The Political Examiner N°10. Rules for the Conduct of Newspaper Editors with respect to Politics and News', *The Examiner*, 10 (6 March): 145–6.

——— (ed.) (1812a) *The Reflector, A Collection of Essays, on Miscellaneous Subjects of Literature and Politics; Originally Published as the Commencement of a Quarterly Magazine*, 2 vols, London: J. Hunt.

——— (1812b) 'Theatrical Examiner N°109', *The Examiner*, 215 (9 February): 91–2.

——— (1812c) 'The Political Examiner N°213. Princely Qualities', *The Examiner*, 219 (8 March): 144–6.

——— (1813a) 'The Political Examiner N°285. Office of Poet-Laureat', *The Examiner*, 294 (15 August): 513–14.

——— (1813b) 'The Political Examiner N°287. The Laureatship', *The Examiner*, 296 (29 August): 545–7.

——— (1813c) 'The Political Examiner N°291. The New Poet-Laureat', *The Examiner*, 300 (26 September): 609–10.

——— (1814a) *The Feast of the Poets, with Notes, and Other Pieces in Verse*, London: James Cawthorn.

——— (1814b) 'The New Year's Ode', *The Examiner*, 316 (16 January): 41–2.

——— (1814c) 'Note upon Note, or a Word or Two on the Passion of Love, in Answer to some Observations in our last week's Examiner', *The Examiner*, 346 (14 August): 525.

——— (1815a) *The Feast of the Poets, with Other Pieces in Verse*, London: Gale and Fenner.

——— (1815b) 'Theatrical Examiner N°191. Sketches of the Performers. The Tragic Actors', *The Examiner*, 371 (5 February): 89–90.

——— (1815c) 'Autograph letter to William Wordsworth', 28 May, Dove Cottage Library, DC MS 170.

——— (1816a) 'The Political Examiner N°411. Men of Talent in Parliament', *The Examiner*, 422 (28 January): 49–51.

——— (1816b) 'The Late Mr. Sheridan', *The Examiner*, 446 (14 July): 433–6.

——— (1817a) 'Death and Funeral of the Late Mr. Southey'. *The Examiner*, 485 (13 April): 236–7.

——— (1817b) 'Extraordinary Case of the Late Mr. Southey', *The Examiner*, 489 (11 May): 300–3.

——— (1817c) 'To Z', *The Examiner*, 516 (16 November 1817) 729.

——— (1818a) *Foliage; or Poems Original and Translated*, London: C. and J. Ollier.

——— (1818b) 'Literary Notices N°43. The Editor of the Quarterly Review', *The Examiner*, 546 (14 June): 378–9.

——— (1819a) 'Literary Notice', *The Examiner*, 580 (7 February): 90.

——— (1819b) 'Literary Notices N°48. Mr. Hazlitt's Letter to Mr. Gifford', *The Examiner*, 584 (7 March): 156.

——— (1819c) 'A Tale for Chimney Corner', *Indicator*, X (15 December): 73–9.

——— (1820a) 'The Political Examiner N°612. Non-Appearance of the Laureat to Celebrate the National Happiness', *The Examiner*, 627 (2 January): 1–3.

——— (1820b) 'Deaths of Little Children', *Indicator*, XXVI (5 April): 201–4.

——— (1820c) 'Of the Sight of Shops', *Indicator*, XXXIV (31 May): 265–72.

——— (1820d) 'Coaches', *Indicator*, XLVI (23 August): 361–8.

——— (ed.) (1822–3) *The Liberal. Verse and Prose from the South*, 2 vols, London: John Hunt.

——— (1823a) 'On the suburbs of Genoa and the Country about London', *The Literary Examiner*, VII (16 August): 97–105.

——— (1823b) 'On the suburbs of Genoa and the Country about London', *The Literary Examiner*, VIII (23 August): 113–20.

——— (1825) *Bacchus in Tuscany*, London: John and H. L. Hunt.

——— (1828a) *Lord Byron and Some of his Contemporaries*, London: Henry Colburn.

——— (1828b) *Lord Byron and Some of his Contemporaries*, 2 vols, second edition, London: Henry Colburn.

——— (1828c) 'To the Editor of the *Morning Chronicle*', *Morning Chronicle* (21 January) 3.

——— (ed.) (1830–32) *The Tatler. A Daily Paper of Literature, Fine Arts, Music, and the Stage*, 4 vols, London: R. Seton.

——— (1835) 'Review of *Letters, Conversations, and Recollections of S. T. Coleridge*', *Leigh Hunt's London Journal and the Printing Machine*, Monthly Supplement (31 December): 457–9.

——— (1844) *The Poetical Works of Leigh Hunt, Containing Many Pieces now First Collected*, London: Edward Moxon.

——— (1846) *Stories from the Italian Poets, with Lives of the Writers*, 2 vols, London: Chapman and Hall.

——— (1848) *A Jar of Honey from Mount Hybla*, London: Smith, Elder, and Co.

——— (1850) *The Autobiography of Leigh Hunt; with Reminiscences of Friends and Contemporaries*, 3 vols., London: Smith, Elder and Co.

——— (1857) *The Poetical Works of Leigh Hunt. Now First Entirely Collected, Revised by himself, and Edited with an Introduction by S. Adams Lee*, ed. S. A. Lee, 2 vols, Boston: Ticknor and Fields.

——— (1859) 'Autograph Letter to George James de Wilde', 6 June, Brewer–Leigh Hunt Collection D52h n°10.

——— (1860) *The Poetical Works of Leigh Hunt, now Finally Collected, Revised by himself, and Edited by his son, Thornton Hunt*, ed. T. Hunt, London: Routledge, Warne, and Routledge.

——— (1862) *The Correspondence of Leigh Hunt*, ed. T. Hunt, 2 vols., London: Smith, Elder and Co.

——— (1867) 'An Essay on the Cultivation, History, and Varieties of the Species of Poem called the Sonnet', in *The Book of the Sonnet*, ed. L. Hunt and S. Adams Lee, 2 vols, London: Sampson Low, Son, & Marston.

——— (1888) 'The Wishing Cap No. VII: Spring', *The Wishing-Cap Papers*, ed. Leigh Hunt, Boston: Lee and Shepard.

——— (1923) *The Poetical Works of Leigh Hunt*, ed. H. S. Milford, Oxford and New York: Oxford UP.

——— (1938) *My Leigh Hunt Library: The Holograph Letters*, ed. L. A. Brewer, Iowa City, Iowa: U of Iowa P.

——— (1949a) *The Autobiography of Leigh Hunt*, ed. J. E. Morpurgo, London: The Cresset P.

——— (1949b) *Leigh Hunt's Dramatic Criticism: 1808–1831*, eds L. Huston Houtchens and C. Washburn Houtchens, London: Geoffrey Cumberlege.

——— (1999) *Leigh Hunt: A Life in Letters, Together with Some Correspondence of William Hazlitt (422 Hunt Letters, 14 Hazlitt Letters)*, ed. E. M. Gates, Essex, Connecticut: Falls River Publications.

——— (2003) *The Selected Writings of Leigh Hunt*, gen. eds M. Eberle-Sinatra and R. Morrison, 6 vols, London: Pickering & Chatto.

Jackson, J. R. de J. (ed.) (1968) *The Critical Heritage: Samuel Taylor Coleridge – Volume I, 1794–1834*, London and New York: Routledge.

[Jeffrey, F.] (1802) '*Thalaba. By Robert Southey*'. *Edinburgh Review*, I (October): 63–83.

[———] (1808) '*Poems. By the Reverend George Crabbe*', *Edinburgh Review*, XII (April): 129–35.

[———] (1814) '*The Excursion. By William Wordsworth*', *Edinburgh Review*, XLVII (November): 1–30.

[———] (1815a) 'Art. X. John Wilson, *The City of the Plague, and Other Poems*', *Edinburgh Review*, XXVI (June): 460–75.

[———] (1815b) '*The White Doe of Rylstone. By William Wordsworth*', *Edinburgh Review*, L (October): 419–30.

[———] (1816a) 'Art. XI. *The Story of Rimini*', *Edinburgh Review*, XXVI (June): 476–91.

——— (1816b) 'Autograph Letter to Leigh Hunt', 20 October, Brewer–Leigh Hunt Collection MsL J46h.

[———] (1818) 'Review of Barry Cornwall's *A Sicilian Story*', *Edinburgh Review*, LXV: 143–6.

Jesson-Dibley, D. (1990) 'Bibliographical Introduction', in Leigh Hunt, *Selected Writings*, ed. D. Jesson-Dibley, Manchester: Carcanet Press Limited.

Johnson, S. (1963) 'New Actors on the Theatre', in *The Yale Edition of the Works of Samuel Johnson*, eds W. J. Bate, J. M. Bullitt, L. F. Powell,. New Haven: Yale UP.

Jones, A. R. (1987) 'Introduction', in *Wordsworth's Poems of 1807: The Text of the Collection Originally Published as Poems, in Two Volumes, together with Poems proposed for Inclusion but not Retained in the 1807 Edition*, ed. A. R. Jones, Basingstoke: Macmillan.

Jones, E. (2003) 'Suburb Sinners: Sex and Disease in the Cockney School', in *Leigh Hunt: Life, Poetics, Politics*, ed. N. Roe, London and New York: Routledge.

Jones, S. (1899) *The Actor and his Art: Some Considerations of the Present Condition of the Stage*, London: Downey & Co. Limited.

Jones, S. (1989) *Hazlitt: A Life, from Winterslow to Frith Street*, Oxford: Clarendon P.

Kandl, J. (1995) 'Private Lyrics in the Public Sphere: Leigh Hunt's *Examiner* and the Construction of a Public "John Keats"', *Keats–Shelley Journal*, XLIV: 84–101.

Kautz, B. D. (2000) 'Mary Shelley's *Rambles in Germany and Italy*: A Journey of Aesthetic Healing', in *Romantic Geographies: Discourses of Travel, 1775–1844*, ed. A. Gilroy, Manchester: Manchester UP.

Keach, W. (1986) 'Cockney Couplets: Keats and the Politics of Style', *Studies in Romanticism*, 25.3: 182–96.

Keats, J. (1958) *The Letters of John Keats, 1814–1821*, ed. H. E. Rollins, 2 vols, Cambridge, Mass.: Harvard UP.

——— (1988) *The Complete Poems*, ed. J. Barnard, London: Penguin Books.

Kelly, L. (1980) *The Kemble Era: John Philip Kemble, Sarah Siddons and the London Stage*, London, Sydney and Toronto: The Bodley Head.

Kemble, J. P. (1786) *Macbeth Reconsidered: An Essay intended as an Answer to Part of the Remarks on Some of the Characters of Shakespeare*, London: T. and J. Egerton.

Kendall, K. E. (1971) *Leigh Hunt's Reflector*, The Hague and Paris: Mouton.

Kilgour, A. (1825) *Anecdotes of Lord Byron, from Authentic Sources; with Remarks Illustrative of his Connection with the Principal Literary Character of the Present Day*, London: Knight and Lacey.

Kirkpatrick, R. (1987) *Dante's Inferno: Difficulty and Dead Poetry*, Cambridge: Cambridge UP.

Kruger, L. (1992) *The National Stage: Theatre and Cultural Legitimation in England, France, and America*, Chicago: U of Chicago P.

Kucich, G. (1992) '"A Haunted Ruin": Romantic Drama, Renaissance Tradition, and the Critical Establishment', *The Wordsworth Circle*, 23.2: 64–76.

——— (1999) '"The Wit in the Dungeon": Leigh Hunt and the Insolent Politics of Cockney Coteries', *Romanticism on the Net*, 14 (May): n. pag. Online. Available HTTP: <http://www.erudit.org/revue/ron/1999/v/n14/005850ar.html> (accessed 12/12/03).

——— (2003) 'Cockney Chivalry: Hunt, Keats and the Aesthetics of Excess', in *Leigh Hunt: Life, Poetics, Politics*, ed. N. Roe, London and New York: Routledge.

Kuhns, O. (1904) *Dante and the English Poets from Chaucer to Tennyson*, New York: Henry Holt and Company.

Lamb, C. and M. Lamb (1903–05) *The Works of Charles and Mary Lamb*, ed. E. V. Lucas, 7 vols, London: Methuen.

——— (1975–78) *The Letters of Charles and Mary Lamb*, ed. E. W. Marrs, Jr. 3 vols, Ithaca and London: Cornell UP.

Landré, L. (1936) *Leigh Hunt (1784–1859) Contributions à l'histoire du romantisme anglais*, 2 vols, Paris: Edition 'Les Belles-Lettres'.

——— (1959) 'Leigh Hunt: A Few Remarks about the Man', *Keats–Shelley Memorial Bulletin*, 10: 1–6.

Laplace-Sinatra, M. (1998) '"A natural piety": Leigh Hunt's *The Religion of the Heart*', *Allen Review*, 19: 18–21.

——— (1999) '"I *will* live beyond this life": Shelley, Prefaces and Reviewers', *Keats–Shelley Review*, 13: 88–104.

[Lockhart, J. G.] (1817) 'On the Cockney School of Poetry. No I', *Blackwood's Edinburgh Magazine*, II, VII (October): 38–41.

[———] (1818a) 'Letter from Z. to Leigh Hunt, King of the Cockneys', *Blackwood's Edinburgh Magazine*, III, XIV (May): 196–201.

[———] (1818b) 'On the Cockney School of Poetry. N°IV', *Blackwood's Edinburgh Magazine*, III, XVIII (August): 519–24.

[———] (1819) 'On the Cockney School of Poetry. N°VI', *Blackwood's Edinburgh Magazine*, VI, XXXI (October): 70–6.

[———] (1820) 'Review of Percy Bysshe Shelley's *Prometheus Unbound*', *Blackwood's Edinburgh Magazine*, VII, XLII (September): 684–7.

[———] (1825) 'The Cockney School of Poetry. N°VIII', *Blackwood's Edinburgh Magazine*, XVIII, CIII (August): 155–60.

[———] (1828) *'Lord Byron and Some of his Contemporaries'*, *Quarterly Review*, XXXVII (March): 402–26.

MacCarthy, F. (2002) *Byron: Life and Legend*, New York: Farrar, Straus and Giroux.

[Maginn, W. and J. G. Lockhart] (1823) 'Review of *Don Juan*, Cantos VI–VIII', *Blackwood's Edinburgh Magazine*, XIII, LXXIV (July): 80–92.

Magnuson, P. (1998) *Reading Public Romanticism*, Princeton, New Jersey: Princeton UP.

Marshall, W. H. (1960) *Byron, Shelley, Hunt, and The Liberal*, Philadelphia: U of Pennsylvania P.

Mazzini, J. (?1851) 'Letter to Leigh Hunt', Brewer–Leigh Hunt Collection MsL M477h.

Medwin, T. (1966) *Medwin's Conversations of Lord Byron. Revised with a New Preface by the Author for a New Edition and Annotated by Lady Byron, John Cam Hobhouse, Sir Walter Scott, Sir Charles Napier, John Murray, John Galt, William Harness, Robert Southey, Lady Caroline Lamb, Leigh Hunt, Mary Shelley, E. J. Trelawny, William Fletcher, Countess Teresa Guiccioli, and Others who Knew the Poet Personally*, ed. E. J. Lovell, Jr. Princeton: Princeton UP.

Mellown, M. J. (1981) 'Francis Jeffrey, Lord Byron, and *English Bards and Scotch Reviewers*', *Studies in Scottish Literature*, XVI: 80–90.

Mezaro, G. (1975) *Vittorio Alfieri: Forerunner of Italian Nationalism*, New York: Octogon Books.

Mikhail, E. H. (ed.) (1989) *Sheridan: Interviews and Recollections*, Basingstoke: Macmillan.

Miller, B. (1910) *Leigh Hunt's Relations with Byron, Shelley and Keats*, New York: Columbia UP.

Mineka, F. E. (1972) *The Dissidence of Dissent: The Monthly Repository, 1806–1838, under the Editorship of Robert Aspland, W. J. Fox, R. H. Horne, and Leigh Hunt*, New York: Octagon Books.

Mitchell, T. (1816) 'Autograph Letter to Leigh Hunt', Brewer–Leigh Hunt Collection MsL M68h n°2.

Mitchell, T. R. (1994) 'Keats's "outlawry" in "Robin Hood"', *Studies in English Literature*, 34 (Autumn): 753–69.

Mitford, W. (1774) *An Essay upon the Harmony of Language, Intended to Illustrate that of the English Language*, London: J. Robson. Brewer–Leigh Hunt Collection 416 M68e.

Mizukoshi, A. (2001) *Keats, Hunt, and the Aesthetics of Pleasure*, Houndsmills, Basingstoke: Macmillan.

Molière, Jean-Baptiste Poquelin (1739) *The Works of Moliere, French and English*, 2 vols, London: John Watt. Brewer–Leigh Hunt Collection 848 M721 1739

Monkhouse, C. (1893) *Life of Leigh Hunt*, London: Walter Scott.

[Montgomery, J.] (1815) 'Review of William Wordsworth, *The Excursion*', *Eclectic Review*, III. (January): 13–39.

Montluzin, E. L. de (1987) 'William Blackwood: The Human Face behind the Mask of 'Ebony'', *Keats–Shelley Journal*, XXXVI: 158–89.

——— (1998) 'Killing the Cockneys: *Blackwood's* Weapons of Choice against Hunt, Hazlitt, and Keats', *Keats–Shelley Journal*, XLVII : 87–107.

Moore, T. (1853–6) *Memoirs, Journals, and Correspondence of Thomas Moore*, ed. J. Russell, 8 vols, London: Longman, Brown, Green, and Longmans.

——— (1854) *Life of Lord Byron: with his Letters and Journals*, 6 vols, London: John Murray.

——— (1910) *The Poetical Works of Thomas Moore*, ed. A. D. Godley, Oxford: Oxford UP.

——— (1964) *The Letters of Thomas Moore*, ed. W. S. Dowden, 2 vols, Oxford: Clarendon P.

Moorman, M. (1965) *William Wordsworth, a Biography – The Later Years 1803–1850*, Oxford: Clarendon P.

Moskal, J. (1995) 'Gender, Nationality, and Textual Authority in Lady Morgan's Travel Books', in *Romantic Women Writers: Voices and Counter-Voices*, ed. P. R. Feldman and T. M. Kelley, London: UP of New England.

——— (1999) 'Gender and Italian Nationalism in Mary Shelley's *Rambles in Germany and Italy*', *Romanticism*, 5.2: 187–98.

——— (2000) 'Politics and the Occupation of a Nurse in Mariana Starke's *Letters*', in *Romantic Geographies: Discourses of Travel, 1775–1844*, ed. A. Gilroy, Manchester: Manchester UP.

Motion, A. (1997) *Keats*, London: Faber & Faber.

Mott, F. L. (1970) *A History of American Magazines, 1741–1850*, Cambridge, Mass.: Harvard UP.

Moxon, E. (1842) 'Autograph Letter to William Wordsworth', Dove Cottage Moxon Letter 1839–1844, WL/Box 6.

Mudford, W. (1812) *The Life of Richard Cumberland*, London: Sherwood, Neely, and Jones, and J. Asperne.

Mulrooney, J. (2001) 'The Subject of Theater: Theatrical Criticism and Poetry in Britain, 1798–1832', unpublished thesis, Boston U.

——— (2003) 'Keats in the Company of Kean', *Studies in Romanticism*, 42.2 (Summer): 227–50.

Newey, V. (1995) 'Keats, History, and the Poets', in *Keats and History*, ed. N. Roe, Cambridge: Cambridge UP.

Newlyn, L. (2000) *Reading, Writing, and Romanticism: The Anxiety of Reception*, Oxford: Oxford UP.

Nichol, J. (1880) *Byron*, London: Macmillan and Co.

O'Connor, M. (1998) *The Romance of Italy and the English Imagination*, Basingstoke: Macmillan.

Oliphant, M. (1897) *William Blackwood and His Sons, Their Magazines and Friends*, 2 vols, Edinburgh and London: William Blackwood and his sons.

O'Neill, Michael (2003) '"Even now while I write": Leigh Hunt and Romantic Spontaneity', in *Leigh Hunt: Life, Poetics, Politics*, ed. N. Roe, London and New York: Routledge.

Orr, C. C. (1998) 'Mary Shelley's *Rambles in Germany and Italy*, the Celebrity Author, and the Undiscovered Country of the Human Heart'. *Romanticism on the Net*, 11 (August): n. pag. Online. Available HTTP: <http://www.erudit.org/revue/ron/1998/v/n11/005813ar.html> (accessed 12/1/04).

Owen, W. J. B. (1957) 'Costs, Sales, and Profits of Longman's Editions of Wordsworth', *Library*, 12: 93–107.

Owenson, S., Lady Morgan (1821) *Italy*, 2 vols, second edition, London: Henry Colburn.

——— (1862) *Lady Morgan's Memoirs: Autobiography, Diaries and Correspondence*, ed. W. Hepworth Dixon, 2 vols, London: Wm. H. Allen & Co.

[Peabody, W. E. O.] (1829) 'Art. I.—*Lord Byron and His [sic] Contemporaries*', *North American Review*, LXII, 37 (January) 1–19.

Peacock, T. L. [as P. M. O'Donovan] (1814) *Sir Proteus: A Satirical Ballad*, London: T. Hookham, Junr. and E. T. Hookham.

Perry, S. (1996) 'Robert J. Griffin, *Wordsworth's Pope*', *Romanticism on the Net*, 4 (November 1996): n. pag. Online. Available HTTP: <http://www.erudit.org/revue/ron/1996/v/n4/005728ar.html> (accessed 12/1/04).

Pinkney, N. (1814) *Travels through the South of France, and in the Interior of the Provinces of Provence and Languedoc, in the Years 1807 and 1808, by a Route never before Performed, being along the Banks of the Loire, the Isere, and the Garonne, through the Greater Part of their Courses*, London: Gale, Curtis, and Fenner. Brewer–Leigh Hunt Collection 944dP65t.

Pite, R. (1994) *The Circle of Our Vision: Dante's Presence in English Romantic Poetry*, Oxford: Clarendon P.

Power, J. (1964) *Shelley in America in the Nineteenth Century: His Relation to American Critical Thought and His Influence*, New York: Haskell House.

Prance, C. A. (1992) *The Characters in the Novels of Thomas Love Peacock, 1785–1866, with Bibliographical Lists*, Lewiston, New York; Queenston, Ontario; Lampeter, England: The Edwin Mellin P.

Read, T. B. (1859) 'Autograph Letter to Leigh Hunt', May, Brewer–Leigh Hunt Collection MsL R28h.

Reiman, D. H. (1972) *The Romantic Reviewed: Contemporary Reviews of British Romantic Writers – Part C: Shelley, Keats, and London Radical Writers*, 2 vols, New York and London: Garland Publishing, Inc.

——— (ed.) (1973–86) *Shelley and His Circle, 1773–1822*: vols 5–8, Cambridge, Mass.: Harvard UP.

Repton, H. (1803) *Observations on the Theory and Practice of Landscape Gardening, including some Remarks on Grecian and Gothic Architecture*, London: Taylor.

Reynolds, J. H. (1816) 'Autograph letter to William Wordsworth', August, Dove Cottage Library DC MS 170.

Richardson, A. (1988) *A Mental Theater: Poetic Drama and Consciousness in the Romantic Age*, University Park and London: The Pennsylvania State UP.

[Roberts, William] (1816) 'Art. XVIII. *The Siege of Corinth. A Poem. Parisina. A Poem.* 8vo. London, 1816. Murray. – *The Story of Rimini. A Poem.* By Leigh Hunt. London, 1816. Murray', *The British Review, and London Critical Journal* (May): 452–69.

Robinson, C. E. (1983) 'Percy Bysshe Shelley, Charles Ollier, and William Blackwood: the Contexts of Early Nineteenth-Century Publishing', in *Shelley Revalued: Essays from the Gregynog Conference*, ed. K. Everest, Totowa, New Jersey: Barnes & Noble Books.

Robinson, H. C. (1869) *Diary, Reminiscences, and Correspondence of Henry Crabb Robinson*, ed. Thomas Sadler, 3 vols, London: Macmillan and Co.

Roe, N. (1981) 'Leigh Hunt and Wordsworth's *Poems*, 1815', *The Wordsworth Circle*, 12.1: 89–91.

——— (1995a) 'Introduction', in *Keats and History*, ed. N. Roe, Cambridge: Cambridge UP.

——— (1995b) 'Keats's Commonwealth', in *Keats and History*, ed. N. Roe. Cambridge: Cambridge UP.

——— (1995c) 'Keats's "Mawkish Fame"', *Notes and Queries*, 240: 185–6.

——— (1997) *John Keats and the Culture of Dissent*, Oxford: Clarendon P.

——— (ed.) (2003) *Leigh Hunt: Life, Poetics, Politics*, London and New York: Routledge.

Rogers, S. (1956) *The Italian Journals of Samuel Rogers*, ed. J. R. Hale, London: Faber and Faber.

Rutherford, A. (1961) 'The Influence of Hobhouse on *Childe Harold's Pilgrimage, Canto IV*', *Review of English Studies*, 12: 391–7.

——— (1961) *Byron: A Critical Study*, Edinburgh and London: Oliver and Boyd.

——— (ed.) (1970) *Byron: The Critical Heritage*, London: Routledge & Kegan Paul; New York: Barnes & Noble Inc.

[Scott, W.] (1818) 'Review of Lord Byron's *Childe Harold's Pilgrimage, Canto IV*', *Quarterly Review*, XIX (April): 215–32.

——— (1932–6) *The Letters of Sir Walter Scott*, ed. H. J. C. Grierson, 10 vols, London: Constable & co. Ltd.

Scott, W. B. (1892) *Autobiographical Notes of the Life of William Bell Scott, and Notices of his Artistic and Poetic Circle of Friends, 1830 to 1882*, ed. W. Minto, 2 vols, New York: Harper & Brothers.

Scott, W. S. (ed.) (1943) *The Athenians: Being Correspondence between Thomas Jefferson Hogg and his Friends Thomas Love Peacock, Leigh Hunt, Percy Bysshe Shelley, and Others*, London: The Golden Cockerel P.

Shelley, M. (1980–88) *The Letters of Mary Wollstonecraft Shelley*, ed. B. T. Bennett, 3 vols, Baltimore and London: Johns Hopkins UP.

——— (1996) *The Novels and Selected Works of Mary Shelley*, gen. ed. N. Crook with P. Clemit, 8 vols, London: Pickering & Chatto.

Shelley, P. B. (1964) *The Letters of Percy Bysshe Shelley*, ed. F. L. Jones, 2 vols, Oxford: Clarendon P.

Shine, H. and H. Chadwick Shine (1949) *The Quarterly Review under Gifford: Identification of Contributors, 1809–1824*, Chapel Hill: The U of North Carolina P.

Short, C. (1972–3) 'The Composition of Hunt's *The Story of Rimini*', *Keats–Shelley Journal*, XXI–XXII: 207–18.

Simond, L. (1828) *A Tour of Italy and Sicily*, London: Longman, Rees, Orme, Brown, and Green.

Smith, J. and H. Smith (1812) *Rejected Addresses, or the New Theatrium Poetarum*, London: John Miller.

Sotheby, W. (1828) *Italy and other Poems*, London: John Murray.

Southey, R. (1832) *Essays, Moral and Political*, 2 vols, London: John Murray.

——— (1965) *New Letters of Robert Southey*, ed. K. Curry, 2 vols, New York and London: Columbia UP.

Springer, C. (1987) *The Marble Wilderness: Ruins and Representation in Italian Romanticism, 1775–1850*, Cambridge: Cambridge UP.

Squier, C. L. (1978) *Sir John Suckling*, Boston: Twayne Publishers.

St Clair, W. (2004) *The Reading Nation in the Romantic Period*, Cambridge: Cambridge UP.

Stabler, J. (2002) *Byron, Poetics and History*, Cambridge: Cambridge UP.

——— (2003) 'Leigh Hunt's Aesthetics of Intimacy', in *Leigh Hunt: Life, Poetics, Politics*, ed. N. Roe, London and New York: Routledge.

Story, P. (1980) 'A Neglected Cockney School Parody of Hazlitt and Hunt', *Keats–Shelley Journal*, XXIX: 191–202.

Stout, G. D. (1925) 'Leigh Hunt's Money Troubles: Some New Light'. *Washington University Studies*, XII, 2: 223–8.

——— (1928) 'Studies toward a Biography of Leigh Hunt', unpublished thesis, Harvard University.

——— (1949) *The Political History of Leigh Hunt's Examiner, together with an Account of 'The Book'*, Saint Louis: Washington University Studies.

——— (1957) 'Leigh Hunt on Wordsworth and Coleridge', *Keats–Shelley Journal*, VI: 59–73.

Strout, A. L. (1937) 'Hunt, Hazlitt, and *Maga*: The Lighter Side of "Cockney-Killing"', *English Literary History*, 4: 151–9.

——— (1946) *The Life and Letters of James Hogg, the Ettrick Shepherd*, Lubbock, Texas: Texas Tech P.

Suckling, J. (1971) *The Works of Sir John Suckling – The Non-Dramatic Works*, ed. Thomas Clayton, Oxford: Clarendon P.

[Talfourd, T. N.] (1815) 'An Attempt to Estimate the Poetical Talent of the Present Age', *Pamphleteer*, 5 (February): 459–65.

Taylor, J. (1832) *Records of my Life*, 2 vols, London: Edward Bull.

Taylor, G. (2000) *The French Revolution and the London Stage, 1789–1805*, Cambridge: Cambridge UP.

Thompson, J. R. (1977) *Leigh Hunt*, Boston: Twayne Publishers.

——— (1984) '"Mild Singing Clothes": The Poetry of Leigh Hunt', *Books at Iowa*, 40: 21–30.

Thomson, P. (1971) 'The Early Career of George Colman the Younger', in *Nineteenth-Century British Theatre*, eds K. Richards and P. Thomson. London: Methuen & Co., Ltd.

Thorpe, C. DeWitt (1956) 'Leigh Hunt as Man of Letters', in *Leigh Hunt's Literary Criticism*, eds L. Huston Houtchens and C. Washburn Houtchens, New York: Columbia UP.

——— (1959) 'The Nymphs', *Keats–Shelley Memorial Bulletin*, 10: 33–47.

Timperley, C. H. (1839) *A Dictionary of Printers and Printing, with the Progress of Literature, Ancient and Modern; Bibliographical Illustrations, etc. etc.*, London: H. Johnson.

Todd, W. B. (1972) *A Directory of Printers and Other in Allied Trades: London and Vicinity, 1800–1840*, London: The Printing Historical Society.

Trollope, A. (1996) *An Autobiography*, ed. D. Skilton, London and New York: Penguin.

Trott, N. (2003) 'Wordsworth and the Parodic School of Criticism', in *The Satiric Eye: Forms of Satire in the Romantic Period*, ed. S. E. Jones, New York: Palgrave.

[Tudor, W.] (1816) *'The Story of Rimini', North American Review and Miscellaneous Journal*, 8 (July): 272–83.

Turley, R. M. (1998) 'Handy Squirrels and Chapman's Homer: Hunt, Keats, and Romantic Philology', *Romanticism*, 4.1: 115–18.

Vail, J. W. (2000) *The Literary Relationship of Lord Byron and Thomas Moore*, Baltimore: Johns Hopkins UP.

——— (2004) 'The Standard of Revolt: Revolution and National Independence in Moore's *Lalla Rookh*', *Romanticism on the Net* 39 (August): n. pag. Online. Available HTTP: <http://www.erudit.org/revue/ron/2005/v/n39/005859ar.html> (accessed 12/5/05).

Vallois, M. (1985) 'Voyage au pays des doubles: ruines et mélancolie chez Mme de Staël', *L'Esprit Créateur*, 25, 3: 71–84.

Vincent, E. R. (1949) *Byron, Hobhouse and Foscolo: New Documents in the History of a Collaboration*, Cambridge: Cambridge UP.

Waldie, C. A. (Mrs Eaton) (1820) *Rome in the Nineteenth Century; containing a Complete Account of the ruins of the Ancient City, the remains of the middle ages, and the monuments of modern times. with Remarks on the fine arts, on the State of Society, and on the Religious ceremonies, manners, and customs, of the modern Romans. In a Series of Letters written during a Residence at Rome, in the years 1817 and 1818*, 3 vols, Edinburgh: Archibald Constable and Co.; London: Hurst, Robinson, and Co.

Waldie, J. (1820) *Sketches Descriptive of Italy in the Years 1816 and 1817*, 4 vols, London: Longman, Orme, and Longmans.

Webb, T. (1992) 'Religion of the Heart: Leigh Hunt's Unpublished Tribute to Shelley', *Keats–Shelley Review*, 7: 1–61.

Weinberg, A. M. (1999) *Shelley's Italian Experience*, Basingstoke: Macmillan.

Whately, T. (1785) *Remarks on Some of the Characters of Shakespeare. By the Author of Observations on Modern Gardening*, London: T. Rayne and son.

Wheatley, K. (1992) 'The *Blackwood's* Attacks on Leigh Hunt', *Nineteenth-Century Literature*, 47, 1: 1–31.

——— (1999) *Shelley and his Readers: Beyond Paranoid Politics*, Columbia and London: U of Missouri P.

——— (2003) 'Conceiving Disgust: Leigh Hunt, William Gifford and the *Quarterly Review*', in *Leigh Hunt: Life, Poetics, Politics*, ed. N. Roe, London and New York: Routledge.

Williams, J. A. (1817) *Memoirs of John Philip Kemble, Esq. with an Original Critique of his Performance*, London: John Bowley Wood.

[Wilson, John] (1817) 'Some Observations on the "Biographia Literaria" of S. T. Coleridge, Esq.–1817', *Blackwood's Edinburgh Magazine*, II, VII (October): 1–18.

[———] (1828) *'Lord Byron and some of his Contemporaries*. By Leigh Hunt', *Blackwood's Edinburgh Magazine*, XXIII, 136 (March): 362–408.

Wolfson, S. (1995) 'Keats enters History: Autopsy, *Adonais*, and the Fame of Keats', in *Keats and History*, ed. N. Roe. Cambridge: Cambridge UP, 1995.

Woodring, C. (1962) 'Leigh Hunt as Political Essayist', in *Leigh Hunt's Political and Occasional Essays*, eds L. Huston Houtchens and C. Washburn Houtchens, New York and London: Columbia UP.

——— (1970) *Politics in English Romantic Poetry*, Cambridge, Mass.: Harvard UP.

Wordsworth, J. (1996) 'Introduction to Leigh Hunt's *The Feast of the Poets*', *Ancestral Voices: Fifty Books from the Romantic Period*, Poole and New York: Woodstock Books.

Wordsworth, W. (1968) *Guide through the District of the Lakes in the North of England*, ed. W. M. Merchant, New York: Greenwood P, Publishers.

——— (1974) *The Prose Works of William Wordsworth*, eds W. J. Owen and J. Worthington Smyser, 3 vols, Oxford: Clarendon P.

——— (1984) *William Wordsworth – The Oxford Authors*, ed. S. Gill, Oxford and New York: Oxford UP.

——— and D. Wordsworth (1969–70) *The Letters of William and Dorothy Wordsworth – The Middle Years 1806–20*, ed. E. de Selincourt, rev. M. Moorman and A. G. Hill, 2 vols, Oxford: Clarendon P.

——— and D. Wordsworth (1978) *The Letters of William and Dorothy Wordsworth – Volume III The Later Years, Part I 1821–1828*, ed. E. de Selincourt, revised, arranged and edited by A. G. Hills, second edition, Oxford: Clarendon P.

——— and D. Wordsworth (1979) *The Letters of William and Dorothy Wordsworth – Volume V The Later Years, Part II 1829–1834*, ed. E. de Selincourt, revised, arranged and edited by A. G. Hill, second edition, Oxford: Clarendon P.

——— and D. Wordsworth (1993) *The Letters of William and Dorothy Wordsworth – Volume VIII: A Supplement of New Letters*, ed. A. G. Hill, Oxford: Clarendon P.

Wu, D. (1995) *Wordsworth's Reading, 1800–1815*, Cambridge: Cambridge UP.

——— (1996) 'Leigh Hunt's 'Cockney' Aesthetics', *Keats–Shelley Review*, 10: 80–1.

Wynn, L. (1951) 'The Reputation of Samuel Taylor Coleridge among his Contemporaries in England', unpublished thesis, Princeton University.

Zani, S. (2004) 'Byronic Biography and the Foundation of Genius', *Byron Journal*, 32, 1: 31–8.

Index

For Product Safety Concerns and Information please contact our EU representative GPSR@taylorandfrancis.com
Taylor & Francis Verlag GmbH, Kaufingerstraße 24, 80331 München, Germany

www.ingramcontent.com/pod-product-compliance
Lightning Source LLC
Chambersburg PA
CBHW071516100726
47908CB00004B/1185

* 9 7 8 0 4 1 5 8 6 0 0 2 4 *